DARWIN
Survival of a City

The 1890s

Derek Pugh

Foreword by The Hon. Sally Thomas AC
20th Administrator of the Northern Territory

Derek Pugh OAM: Author.
DARWIN: Survival of a City: The 1890s.
Text © Derek Pugh 2023.
Original Photographs © Derek Pugh 2022, unless otherwise attributed.

ISBN: 978-0-6457374-0-0
All rights reserved. No part of this publication may be reproduced, stored in a retrieval system, or transmitted in any form by any means, electronic, mechanical, photocopying, recording, or otherwise, without the prior written permission of the author.

Design and layout by Mikaela Pugh: mikaelaapughh@gmail.com

Subjects:
Palmerston: Darwin, Port Darwin.
Northern Territory: History—British military attempts at settlement.
Australian Aborigines: Larrakia, Woolwonga, Tiwi, Wulna.
Chinese people in North Australia in the 19th Century.
Pioneers: Northern Territory—social conditions—health.
Cyclone destruction Northern Territory

Other books in this series:
Darwin 1869: The Second Northern Territory Expedition
Darwin: Origin of a City: The 1870s
Twenty to the Mile: The Overland Telegraph Line
Darwin: Growth of a City: The 1880s

Front Cover: Darwin Railway Station, c 1898 (SLSA, B30548)

Contact: derekpugh1@gmail.com
www.derekpugh.com.au

A catalogue record for this book is available from the National Library of Australia

Acknowledgements

My thanks go to the 20th Administrator of the Northern Territory, the Honourable Sally Thomas AC, who was a willing reader of the manuscript and was happy to pen an inciteful foreword.

Also, to my late brother, Michael Pugh, for his design work, and his daughter Mikaela, who so ably took over from him as a designer when needs arose.

And to my companions in the exploration of what's left of 1890s Darwin, Paddy Coleman and Peter Whelan.

As usual, thanks also to the staff at the Library and Archives of the Northern Territory and the State Library of South Australia. I am grateful for the support of the NT Government and the NT history grants program that generously covered many of the production costs of this book.

Aboriginal people should be aware that as this is a history, it contains the names of long-deceased individuals.

Note also that language is quoted that is now considered offensive. It is presented as a part of the truth-telling of our history, and I am aware that some might find it painful. If this is the case, I apologise.

Contents

Acknowledgements	iii
Contents	iv
Maps	vii
Timeline	xi
Foreword	xv
Preface	xvii
Chapter 1: Management	1
Chapter 2: Representation: Parsons, Solomon, and Griffiths	37
Gallery: Palmerston in the 1890s	45
Chapter 3: The Larrakia	53
Chapter 4: Asian Settlers	63
Chapter 5: Communication	79
Chapter 6: Daily Life in Palmerston: Clubs and Societies	85
Chapter 7: Alcohol and Opium	119
Chapter 8: Industry	125
Chapter 9: The Railway	149
Chapter 10: The Charles Point Lighthouse	155
Chapter 11: Territory Women	163
Chapter 12: Capital Crimes	177
Chapter 13: Health	195
Chapter 14: The Overlander	205
Chapter 15: Palmerstonian Souls	209
Chapter 16: A Royal Commission for a White Elephant	219
Chapter 17: The Great Hurricane	229
Gallery: The Great Hurricane of 1897	243
Chapter 18: And Now?	251

Appendices 259
Bibliography 265
Index 273
Further reading

Abbreviations

LANT	Library and Archives of the Northern Territory.
NA	North Australian (a newspaper)
NLA	National Library of Australia.
NTTG	Northern Territory Times and (Government) Gazette.
SAPP	South Australian Parliamentary Papers.
SLSA	State Library of South Australia.

Darwin: Survival of a City

Maps

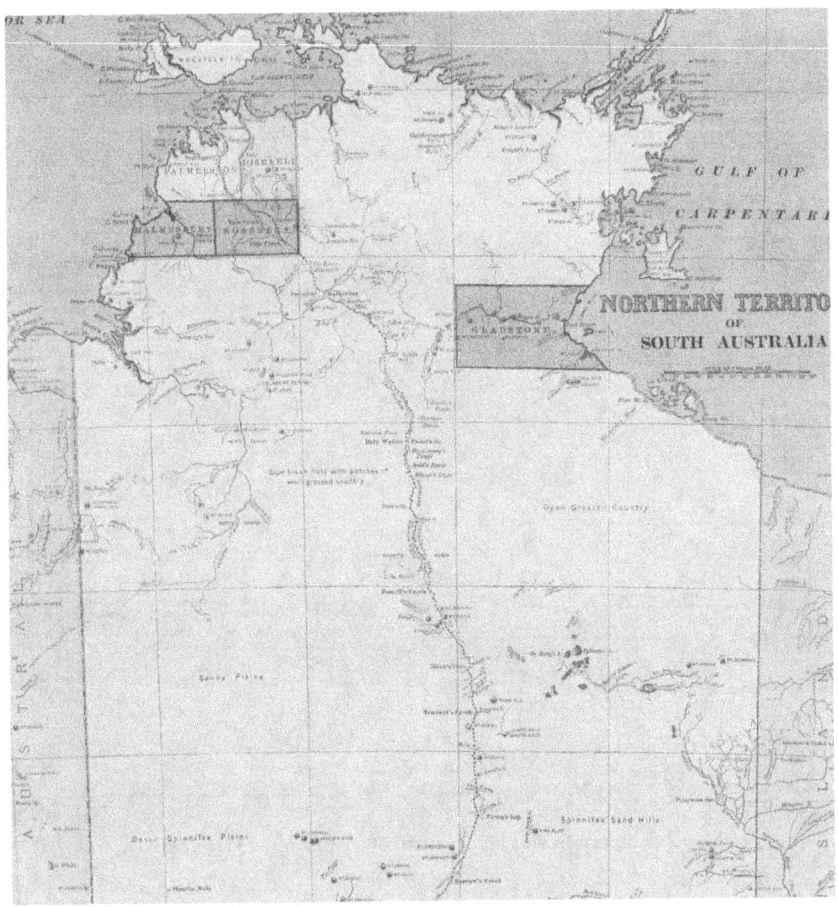

Map 1: The Northern Territory of South Australia, from *The Picturesque Atlas Publishing Company*, 1886 (nla.obj-148379306).

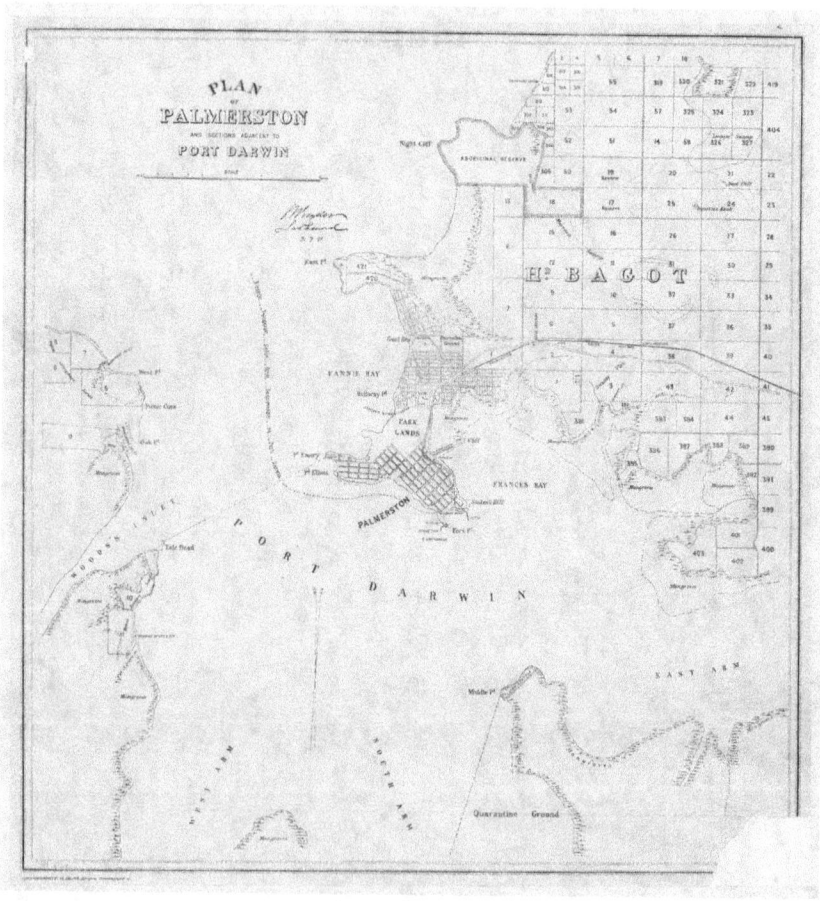

Map 2: Palmerston and Port Darwin 1891 (nla.obj-231764246-1).

Maps

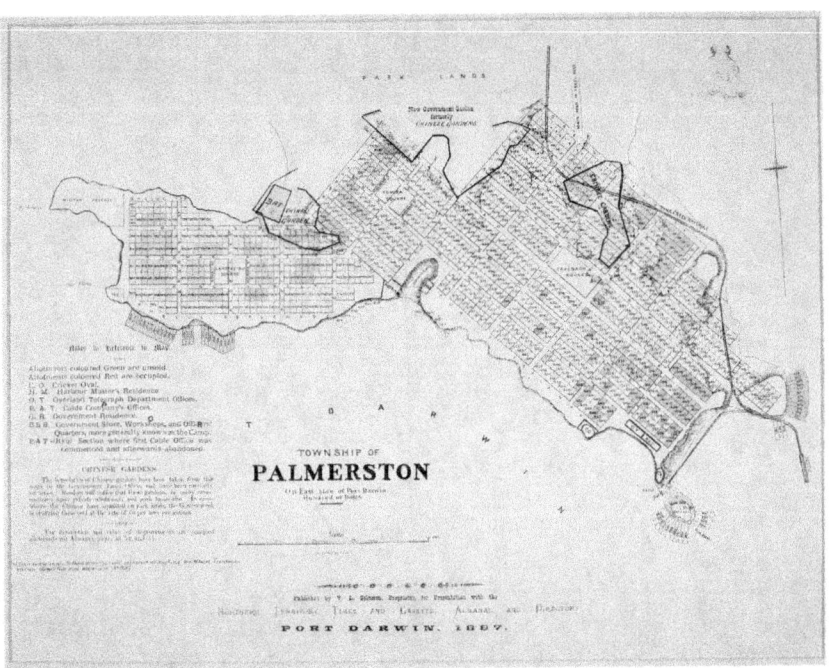

Map 3: Palmerston map published in colour by V.V. Solomon 1887. The dark shaded blocks were occupied, the light shaded blocks were unsold. (LANT rare_map_36).

Darwin: Survival of a City

Timeline

1869	Palmerston and Port Darwin are surveyed.
21 January 1870	*Kohinoor* arrives in Port Darwin with the first settlers. They include Paul Foelsche and six policemen.
5 February 1870	The Larrakia offer a friendly welcome to George Goyder and The Second Northern Territory Survey Expedition on the *Moonta*. The Darwin region has been home to the Larrakia people since the Dreamtime.
1 August 1871	John Little is appointed to the Northern Territory as Post and Telegraph Master.
22 August 1872	First telegram is sent from Palmerston to Adelaide after the Overland Telegraph Line is connected at Frew's Ponds.
2 November 1873	First church service is held in the new Wesleyan Church building, led by Reverend Bogle.
7 November 1873	Issue 1 of *The Northern Territory Times and Gazette* (*NTTG*) is published by Richard Wells. It runs until 1932.
March 1883	Palmerston Town Hall opens with the first performance of the Dramatic and Musical Society.
1 June 1883	*North Australian*, Palmerston's second newspaper begins.
August 1887	First case of smallpox in Palmerston is diagnosed. The victim and his close contacts are taken to quarantine.
2 March, 1888	A South Australian Parliamentary Party arrive to tour the goldfields and assess agricultural and pastoral opportunities, under Education Minister, Joseph C.F. Johnson.
16 July 1888	The first passenger trains travel between Darwin and Adelaide River.

1888	The *Chinese Immigration and Restriction Bill* is passed in the South Australian Parliament. There are 6,122 Chinese living in and around Darwin.
16 July 1888	Railway service to Adelaide River begins.
1889	30 per cent of land held under pastoral leases in the Northern Territory is rescinded as stations collapsed.
1889	Mud Island Leprosy Station is established.
30 September 1889	The railway line is completed as far as Pine Creek (145 miles) and the contractors hand it over to the Government without fanfare.
1890	John George Knight is appointed to the position of Government Resident in Palmerston.
1890	John Langdon Parsons and Vaiben Solomon win the election to represent the Northern Territory in the South Australian Parliament.
1890	Mrs Ryan's *North Australian Hotel* opens. It is renamed *Victoria Hotel* in 1896.
1891	The Jesuit Mission at Rapid Creek is closed. The missionaries then focus on Daly River Mission.
1891	Government census lists the name, age, occupation, country of origin, and religion of every white person in the Territory. Aboriginal and Chinese people are counted but not named.
31 March 1891	Governor Kintore arrives in Palmerston and travels back to Adelaide overland.
1892	The pearl shell industry is revived by Japanese pearlers.
10 January 1892	John George Knight dies of an asthma attack.
1 April 1892	Premier Thomas Playford visits Palmerston, arriving quietly on the *Taiyuan*.
27 April 1892	Charles Dashwood arrives as the new Government Resident. He remains in office for 13 years.
1893	Walter Griffiths is elected to represent the N.T. and, at 25 years old, he is the youngest Member of Parliament. Vaiben Solomon is re-elected.
1893	The Dingo Glee Club begins regular meetings.

Timeline

February 1893	The Charles Point Lighthouse opens.
15 July 1893	Charlie Flannigan is hanged at Fannie Bay Gaol for the murder of Samuel Burns Croker at Auvergne Station.
25 July 1893	Wandi Wandi is hanged for the murder of some Malay fishermen.
18 December 1894	South Australian women earn the right to vote in elections, and 82 Territory women enroll.
1895	The South Australian Government holds a Royal Commission into Territory affairs.
1895	E.O. Robinson and Joe Cooper return to Melville Island with a party of about 20 Iwaidja workers to harvest buffalo.
1896	Port Darwin's new jetty is built at Stokes Hill by Chinese labour.
1896-1903	The live export market for cattle is closed to Java and Singapore due to Redwater fever infestations.
6 May 1896	The Port Darwin Lodge of Freemasons begins.
July 1896	Chinese-born Reverend Tack, his wife Emma Lee Young, and their five children arrived in Port Darwin in July 1896 to lead the Wesleyan Church.
6 January 1897	The 'Great Hurricane' destroys the town of Palmerston. It kills at least 28 people.
1897	The Palmerston Brass Band has its debut.
21 May 1897	Jerome Murif arrives in Palmerston after riding across the continent on a bicycle.
16 August 1897	The new Wesleyan Church is built from a kit and opens for service.
1899	Daly River Mission is closed.
December 1899	Vaiben Solomon is Premier of South Australia for 8 days.
10 August 1899	Chung Yeung and Lem Kai are hanged at Fannie Bay Gaol for murder.
12 August 1899	Moolooloorun is hanged in front of his countrymen, for murder.

Foreword

The Honourable Sally Thomas AC, 20th Administrator of the Northern Territory

Derek Pugh brings the Darwin of the 1890s alive.

They were depressing times: a devastating cyclone in 1897; a Royal Commission to address concerns about the financial future of the Northern Territory; the execution of murderers; the difficulty in conducting criminal trials; the struggles of the cattle industry and developments in mining.

In 1897, Banjo Paterson visited and described Darwin as a city of 'booze, blow and blasphemy', but went on to tell how visitors to Darwin [Palmerston] always 'had a hankering to get back there'. The cyclist, Jerome Murif, who also visited in 1897 found the European Palmerstonians to be a 'laughter loving generously hospitable people' whose lives were 'rounds of light gaieties and small pleasures'. They found 'a picnic, dance, a sports day, or a concert' to be an 'ever-absorbing topic'.

Derek's description of the various religions practiced in Darwin highlights the range of nationalities and beliefs. The Chinese were mainly Taoists and Buddhists, for Europeans there were three Christian churches, and the Aboriginal population stuck to their traditional beliefs – resisting the attempts of the Jesuit missionaries to convert them to Catholicism. The Chinese temple was already in existence in Woods Street and there is a wonderful description of the building of the Wesleyan Church.

In 1890, the Chinese were more than 80 percent of the non-Aboriginal population of Darwin. They were railway workers, agriculturalists, shopkeepers, miners, and members of the service industries. Despite their value in these capacities, they were often shunned and excluded by European society and the South Australian Government actively discriminated against them. The Chinese focused on their own activities. The author includes the description of the Chinese New Festivals and the joyous and colourful New Year celebration in 1893.

Through all these activities we find insightful descriptions of the various characters who dominated society in the 1890s: Government Resident Dashwood, Vaiben Solomon of Brown's Mart fame; Ellen Ryan who built the Vic Hotel; Wandi Wandi, convicted of murder; and many others.

The 1890s were a time of depression in the Northern Territory, but Derek Pugh's book is far from depressing. It is a wonderful story of the vigour of the residents, of the personalities, the cruelty, and the kindness that occurred in the day-to-day lives of the people of Darwin in the 1890s.

Preface

The last decade of the nineteenth century was very different to the exciting times of the 1880s in the Territory. Then, furious growth in mining, pastoralism and even agricultural pursuits looked very promising and the Territory's population soared, although not in the way the colony's South Australian pioneers had hoped. The majority of Territory residents were Chinese. The original inhabitants, the local Aboriginal people, were uncounted and misunderstood, and white settlers thought they were a dying race anyway – it was only a matter of time before they would be gone.

Of the thousands of Chinese 'coolie' workers that came to work in the mines and in railway construction, few spoke English, and even fewer wanted anything to do with Europeans or Aboriginal people. They were here to work, make their fortunes, and return home to their families in triumph. In 1888, there were 6,122 Chinese people in the Territory,* mostly from Hong Kong, Canton, and Singapore, but with the demise of the mines and completion of the railway and its jetty in the final years of the 1880s, they started to leave. Thousands went home in 1889 and the next year just 4,141 Chinese people remained (or were newly arrived) in the Territory.

The legacy of those people lives on in the Territory. The Territory of the 1880s was literally built by Chinese workers. They had dominated work parties on both the railways and the goldfields, grown fresh vegetables for the Palmerston and goldfields markets, constructed the town roads, built bridges, run shops, and worked as

---

* Jones, 1987.

domestic servants for the Europeans. For all that, the white residents worried about them, derided their culture, and pilloried their work ethic in the newspapers. Many hardworking Chinese suffered such extraordinary racism it was little wonder that they wanted to go home.

The two important industries of mining and pastoralism needed access to Palmerston's port and other markets, and the completion of the Pine Creek to Palmerston railway was a step in the right direction. Many South Australians dreamed of a transcontinental railway, following the American model, which would open the country and allow easy access to the spoils of the interior. Railway lines were laid from Port Augusta to Oodnadatta in the south, with hopes of eventually reaching the line that ended Pine Creek. But as South Australians watched their debts swell to more £20 million, the Government lost interest. The northern lines stopped in Pine Creek in 1887 and stayed there until a burst of optimism 42 years later extended it via Katherine to Birdum. But there it stopped again, and the whole system was at last scrapped in 1976.

At the same time, mining activity declined. Between 1886 and 1888, gold production more than halved. A sudden spike in 1889 gave hope, but the old problems of the high costs of isolation, shortage of labour, lack of capital, and poor local knowledge continued to plague the industry.* Even though the mining industry was supported by a variety of ores – gold, copper, tin, and silver – they all suffered the same problems.

Meanwhile, pastoralists battled outbreaks of a disease that was hard to understand, let alone fight. The cattle tick, *Boophilus microplus*, almost destroyed the industry before it began. *Boophilus* carried Redwater fever, and cattle herds across the Top End were decimated. Nearly 30 per cent of land leased to pastoralists was rescinded by 1889 as cattle stations collapsed, particularly in the Top End.

As the 1890s progressed, the South Australian Government and their wealthy lobbyists grew tired of supporting their poor northern

---

* Powell, 1982.

lands. The Territory was a 'white elephant', and more and more came the calls to cut ties and give the land back to British Colonial Government control, and then, after Federation in 1901, to the Australian Commonwealth Government.

The hope and sweet optimism seen in the Territory in the 1870s and 1880s turned to depression in the 1890s. Nevertheless, many men and women continued to live in the Top End and fully believed in a bright future. In these pages you will find 'warts and all' stories of economic malaise, murder and mayhem, and death and disease. But don't despair, the gloom was tempered by good times, personal successes, and stories of some amazing people. You will meet, among others: Murif, who arrived from Adelaide by bicycle in a time before roads; cricket players whose biggest complaint was the upkeep of the fence around The Oval; extraordinary women; government residents in fancy dress; glee club singers; pearlers, publicans, and politicians.

The stories start with a rundown on some of the VIPs and leading businessmen operating in the Top End during the 1890s. Records of who they were and what they did are mostly written by European men of course, and the inhabitants of Palmerston were not necessarily equal in terms of social status, income, government role and access to the media. The businessmen and their businesses who were the backbone of the community include the Adcock Brothers; P.R. Allen and Co; Baines and Hughes; Aplin, Brown and Co; Rundle Brothers and Co; and Jolly and Luxton. They are easier to research than the 15 Chinese storekeepers who rarely, if ever, felt the need to advertise in the *North Australian* or the *NT Times*, never wrote letters to the editors, and mostly kept to themselves and maintained 'commercial in confidence'. Men like Cheong Wo, Chin Pack Sue, Yuen Ng Kan, Ah San, Chin Toy, Wing Wah Loong, Chin Yam Yan, Yet Loong, Wing Chong Sing, were in competition with Solomon, V.V. Brown, and H.H. Adcock. The Chinese were a significant part of the community. They were, after all, the majority of the population, and their lives ran parallel to that of their European neighbours.

The same goes for the Larrakia people and other Aboriginal groups from neighbouring areas, as well as minority populations like Filipino 'Manila-men', Japanese pearl divers and 'coolie' laborers from the sub-continent. This book is not a full history of these people, although it must touch on all of them. There are books and papers on some, but we have only scratched the surface of their lives and their contributions to the Territory – their histories are yet to be fully written.[*]

I have previously described history as a bowl of spaghetti – each strand lies entangled with a hundred others, each with its own story. Any work on history follows strands, selects stories, and promotes individuals. This book, my ninth on nineteenth century Northern Territory settlement history, completes my series – or does it? Already I am discovering many more stories and personalities that need an airing. The spaghetti bowl is still full.

---

[*] See, for example, Jones, 1990, Reid 1990, Read and Read 1991.

Chapter 1

Management

Government Resident John George Knight

Figure 1: John George Knight.

John Knight was an architect who originally arrived in the Northern Territory as part of the gold rush in 1873 but was quickly recruited to the public service. He was a man of many skills and over the next 20 years worked in most of the important senior positions in the Territory, including: Secretary and Accountant to the Government Resident; Superintendent of Works; Gold Warden; Clerk of the Court; Deputy Sherriff; Clerk of the Licensing Bench; Curator of the Property of Convicts; Registrar; Accountant; Special Magistrate; Justice of the Peace; Crown Prosecutor; Official Receiving and Returning Officer; and Architect.*

As part of Palmerston society, Knight also performed in amateur dramatics and debating clubs, and in 1887, he was awarded a first Order of Merit medal for the 'mineral trophy and ball of Territory gold' at his well-received Territory display at the Adelaide Jubilee Exhibition in 1887 and the Melbourne International Exhibition in 1888.

Knight's family never joined him in the Territory, except for

---

* Carment, 1990.

Figure 2: Theatricals at The Residence 1886 (L to R) Mr John Knight, Mrs Hilson, Mr Green, Miss Parsons, Mr Ward, Mr Whitelaw, Mr Howse (LANT ph1060-0074).

one adult son, Walter, who arrived in Palmerston shortly before his father's death. A collection of letters from Knight to family members suggest he was a lonely man, intent on finding a position in Victoria or elsewhere in the south, closer to his family, but he was financially scuttled by collapses in the price of his shares in 'Broken' (BHP) and Melbourne Trams. He wrote that the northern climate was 'hell', but nevertheless agreed to act as the Government Resident and judge after John Langdon Parsons resigned in 1889, even though he had no legal training and was, at 65, approaching old age. Knight was appointed to the position in 1890, but two years later, on 10 January 1892, he died of an asthma attack brought on by bronchitis and influenza. Walter was by his side. He was about 68 years old, and his remains lie in the Goyder Road Cemetery.*

---

* At one time the family thought his body would be shipped home to Melbourne, though it never happened. Walter wrote: 'I need not say how glad I am that our poor old dad's remains are to be removed. This is an awful place to remain in – the heat is terrific today and I am in a bath of perspiration' Walter Knight, 5 April 1892 (Wilson et al, 1994).

John Knight was originally an architect, and he was one of the designers of Victoria's Houses of Parliament. In Darwin he left his mark in several of the city's oldest buildings, such as the Town Hall (1883) and Brown's Mart, a commercial premise originally built for Vaiben Solomon in 1885, out of the local porcellanite stone.

Famously, John Knight built a house for himself that appeared to be ahead of its time. It sat on a sloping block above Kitchener Bay and was designed to suit the climate. Constructed of 'Egyptian' bricks and concrete, it was an imposing two-storey, one-room-wide residence, with large verandas on each side. It was a 'novel residence'[*] that was dubbed the 'Mud Hut' or, just as disparagingly, 'Knight's Folly' by the gossip mongers of the settlement. Controversially, Knight used prison labour to build the house – 'blackfellows and Chinese, under the direction of the European prisoner' named Fergusson.[†] The house survived the 1897 cyclone almost unscathed, but unfortunately, it burned down in 1933.

Knight's short term in the office of Government Resident left only a single annual report under his name – that of 1890. In it, Knight clearly articulated many concerns about the directions the Territory was taking, and he offered solutions to the problems. Firstly, he emphasised how important it was to unite the existing railway lines to Pine Creek and Oodnadatta into a transcontinental railway – and work should start immediately! Other projects he suggested included: the sinking of wells across the country; the clearing of roads through the bush; the establishment of a meat preserving works; maintaining bonuses for agriculture and the discovery of new minerals; and the fostering of mining 'in every way possible'.[‡] To encourage settlement, he suggested that 'working men, Europeans', after they had settled for seven years, be given 100 acres of land on a 99-year lease.

---

[*] *NTTG*, 5 January 1884.

[†] See Pugh, 2021. Ex-constable Ferguson was arrested and tried for stealing a gold shipment he was entrusted to guard as it travelled from Yam Creek to Southport. He was sentenced to seven years hard labour.

[‡] Knight, 1890.

Figure 3: 'Knight's Folly' or the 'Mud Hut' was built by John Knight using prison labour in 1884. It was destroyed by fire on New Year's Eve in 1933. The Government Offices are on the high ground above the house (Foelsche 1887, SLSA B-5060).

Above all, he wanted understood in his report that he had 'not lost faith in the Territory as a whole' and he believed that 'a bold, liberal and comprehensive administration of its affairs in the future' would 'bring about such a grand change for the better, which we all desire, though some despair of'. Unfortunately, he did not live long enough to see it.

Management

Figure 4: Palmerston Town Hall and Solomon's Mart (later Brown's Mart) buildings were designed by John George Knight (Anon, Roger Knott Collection, LANT, ph0002-0080).

Government Resident Charles James Dashwood

Figure 5: Charles Dashwood in 1899 (Searcy 1912).

When he was appointed to the Northern Territory in 1892, His Honour Mr Justice Charles James Dashwood was a 49-year-old civil engineer, turned lawyer and politician. His official title was 'Judge of the Territory, Special Magistrate, and Government Resident' and his salary was £1,000 plus £100 allowance per annum.

Dashwood left Adelaide with the hopes and good wishes of the establishment:

… There is reason to believe that Mr. Dashwood will discharge the new duties that devolve upon him with intelligence and conscientiousness. His long legal experience ought to admirably fit him for the discharge of his judicial functions.*

---

* *Evening Journal*, 9 April 1892

But at 49, he was an aging man. This didn't go unnoticed by the editor of the *Northern Territory Times*, who preferred a 'young man, firm in all things, independent as to whom he pleases or offends... and prepared to abolish red-tapeism'.* The editor was concerned about 'fogeyism' – perhaps from experience – John Knight was about 68 years old when he died.

Dashwood was unmarried and a confirmed bachelor with an illegitimate child, named Robert, born just before he left for the north. He arrived in Port Darwin on 27 April 1892 on the S.S. *Catterthun*, with two sisters – Margaret and Augusta – whom he supported, travelling with him. The sisters soon became well known as the 'Misses Dashwood'. The *Times* noticed the Dashwoods' arrival, but few others seemed to care. No bunting decorated the jetty or the ships in the harbour, and no greeting parties sailed out to meet the new G.R. like they had for his predecessors. It was no one's fault – they *meant* to offer Dashwood a welcome, however:

> ... It was not, we may say, through any unfriendly feelings towards Mr. Dashwood, far from it; but it was because we are at all times a difficult community to set going, and while we were all cogitating and wondering what form of welcome we should extend, lo, and behold, the *Catterthun* arrives and the gentleman himself is amongst us.†

The 'difficulty to get going' was apathy. The three major industries of the Northern Territory – mining, pastoralism, and agriculture – were all in the doldrums and the growing debt, which was costing at least £50,000 a year to service, was on the mind of anyone with an eye to the future. Few people remained optimistic, and the name-calling by southern politicians, and demands to release South Australia from her commitments to the Territory increased.

Perhaps things would change with a new resident. Once on shore, Dashwood and his sisters were driven to Mrs Ryan's North Australian Hotel, where they were to stay until The Residency was

---

* *NTTG*, 5 February 1892
† *NTTG*, 29 April 1892

ready. This gave the townsfolk time to raise themselves from lethargy and gather at the Court House to hear the Chairman of the District Council, Herbert Adcock, read the Resident's commission and lead the crowd through three hearty cheers for the Queen and three for Dashwood. They then listened to their new leader's opening speech, which was reported faithfully by the *Times*. Dashwood promised:

> ... if there was anything that he could do for the advancement of this great part of the province of South Australia it would give him great pleasure to do it, and if he succeeded, he would have the satisfaction of knowing that he was doing a good work. It was not in mortals to command success... he could only assure those present that he would do whatever lay in his power to foster the development of the Territory.

After that, Inspector Foelsche invited him and the senior public servants to his home for a 'friendly glass of welcome'[*] and then, more austerely, that evening he was also welcomed by the Chinese community with an 'address of welcome'.

Within days, Dashwood and his sisters had moved into The Residency but, annoyed by the open grounds of the house welcoming every stray animal, one of the new Resident's earliest decrees was 'ALL Pigs, Dogs, Goats, and Poultry found trespassing on the Residence grounds will be destroyed'.[†] It was his home, after all.

Dashwood settled quietly into his life in Palmerston. Historians consider his time as Resident as 'mediocre'[‡] and he a 'genial second-rater'.[§] Banjo Paterson wrote that he was a 'good man for the position as he doesn't care a damn for anybody, and starting from that safe basis, discharges his varied duties with a light heart'.[¶] However, the 13 years he lasted in the role – more than any other government resident – saw the Territory through some of its toughest times. His report of 1895 perhaps summarises his time:

---

[*] *NTTG*, 29 April 1892.
[†] *NTTG*, 15 July 1892.
[‡] Donovan, 1981.
[§] Elder, 1990
[¶] Paterson, 1898

> ... There is not a great deal of pleasure, or even satisfaction, to be gained from a glance backward at the operations of 1895 so far as they affected the Northern Territory. Taking the actual results in their brightest light, it cannot be said that we have made the headway hoped for, and the one consolation left to us is consideration of the fact that the country has not got further behind.[*]

Historian Kathy De La Rue concluded that he was the most successful of all the government residents, but she could not decide whether the lack of controversy he enjoyed was due to his diplomacy, or the lack-lustre community that surrounded him.[†]

Dashwood was interested in the Territory's history. In 1893, he and Alfred Searcy made an expedition to the tree marked by John McDouall Stuart some 30 years after the great explorer had crossed the continent.[‡] The tree – which had been lost for about 20 years but rediscovered in 1883 – was remarkable healthy, and they hoped it would last another fifty years. Dashwood:

> ... forwarded to the Treasurer two pieces of the memorable tree marked by the great explorer Stuart on reaching the shores of the Indian Ocean. They are portions of a limb which showed signs of decay, and which Mr Dashwood had lopped off. He had engraved on them the letters and figures which appeared on the trunk of the tree, viz. – 'J. McD. S., 1862'. One of the pieces of wood will be sent by the Treasurer to the Museum.[§]

Unfortunately, the tree burned down in 1902.[¶]

---

[*] Dashwood, Government Resident's Report 1895.
[†] De La Rue, 2004.
[‡] See '*A Cruise in the S.S. Maggie,*' *NTTG* 30 June 1893.
[§] *Adelaide Observer*, 23 October 1893.
[¶] The Administrator, His Honour Justice Mitchell visited the site in 1911 and found a burned-out stump. A three-metre length of railway line was inserted into the stump's hole as a memorial and a canister was buried in cement with a note that read: "Aug. 24, 1911 – Upon this spot there grew a tree upon which the explorer John McDouall Stuart carved his initials on the 24th day of July 1862, after his venturesome and successful journey across the continent of Australia. The tree was burned down in 1902. Shortly afterwards the spot was marked by Mr. Justice Dashwood... Mr. Justice Mitchell, the Acting Administrator of the Northern

Figure 6: Dashwood (left) with Alfred Searcy and John Darby (SLSA, PRG280-1-44-36).

Dashwood resigned his post in Darwin in 1905 to make way for his successor, Charles Edward Herbert. He returned to Adelaide and was appointed King's Council in 1906, then served in the position of Crown Solicitor until he retired in 1916, aged 74.

Dashwood married for the first time in February 1916. His bride was a 41-year-old spinster named Martha Klevesahl. He died three years later, in July 1919 aged 77, of heart failure, with an estate that was worth £3,867.*

Territory is now visiting the spot in company with Mr. Walter S. Chap-bell [sic] and Mr. Thomas, of the Eastern Extension Telegraph Cable Company, and will place this writing in a cemented tin box and bury it at the foot of an iron post brought by His Honour to erect on the place where formerly the tree grew. God save the King." The site is now a part of the Point Stuart Coastal Reserve with a memorial cairn placed there by The Reserves Board of the NT in 1971.

* Elder, 1990.

Inspector Paul Foelsche

Figure 7: Inspector Paul Foelsche.

Paul Foelsche arrived in Port Darwin with six police officers and the first settlers on the *Kohinoor* in February 1870 and remained in the Northern Territory for the rest of his long life. On arrival, he built himself a house, then sent for his wife, Charlotte,* and their two daughters.

As Chief of Police in the Territory his family enjoyed high status and Foelsche's unending cheerfulness, optimism, and skills in a wide range of activities – from photography to dentistry – made him a driving force of the embryonic community and gave him the respect of the population. Foelsche was an excellent police officer with an extraordinary working knowledge of the law which, it was said, made him the 'best lawyer outside the South Australian Bar'.†

All British subjects in the Northern Territory lived under South Australian Law. This included Aboriginal people who had no knowledge of the white man's law. They were answerable to their own traditional laws, and few understood that they had also become 'South Australians' and were subject to the British Queen, with all the obligations that theoretically entailed. Inevitably, conflict and misunderstanding easily arose.

Foelsche developed a greater understanding of the tribes than most of the white inhabitants of the Territory. He wrote an authoritative 'anthropological' paper in 1881 titled 'Notes on the Aborigines of North Australia', which was read to the Royal Society of South Australia.‡ He was, nevertheless, a man of his times, and

---

* Charlotte arrived in May 1871 and was a leading member of the Palmerston Wesleyan Church. She was well known for her charity work, and most residents of Palmerston made a point of attending her funeral after her death by cerebral haemorrhage in 1899.
† Noye, 1972.
‡ Foelsche, 1882.

his role in shocking ill-treatment of Aboriginal 'criminals' on several occasions seems extraordinary to modern minds.*

Foelsche became a dedicated and skilled photographer. He owned the only camera in the Northern Territory for many years, so his photographs are the major pictorial record of those years. He used them to passionately promote the Northern Territory at every opportunity. He was also a botanical collector for noted botanist Ferdinand Mueller, and the broad-leafed bloodwood tree, *Corymbia foelscheana* subsequently bears his name. He was an active Freemason, installed as the first Master of the Port Darwin Lodge in May 1896.†

Foelsche ran the Police Court in his role as stipendiary magistrate and it was a rare copy of a Territory newspaper that failed to recount the events in his court. For example, the following is taken almost randomly from the *North Australian* of 14 March 1890. It illustrates an average week for Inspector Foelsche:

> Legal Information
> POLICE COURT.
> (Before Paul Foelsche Esq.. S.M)
> Saturday, 10th May. Chin Tuck, a Chinaman, was charged with trespassing on the Railway Yard without authority. Pleaded guilty.
> V. V. Brown, sworn, stated that on the 9th instant he saw the prisoner in the railway yard; directly prisoner saw witness he ran away towards China Town; this was about half-past 9 a.m.; witness saw him again about five minutes past 12 (noon); on the morning of the 10th he was there again and came up to the goods shed; witness asked what he wanted and what

---

* For example, Inspector Foelsche's response to the murder of Charles Johnstone at Roper River in 1875 was to send his men to 'have a picnic with the natives' (Reid G., 1990). He told his officers: 'I cannot give you orders to shoot all natives you come across, but circumstances may occur for which I cannot provide definite instructions.' He had official warrants for four named suspects and a warrant for 'those unknown', which he explained was a loophole. The suspects were hunted down, and many innocent men and women died during the process (see Pugh 2019).

† *NTTG*, 15 May 1896.

he came there for but prisoner said "no savvee"; he is not employed on the railway, nor had he any business there. Fined £5, with £1 costs, and 10s. interpreter's fee.

Prisoner stated that he had no means to pay the fine and he was then sent to gaol for three months to work for his living.

MAY 12TH. Patrick Lynn, a pauper lunatic, was brought up on remand.

Leonard Smith O'Flaherty deposed: I am a duly qualified medical practitioner; I have had prisoner under my care since the 1st of May; he is no better and should be sent to an asylum for proper treatment. The Bench decided to send him to the Adelaide lunatic asylum.

Low Gow, Lung Sen, and Sam Wong, three Chinese, were charged with being found wandering about and unable to give a good account of themselves.

Pleaded not guilty. Mounted Constable Brooks, sworn, said: I was on duty in Cavenagh Street about half-past 1 on Sunday morning; I saw Sam Wong going out of town; I asked what he was doing out at that time in the morning, and he replied "no savvee"; asked where he was going and he repeated "no savvee"; I have spoken to him since and he speaks good English; about half past 2, I saw the other prisoners going out of town; asked where they were going and they both replied "no savvee"; they had some liquor with them, gin or whisky; they speak fairly good English; it has been reported to me that frequent robberies have been committed in town recently. Prisoners made no defence and were fined 10s. each, which they paid.[*]

Foelsche travelled to the goldfields to sit on the benches of the rural Police Courts on many occasions for crimes ranging from horse stealing to using obscene language in a public place (which drew a fine of £1). Alcohol or opium was often an issue because being 'drunk in a public place' was a crime, and it was also illegal to supply alcohol or opium to Aboriginal people. These laws meant that most inmates in Fannie Bay Gaol were Aboriginal or Chinese. The guilty were usually fined but would often end up in Fannie Bay Gaol for two or three

---

[*] *North Australian*, 14 March 1890

Figure 8: The Foelsche family on Mindil Beach in the early 1900s. Mary Andrews (nee Foelsche) sits with her two daughters, Rita (b 1900) and Dorothy (b 1895). The man holding the kite is businessman Hildebrand Stevens, husband of Rosie Emma Foelsche, the eldest daughter (holding an umbrella). The man in dark trousers is Mary's husband, railway engineer William Wallace Andrews. The Aboriginal boy, Chinese servant, the seated European man, and the woman on the left are all unidentified (Foelsche, c 1900, SLSA B-46851).

months when they were unable to pay the pound or two required. Reading the Police Court reports and their litany of repeated issues is exhausting. Foelsche must have been a patient man to sit through them year after year.

Probably of greater interest to the Inspector were trials for more serious crimes such as murder, which may have started in the Police Court before moving up to be tried by the Government Resident. These are discussed in Chapter 12.

Throughout the 1870s, 1880s and 1890s, Foelsche joined Post and Telegraphmaster General John Little as one of the most constant and stable public service personalities in the north. On retirement in January 1904, Foelsche left the force with an Imperial Service Order. He stayed in the northern town he was such a part of until his health finally began to deteriorate from about 1912. He finally passed away at the age of 83, in January 1914. He and Charlotte share a grave in the Goyder Road Cemetery in Darwin under two splendidly carved marble crosses that stand proudly as headstones. Charlotte had died in 1899, aged 59 years. Paul lived alone for a further 15 years.

Foelsche's legacy is his collection of photographs, taken almost from the first years of the settlement until his death. His photographs were always carefully orchestrated with the subjects ranging from portraits of Aboriginal people to picnics with his family.

John Archibald Graham Little

Figure 9: John Little (LANT, ph1134-0001).

John Little was appointed to the Northern Territory on 1 August 1871 as the Superintendent of the Telegraph Department for the South Australian Government in Palmerston, and soon after sailed for Port Darwin on the *Bengal*. In the early days he would not have known that his transfer to the Top End would be his last, for he was to spend the rest of his life living and working there. He was a family man, married to Matilda Cecily Johnstone who gave birth to infant daughter, Edith, in May that same year.*

Little came with high recommendations:

> ... We may mention that Mr. Little has been in the telegraph department since 1857, and during the whole of the time, wherever he has been stationed, he has by his untiring zeal in the execution of his duties, won the deserved esteem of his chief and the public with whom he has come in contact, so that his appointment to the Port Darwin Station is but a just

---

* *Evening Journal*, 23 May 1871. The Little's children were Edith (30 August 1869), Blanche (May 1871), Egbert (13 September 1974) and Maud (September 1876). Egbert Little became a lawyer and a partner in Herbert and Little (Palmerston) in 1900. He was appointed crown prosecutor in the Palmerston Court in 1906 (*NTTG* 13 July 2006). He also ran as a candidate for election to the House of Assembly several times, without success. He married Jean Horrocks in April 1908.

recognition of his merits.*

On 19 April 1877, Matilda died of 'erysipelas of the brain', and Little was left with four young children to rear: Edith, Blanche, Egbert, and Maud. He sent them to be cared for in Adelaide but chose to stay in Palmerston to avoid an inevitable demotion. As they grew up, the children re-joined their father in Palmerston. The girls made the 'social pages' of the *Times* and *North Australian* numerous times during the 1880s and 1890s, as might be expected of eligible young women in a frontier town. When she was 22 years old, Edith married the local bank manager, and their wedding story was one of the momentous occasions in Palmerston society that year:

> ... True to anticipation, an immense gathering of townspeople assembled at the Catholic Church on Sunday morning last to witness the ceremony of uniting Mr. J. J. Lawrie, manager of the Palmerston branch of the English, Scottish, and Australian Chartered Bank, to Edith Matilda Little, eldest daughter of Mr. J. A. G. Little... the little church was filled to its utmost capacity, whilst perhaps as many more citizens... crowded in the verandas of the sacred edifice, resolved to obtain a glance at the principals and to hear the happy sentence passed upon the pair to be "in love and mutual honour joined.
>
> The bridegroom arrived first, attended only by the best man, Mr. J. C. Hendry, and a few minutes later the bride drove up, accompanied by her father and sister (Miss Blanche Little†) – the desire being to have the solemn rite performed with as little show of ostentation, and with as few of the rules and regulations of conventional society as possible. Both bride and bridesmaid were attired in simple yet rich and quietly elegant costumes, and the bridegroom, dressed in becoming spotless white, showed remarkable good sense in securing ease and comfort at no sacrifice of elegance.‡

Little's career prospered and by the 1890s he was at the height of his powers – with a civil income second only to that of Charles Todd,

---

* *The Express and Telegraph*, 24 August 1871.

† Blanche Little married John Kennedy Gibson of the E.E.A. and C. Telegraph Company on 9 May 1899 when she was 28 years old (*NTTG*, 12 May 1899).

‡ *NTTG*, 4 March 1892

his boss in Adelaide. Apart from Superintendent of Telegraphs and Postmaster, Little was a Justice of the Peace and Deputy Sheriff with duties that included the clean and efficient legal execution of those on death-row.

Little was also the Chief Inspecting Officer for the northern part of the Overland Telegraph Line and part of his outstanding record of service was the annual line inspection of his entire section. He personally supervised the replacement of old wooden telegraph poles with metal *Oppenheimer* poles and the installation of a copper wire in 1898. The latter was necessary to manage the increasing telegraphic traffic to and from Europe, and the efficiency of copper, compared to the original galvanised steel wire made it worth the extra expense. Copper is a soft metal, and it needed a 'new patent process for binding it round the insulator so as to reduce breakages to a minimum'.§ It was installed by departmental employees,¶ rather than contractors, because 'copper wire requires more delicate handling than iron, and skilled wiremen [were] employed for the work'.** This also allowed Little to maintain control of the process.

Each annual inspection required travelling by horse for 1,500 kilometres or more, as far south as Attack Creek and this was, according to his obituary, a 'feat which spoke volumes for his energy and vitality'.†† In fact, it was no mean feat at all: Little was not small, eventually weighing in at more than 17 stone (109 kilograms) and it was said that it took two men to get him into his saddle – one for a leg-up, and the other to stop the saddle from slipping around the horse.

Considering how unforgiving the Territory bush is to those who are ill-prepared, Little's success is remarkable. Others, like a traveller named Charles Sayle for example, found themselves in difficulties.

---

§ *NTTG*, 19 August 1898.
¶ One of whom, Alfred Pybus, lies in a lonely grave near Powell Creek Telegraph Station. Pybus worked on the OTL for 29 years.
** *South Australian Register*, 5 July 1898.
†† *Observer*, 26 May 1906.

Sayle died of thirst near Attack Creek in 1893 and Little recorded that the 'deceased had apparently tried to cut the wire, as the insulator was much broken'.*

Little died in 1906, at the age of 63, after nearly 50 years of public service. An injury caused by the chaffing of a boot nail to his foot became gangrenous:

> ... two doctors arrived at the conclusion that Mr. Little was sinking and could not live more than a few days. The verdict came as a shock to his family and many friends, as he had never complained, and was generally regarded as being an exceptionally robust and strong man for his years. Mr. Little received the news of his serious state with courage and resignation, and as stated, he passed away calmly and peacefully a few minutes after 1 p.m. on Monday, the 21st inst… Immediately upon the news of Mr. Little's death becoming known all the flags in town were half masted.†

His remains lie in the Pioneer Cemetery on Goyder Road in Darwin not far from Paul Foelsche. His gravestone, which lies flat on the ground under a large marble carved cross, is now stained black from the annual wet season algal growth.

Governor Kintore

Figure 10: Lord Kintore 1890 (SLSA B-5986).

The South Australian Governor of the early 1890s was not an ordinary man.‡ His Excellency the Right Honourable Algernon Hawkins Thomond was the Earl of Kintore, Lord Falconer of Halkerton, Lord Keith of Inverurie, Knight Grand Cross of the Most Distinguished Order of St. Michael and St. George, Governor, and Commander-in-Chief in and over the Province of South Australia and the Dependencies thereof, etcetera. He was the only governor to visit the

---

* *South Australian Register*, 3 October 1893.
† *NTTG*, 25 May 1906.
‡ Lord Kintore was in office from April 1889 to April 1895.

Northern Territory in the nineteenth century – and what a visit! He arrived in Port Darwin by steamer, then travelled overland back to Adelaide in what was, for the time, a remarkable feat for anyone, let alone the Queen's representative in the colony.

Kintore arrived in Palmerston on 31 March 1891. The lookout at the Fannie Bay Gaol saw the S.S. *Chingtu* approaching just before noon and raised his flag. Government Resident Knight then steamed out in the *Victoria* to meet her, and by the time the party arrived at the jetty, every flag and bunting in the colony was 'having an airing' to welcome the distinguished visitor. On the jetty, the governor was bundled into a railway carriage and shunted 300 metres to a welcome reception at Palmerston's tiny railway station, which was so heavily festooned there were quips about 'so much decoration for so little house.'

A large crowd had gathered for the welcome. All the heads of the civil departments were there with their staff, plus the merchants, railwaymen, businesspeople, and the society ladies of the town. Importantly, the crowd included many Chinese residents, because they saw the governor's visit as an opportunity to present their case for greater acceptance and equality in the community. A Chinese procession of 'gorgeous concomitants added great colour to the scene.'

A reception committee had been organised a week or so before and its chairperson, Herbert Adcock, was ready with his welcome speech:

> … We congratulate your Excellency on being the first Australian Governor who has undertaken a journey of such magnitude, and we cannot refrain from admiring your determination to enter upon a labour which will not fail to produce results of material advantage, not only to this Territory, but also to South Australia as a whole.*

His Excellency was, of course, pleased to receive such a welcome and 'conveyed a hope that the acquaintance so happily begun would ripen during his stay here and continue harmoniously to the end' and

---

* *NTTG*, 3 April 1891.

he was:

> ... sincerely thankful for the loyal sentiments expressed in the address towards the gracious lady whom he had the honour to represent as Governor of this colony and who had guided the destinies of the British Empire for so long and with such true devotion to the interests of her subjects in all parts of the world.*

The Governor spent the first few days of his tour inspecting the government departments and sites of interest around Palmerston. He was escorted through the Overland Telegraph Office by Superintendent John Little, visited the leper colony in the harbour and the Botanic Gardens, and attended a meeting of the Archery Club. Then a banquet was held in his honour at The Residency,† and the Governor enjoyed the entertainment provided by an Aboriginal dance group. When he spoke, Governor Kintore was upbeat about the Territory's future, and particularly encouraged the farming of horses. Shipments of 500 horses were already being sent to the British military in India from Adelaide. Kintore:

> ... it seems to me, gentlemen, that what Adelaide can do you ought to be able to do better.‡

Governor Kintore was aware of the Territory's predicament when it came to distances involved and the climate. He knew, for instance, that imported workers were needed to cultivate tobacco, sugar and 'tropical products generally', because 'white labour cannot work with profit.' But most South Australians, 2,000 miles to the south, were unaware of the Territory's difficulties. His advice to the Territorians was to work with the coming federal government which he believed would be 'in existence ere long'. The Territory would, he assured them, be advantaged by a federal government in the place of

---

* *NTTG*, 3 April 1891.
† Mrs Margaret Hopewell won the tender to supply the banquet at 27s. per head. The tickets cost 30s. Chinese people were excluded but they solved this by having their own banquet a few days later (*NTTG* 13 March 1891).
‡ *NTTG*, 3 April 1891.

Figure 11: Earl Kintore (seated near the middle of the boat) on a trip to the Adelaide River on the S.S. *Victoria*, 1891. The boat's owner, Hildebrand Stevens is at the stern, while Dr Stirling is in the bow (Foelsche, SLSA B-5054).

the South Australian State Government.*

A trip to the Adelaide River on the S.S. *Victoria* over the weekend followed and, as soon as the Governor returned, he agreed to attend another banquet, this time presented by Chinese community leaders, who had not been invited to the earlier welcome.

The *North Australian* reported that the Chinese banquet was 'an exact counterpart of the European treat, allowing, of course, for the racial exception'.† The paper was magnanimous in its praise for the banquet's organisation, particularly by the chairman, Arthur Hang

---

* This is the earliest comment from a high official about the Territory being taken over by the Federal Government I can find. It was 10 years before federation, and 20 years before South Australia relinquished control of Territory affairs.

† *North Australian*, 17 April 1891. The 20 Chinese in attendance were: Kwong Yee Loong, Yet Loong, Doong Hing Chong, A. Hang Gong, Wing Sang Tong, Yot Sing, Hem Hai Yick, Quon Chong Chan, Kung Hing, Sin Mow Loong, T. Hang Gong, Kwong Wah Shing, Kwong Hang Foong, Kwong Lee Chong, Sin Tee Lee, Sue Loong, Sin Wah Loong, Mau Fong Law, Wing Woh Loong, and Wo Yuen.

Gong, and vice chair, Thomas Chock Tong, but it was dismissive of their orations:

> ... With the exception of the Governor's speech none of the oratory was worth much, and our time and space being both pretty fully occupied this week with other matters.[*]

The next week's paper was more forthcoming. Hang Gong had toasted the governor, and in his speech reminded the Europeans present of the contribution the Chinese were making to the colony:

> ... although the Chinese form the bulk of the population and contribute in large measure to the finances of the colony, they do not seek a voice in the Government of the place, being satisfied that the common fairness and justice worldwide attributed to the British, and of which they as a nation are so justly proud, will be extended to themselves...

Earl Kintore was grateful for the time and expense the Chinese had undertaken to entertain him. He offered his sympathy for the difficulties their compatriots were facing in the eastern states, where governments were placing limits on their numbers and passing increasingly anti-Chinese legislation in an attempt for Australians to remain a white society. But he consoled them:

> ... at least you can take pleasure in remembering that there exist no more honourable, law-abiding, and industrious citizens than the Chinese, and that you heard the head of the Government cheerfully own the fact; you may pride yourselves on having had the greatest share in the development of the Northern Territory, so far as it has gone; you can assure your friends that, but for you, Palmerston would have but few European residents; and you can go forward in the prosecution of your several callings remembering that the assistance of those Chinese who are here is becoming more valued than ever.[†]

Kintore was a proponent for Asiatic Labour. In a later report, he wrote that the development of the Territory depended on Asians. 'Indian coolie or other Asiatic labour' was essential, although he

---

[*] *North Australian*, 10 April 1891.
[†] *NTTG*, 10 April 1891.

Figure 12: Earl Kintore's travelling party at the Hotel Playford in Pine Creek. The Governor is wearing a solar topee beside the first buggy. Dr. E.C. Stirling stands beside the second buggy (9 April 1891, Foelsche, SLSA, B 5057).

agreed with the notion that numbers had to be limited. After all, he concluded, the white colonists across Australia had to be careful not to be 'overrun by an alien race'.*

If the Governor was in the Territory to see what was wrong within it, 'and report to the Imperial authorities his deductions', the *Times* was disappointed. The newspaper complained that the Governor saw little of the settled districts of the Territory other than Goldsborough's station on the Adelaide River.

The Governor left Palmerston on 8 April. He was joined by Professor Stirling, Inspector Foelsche, and Alfred Pybus, who was in charge of the expedition,† in a special train to the Union Goldfield. Foelsche was there as much in the role as photographer as head of the police.

Kintore spent an hour inspecting the Union mines before moving to Pine Creek, and that was all – the *Times* complained that the districts between Palmerston and the Union:

... were inspected from the railway carriages going at a special

---

* SAPP, 75/1891.
† Alfred Pybus was an experienced Territorian who was an original worker on the Overland Telegraph Line in 1872, and who had subsequently been a member of the Telegraph Department since 1873. He worked 'on the line' for 29 years and is buried next to Powell Creek Telegraph Station, where he died in 1900 (see obituary *NTTG*, 13 April 1900).

rate of about 20 miles an hour. His Excellency's report to the Home authorities should, therefore, as far as his personal observations go, be worth, very little. Let us hope he will not go the length of writing a book on the Territory.*

In Katherine, the Governor and his party stayed with Alfred Giles at Springvale Homestead. Whilst there, Kintore was approached by a steward from the Katherine River Sportsmen's Club and asked for financial patronage of a forthcoming race in the annual horse races. Kintore agreed and promised he would supply some funds the next day, but Kintore had already left by the time the steward returned, so his companion, Professor Stirling handed him some cash in Kintore's name.† The steward's jaw must have dropped in surprise. It was just thirty shillings – a paltry amount for a horserace prize. Nevertheless, it was posted, and in recognition of Kintore's poor generosity, the club organised a donkey race called the Kintore Stakes. It was advertised in the *Times*:

> Notice Extraordinary: Katherine Donkey Race, value 30s., donated jointly by Lord Kintore and Dr. Stirling. Last horse, £1; first horse, 10s. Distance 1 mile; catch weights.

In the same edition the *Times* published a poem outlining Kintore's journey that made mention of the race:

> But they, rising to the occasion, and taking heart of grace,
> Included in their programme a 'novel Donkey Race'
> Where the winner of the *Kintore Stakes* should be adjudged to be
> The animal that came in last – and furthermore that he
> Should from the fund receive one pound, and the unlucky moke,
> that came in first, should get ten bob to emphasize the joke!‡

Many were convinced that Kintore must have been insulted and something should be done. *The Advertiser* called for Government

---

* *NTTG*, 10 April 1891.
† Thirty shillings, coincidentally, was also the cost of a ticket for attending the public banquet held in Kintore's honour in Port Darwin just weeks earlier.
‡ 'A Taxpayer' *NTTG*, 15 May 1891. See Appendix 1 for the entire ballad.

Figure 13: Earl Kintore and party at Union Reef Goldfield, Northern Territory: 8 April 1891. Kintore on extreme right and Dr E.C. Stirling fourth from right (Foelsche, SLSA B-17094).

Resident Knight to cancel his patronage of the Katherine Turf Club,* but Kintore refused to recognise the insult – he was, after all, travelling across the continent while the arguments raged.

John Knight had been pleased to see the back of the Governor. In letters to his family, he complained of the expense of the visit – much of the banquet had been paid for out of his 'salary', and he also had to pay for the renovations and furnishings of The Residency so that it would be a suitable accommodation for a Queen's representative.†

Professor Edward Stirling

Figure 14: Professor Edward Stirling (SASL).

Professor Edward Charles Stirling, the Governor's travelling companion, joined the journey on a scientific mission. Dr Stirling was, among many other things, a medical doctor, surgeon, university lecturer, a member of the South Australian Legislative Assembly, the first President of the State Children's Council, chairman of the South Australian Museum committee and honorary

---

* *The Advertiser*, 30 May 1891.
† Letter to Emily, daughter-in-law, 31 December 1890 (Wilson et al 1994).

Figure 15: Dr Edward Stirling, holding the rifle, 'alligator' shooting on the Adelaide River in March 1891. Museum collector Thomas Cormack holds the axe, Hildebrand Stevens (Foelsche's future son-in-law) has the pipe, a Djerimanga elder named Lamaby stands on the right, the man on the left is unidentified (Foelsche, SLSA B-5058).

director of the museum.

Stirling arrived in Port Darwin early. He had several weeks to fill before the Governor arrived, and he was 'fully determined to make the most of his time before His Excellency the Governor call[ed] him to attention'.* He made several field trips and his enthusiasm for the north was soon legendary. The longest excursion was a trip with Inspector Foelsche to the Adelaide River and Port Essington in the S.S. *Victoria*, owned by Hildebrand Stevens.

Stirling was accompanied by a taxidermist and collector named Thomas Cormack, and they went 'to shoot everything that can walk, creep or fly'.† This, of course, included 'alligators' (crocodiles), 'numerous members of the feathered creation, fish of many varieties, reptiles, insects, shells, and the indispensable bundles of native implements, domestic as well as war like'.

During the journey overland, Stirling continued to collect flora and fauna. He made several notable discoveries, such as the marsupial mole (*Notoryctes typhlops*), and a large deposit of fossil bones in Lake

---

*   *NTTG*, 27 March 1871.
†   *NTTG*, 6 March 1891.

Figure 16: Professor Edward Stirling and an unidentified man in the spear grass at Knuckey's Lagoon on 14 March 1891 (Foelsche, SLSA, B 5055).

Callabonna, from which he later reconstructed a complete diprotodon skeleton.* He also collected human remains from Aboriginal burial sites, some of which were shipped to overseas institutions.†

Premier Thomas Playford

Figure 17: Thomas 'Honest Tom' Playford, (1900 SLSA, B-11139).

The Honourable Thomas 'Honest Tom' Playford, Premier of South Australia and the Northern Territory in 1891-2, was a traveller. He had not long been in office, for this, his second time in the role, when he and Mrs Playford went on a study tour of India, Hong Kong, Singapore, and Canton. They returned to Australia on the S.S. *Taiyuan* and arrived in Palmerston unexpectedly – no one knew that he was on the *Taiyuan* when she slipped quietly into Port Darwin on 1 April 1892, a full day before she was due.

---

*   Stirling's career was long. In 1894 he was the medical officer and anthropologist of the Horn Scientific Expedition to Central Australia. In 1895 he was appointed director of the Adelaide Museum in 1895, and professor of physiology at Adelaide university 1900. He died on 20 March 1919.

†   Times have changed, and many of these are now being repatriated to their descendants for burial, 130 years after their 'collection.'

Management

His presence put the senior public servants in a fluster. They missed hosting a formal welcome, but managed to rally round and introduce themselves, nevertheless. Inspector Foelsche loaned the premier the police dray, and he and Mrs Playford then drove themselves 'from sea to shore' and 'were soon in top-storey lodgings at Mrs Ryan's North Australian Hotel, where they propose to remain until they depart for home'.*

Playford presented himself as an expert on soil and spent several days travelling about with Inspector Foelsche and Government Gardener Nicholas Holtze to inspect it. When they visited the defunct sugar plantations at Delissaville on the Government launch, *Maggie*, the Premier ran the clay through his hands and tut-tutted about the foolhardiness of trying to grow sugar in such poor soils. The same happened at Sergison's plantations on the Adelaide River floodplain. Playford wrote: 'Considering that sugarcane requires the richest of soil if it is to be grown successfully, it was simply throwing away the money of the shareholders to attempt to grow sugarcane on such land'.

The plantations were long gone, so his conclusions were correct, but unnecessary. While on the floodplains he also toured the abandoned Beatrice Hill Coffee Plantation and made similar disparaging comments about the folly of planting coffee in that area.

More usefully, Playford was interested in enterprises that had not failed. He was thrilled to see the Botanic Gardens which reflected 'great credit upon the late curator and his son, who is at present in charge'. He was particularly impressed with the new plantations of coconut trees. He reported:

> ... I was pleased to see the excellent growth made by the cocoanut palm, which should be extensively planted on the sandy beaches, of which there is a large area near Palmerston.
>
> The curator informed me that he is growing, and intends in future to grow, a large quantity and as they transplant well, to

---

* *NTTG*, 8 April 1892

plant them on suitable sites. This is the most valuable of all the palms, bears seven years from planting, and would become an important export in future years if extensively planted. I would recommend that the Government encourage the planting of this palm by a liberal supply of funds to the curator.*

He went to the Daly River area in the *Maggie* to view the Jesuit Mission, the Daly Copper Mine, and the Chinese gardens belonging to 'some members of the great An family' who were 'working a lovely plot of land'.† At last, Playford was impressed with the soil. He saw a strip of excellent sandy alluvial soil along the river which he thought would be good for rice. It was rich and easily irrigated from the river and he expressed a hope that promoting agriculture there would pull the Territory from its economic malaise.

Playford then visited the Katherine region, including the gold mining areas of Maude Creek and Pine Creek, 'the beautiful Katherine Gorge', Springvale, the Kintore Caves, and Rum Jungle. He recommended that £200 be expended to repair the roads and creek crossings he experienced near Pine Creek. He caught the train back to Palmerston, via Rum Jungle (now Batchelor), where he viewed more failed ventures – Poett's Coffee Plantation and Brandt's 'equally defunct tobacco farm'. They had been grown in soils that were patently no good without 'heavy manuring', although the 'rubber and mango trees [were] looking well', he thought. Playford concluded that plantation agriculture in most of the Top End had an unlikely future:

> ... There are numerous small areas of good land scattered through the Territory fit for gardens, but they are limited in size from one acre to thirty or forty, and are in no one place, except the one marked upon the map, sufficient for a good-sized plantation.‡

Playford had high hopes for agriculture in the lower Daly River region, but he thought pastoralism would be more 'profitable and

---

* *NTTG*, 11 November 1892.
† *NTTG*, 15 April 1892.
‡ *NTTG*, 15 April 1892.

the mainstay of the Territory' in the years to come. Both industries, however, needed people to work them.

Having only just visited India, Playford proposed populating the area with Indian plantation workers. An experimental colony of Indian farmers might have proved fruitful and Playford could see no difficulty in recruiting any number of 'good practical Hindu farmers to cultivate blocks in the Territory', although their supervisors would need to be chosen carefully:

> ... the success of the undertaking rested a great deal in the fitness and reliability of the overseer who will have charge of the black colony. If we secure a good man, the settlement will be a success; if we happen to get a bad supervisor it will result in failure. As to the right class of Hindu for the purpose... the Tamil from Madras was far and away the most suitable. These were intelligent, industrious, cleanly in habits, and persevering, and were in every sense well qualified to test the experiment that South Australia has set her heart so much upon.*

The Playfords travelled back to Adelaide by steamer in early May after a month in the Top End. The cut and thrust of the South Australian Government being what it was in the late nineteenth century, 'Honest Tom' was deposed as Premier a few weeks later, so nothing ever came from his musings on an Indian colony at Daly River.† Nor was it likely to: the Indian Government was not keen on letting their citizens be shipped to a foreign shore, at least not without the appointment of an Agent-General selected by themselves. They would not legalize emigration to the Northern Territory if the Government Resident was to oversee the migrants there:

> ... It is considered necessary for the welfare of Indian labourers that the officer appointed to be Immigration Agent-General

---

* *NTTG*, 15 April 1892.
† The idea of building a colony of workers continued. In 1898, a plan to colonize land at Victoria River with Japanese workers was canned after the introduction 'White Australia Policies' brought in after Federation that included English (or other European) Language tests for immigrants, designed to ensure that only white men and women made it to Australia (*Evening News*, 18 June 1898).

should be responsible to the Indian Government, and that he should so fully understand the language, the customs, and the prejudices of the immigrants as to be able by timely and intelligent representations to protect them against any kind of oppression or ill-treatment.*

Brown, Adcock, and Brown

Community leaders in the 1890s include several merchants who are worth mentioning because their business interests and involvement in the community touched every aspect of life in the young colony. It is a rare Territory newspaper of the 1800s that does not mention one or all of them. They appear everywhere from court reports as jury members, to committee notices ranging from the Debating Society to the Northern Territory Racing Club.

By 1890, Victor Voules 'Daddy' Brown, Herbert Henry Adcock, and John Alexander Voules Brown were three of the leading merchants in Palmerston, with decades of experience behind them. V.V. Brown arrived in 1876 to manage the business affairs of V.L. Solomon's brother, M. J. Solomon, but in 1879 he set up his own business. In 1880, he also became a junior partner in H.H. Adcock and Co, which Herbert started in Southport with his brother William (who had also worked for Solomon).

Victor Brown's younger brother John came to help when Victor contracted to build Fannie Bay Gaol in 1882. Five years later, John joined a new company, *Brown, Adcock, and Brown*, and they took over Solomon's Mart. The brothers and Herbert Adcock were importers, customs and shipping agents, insurance agents for Lloyds, auctioneers, and from January 1888, their store also became a bonded warehouse for Her Majesty's Customs. By 1891, their business interests grew to include the AMP Society, Leviathan Tin Co, Daly Proprietary Copper Co, and the Alice Hills Gold Mine. When a depression loomed on the horizon in 1894, John decided to leave the partnership and return to

---

* Governor-General of India to Lord Kintore, *Evening Journal*, 21 September 1891.

Western Australia.* Two years later the business went into voluntary liquidation:

> … As a trading concern the company is now, to all intents and purposes dead, and it is a serious reflection on the colony that such concerns should find it necessary to close their doors… at one time it gave great promise of returning large profits… however, of late, dull times attacked the company in a vital part and hence its downfall.†

There was an insolvency hearing where Adcock and V.V. Brown were criticised by the judge for their business dealings and they were both punished; Adcock was suspended from business for nine months, Brown for six months, and the company's assets were sold off. The Brown's Mart building was advertised either for sale or rent at £50 per annum and E.O. Robinson seems to have held the lease for this period. But after his six months suspension, Brown returned to the Mart:

> …Our estimable townsman Mr Victor Voules Brown has arisen superior to his recent misfortune and this week presents his business card to all and sundry. This time he is launching out 'on his own' in a line well within his experience and his undoubted popularity should guarantee him a solid slice of whatever trade is going.‡

Figure 18: V.V. Brown.

V.V. Brown lived in the Territory for 34 years. Jenny Rich, in a history of Brown's Mart, listed his achievements. He:

> …built Fannie Bay Gaol (in 1882) and Christ Church (in 1902); he was also a Councillor, Chairman and Clerk of Palmerston District Council, local agent for Eastern and Australian Steam Ship Co., President of the Northern Territory Reform Association, foundation

---

* J.A.V. Brown, who already had business interests in Western Australia, opened a branch of Adcock's Store in Derby in 1885. Years later, he returned to Palmerston and was elected to represent the Northern Territory in the South Australian Parliament in 1910, following the path of V.L. Solomon. He died in 1945.

† *NTTG*, 28 February 1896.

‡ *NTTG*, 28 February 1896.

President of the Northern Territory Racing Club…member of the Board of Advice for the local school, member of the local Church of England congregation and an office bearer of many local sporting and community groups….In the early 1900s he became known as 'Daddy Brown'.*

Browns Mart was damaged during the 1897 cyclone, losing its roof and part of a wall, but within six months it was repaired and again open for business. Brown remained in business until his death in 1910, aged 69, when his eldest son, Emanuel Victor Voules Brown (1866-1950) took over. V.V. Brown was described in his obituary as 'the most popular and widely known resident of the Northern Territory':

> … Mr. Brown had been ailing for a few days, but the end was quite unexpected. The deceased was a leading spirit in sport and athletics and identified himself with all matters pertaining to the welfare of the Northern Territory. His death is lamented by a wide circle of friends throughout Australia. Mr. Brown left a widow, six sons, and four daughters… He was equally beloved by the Asiatics and the natives.†

Herbert Adcock's life in the Top End was also one of community engagement. He was Palmerston District Council Chairman and Counsellor for many years between 1884 and 1892, and a member of the Board of Health for seven years. As secretary for the North Australian League, Adcock was at the forefront of the fight to get Territory representatives in the South Australian Parliament, and he stood for election himself in 1901 (though he was defeated by Samuel Mitchell). He was also chairman of the Reform Association that examined schools in Palmerston, worked as secretary on many committees, such as the Cricket Club, Melbourne Centenary Exhibition Committee, the Palmerston Institute and Northern Territory Racing Club. He was also a relief-editor and sub-editor of the *Northern Territory Times*.

---

* Rich, 1988.
† *Chronicle*, 26 February 1910.

Adcock's biographer* concludes that his businesses were never outstanding in their success, but his was a life of public-spirited optimism. His last few months were unfortunately spent in Palmerston hospital. He died there, on 28 February 1908, lauded by the citizens of Palmerston.

Kirkland, Mayhew, and The Newspapers

Editors of newspapers have a unique chance to voice their opinions on any matters they wish. Everything from editorials to headlines and the choice of articles for publication sets the agenda for a wide audience. They can therefore influence the thoughts and behavior of a population, even to the extent of influencing the outcomes of elections – as modern politicians certainly know. They also report the news and supply a record of events in their community that we can easily access many decades later.

Editors with integrity certainly respect their power. As Charles Kirkland was to reminisce in 1930:

> ... During the whole of my career as a journalist I endeavoured to conduct the paper in accord with the best traditions of honest journalism and I never knowingly published a malicious or misleading statement designed to hurt the feelings or injure the reputation of anyone. Any criticism of public affairs in which I indulged was so far as my limited capacity permitted conferred within the bounds of common sense and reason.†

Two newspapers vied for supremacy in Palmerston at the beginning of the 1890s: the *Northern Territory Times* and *Government Gazette* and the *North Australian*. The *Times* was the elder of the two, having been established by Richard Wells as the first mechanically printed N.T. newspaper, in November 1873.‡ The *Times* was

---

* Wilson, 2008, *NT Dictionary of Biography*.
† *Northern Territory Times*, 18 July 1930.
‡ There was an earlier paper. Two members of the survey party of 1869 produced a small hand-written and 'roneoed' broadsheet called *The Moonta Herald* and *Northern Territory Gazette*. Six issues were printed, five of them on the way to

Palmerston's sole newspaper for a decade, owned and edited for most of that time by Joseph Skelton. It had the contract to print the *Government Gazette*.

In 1881, with failing eyesight, Skelton employed two young 'journalists' to run the paper for him; Charles Kirkland,* and an 18-year-old 'compositor' named George Washington Mayhew, as his assistant. Joseph Skelton sold the *Times* to Vaiben L. Solomon due to ill-health in 1885.

The *North Australian* was launched in competition to the *Times* by E.O. Echlin on 1 June 1883 and Echlin recruited Mayhew to work with him. Echlin left in 1886, and Mayhew was joined by Kirkland in a partnership that lasted about 10 years. In June 1889, they managed to wrestle the contract for the *Gazette* from the *Times* to become the *North Australian and Northern Territory Government Gazette*, which ran until 1890. Solomon relinquished his control of the *Times* when he ran for parliament to his partner, Walter Griffiths, who then quickly joined forces with his brother-in-law, George Washington Mayhew and his partner Charles Kirkland and merged the two Palmerston papers together. Griffiths withdrew when he also ran for parliament in 1893.

The Mayhew-Kirkland partnership worked well until 1896, when Kirkland joined the pearl shell industry. George Mayhew stayed at the helm of the *Times* until ill health from 'rheumatics' drove him south in 1900. He was farewelled in style by his friends, the leading businessmen of the town and others, who showed their appreciation with speeches and a useful purse of donated sovereigns, presented by members of the Palmerston Brass Band and the Racing Club. After Mayhew's departure, Kirkland once again became the sole editor and proprietor of the paper, a position he then held for the next 17 years.

Darwin Harbour in the S.S. *Moonta*, and the sixth on 24 February 1869, three weeks after arrival. Each issue was later professionally typeset and re-published in Adelaide.

* Farram, 2017.

Mayhew and Kirkland did not necessarily agree on every subject the newspapers broached, but they were united in their racist views on Chinese residents and Aboriginal people. As we shall see in a later chapter, they reflected the Euro-centric racism of the times, but more than that, as newspaper editors, they gave it currency and a legitimacy that we find shocking over a century later.

Darwin: Survival of a City

Chapter 2

Representation: Parsons, Solomon, and Griffiths

As Premier of South Australia, Thomas Playford's management of the Northern Territory fell during its 'white elephant' days. While the opposition to the cost of the Territory's development and its growing debt became insurmountable, Playford exhibited scant political interest. There were, however, three politicians who had a greater and longer lasting influence on the Territory than the peripatetic Premier Playford. Each of Parsons, Solomon, and Griffiths had lived long in the Territory before winning elections to represent it in parliament. They therefore led, for better or worse, from the heart:

John Langdon Parsons

Figure 19: John Langdon Parsons (SLSA B-6725-9).

John Langdon Parsons was an ex-clergyman and career politician who was a conscientious and enthusiastic supporter of the Territory's development. As South Australian Minister for Education and the Territory, he made a horseback journey around the colony in 1882 that lay the groundwork for his appointment as the Government Resident, announced on 15 March 1884.*

---

* For the full story see *Darwin: Growth of a City* (Pugh, 2021).

Parsons' support was a key element of many of the developments such as the railway, throughout the 1880s. He personally introduced the *Palmerston and Pine Creek Railway Bill* to the Legislative Assembly on 17 July 1884, and two years later, after he was appointed Government Resident, the railway was built on his watch. Some historians consider Parsons to be the best of all the government residents[*] but unfortunately, he was not a lawyer or judge. That role, during Parsons' tenure, needed to be filled by a second highly paid public servant – Justice Thomas Pater.

As South Australia entered a recession towards the end of the 1880s, issues arose about the cost of the senior management in the Territory and the Northern Territory budget and salary costs were radically trimmed. For example: the Survey Department budget lost £1,250; the Government cutter, the S.S. *Palmerston* was sold; all civil servants lost their professional allowances; and the Protector of Aborigines, Dr Morice was retrenched. The Government also planned to save money by combining the roles of resident and judge, so both Parsons and Pater were recalled. The plan was delayed when the architect John Knight took the role, but Justice Dashwood was a better fit, and he remained in charge for 13 years.

Once again free to enter the House, Parsons won a seat to represent the Northern Territory, along with Vaiben Solomon. He held the seat for a single term, from 1890 to 1893 and his most important endeavour, in those years, was to consider Aboriginal land rights. He unsuccessfully tried to convince the Government to create Aboriginal reserves, and to ensure fair payment and conditions for Aboriginal workers.

In later years, Parsons spent time as ambassador to Japan, and worked as a member of the United Labour Party and Australasian National League. Parsons died suddenly in Adelaide in 1903 of 'heart trouble'[†] and the Territory lost a great friend and a talented

---

[*] De la rue, 2004.

[†] In his later years, Parsons spent time as ambassador to Japan, and worked as a

man, was considered one of the best speakers in the South Australian Parliament.

Vaiben L. Solomon

Figure 20: Vaiben Louis Solomon.

Vaiben Louis Solomon arrived in the Territory in 1873, initially as part of the goldrush, and quickly joined the social elite of the new colony. He was a popular man, and as a founding member of the Palmerston District Council, he had his first taste of politics.

Solomon was an energetic man whose business ventures began to enter every part of the colony. In 1877, he went into business on Mitchell Street as an auctioneer and shipping agent importing anything that the settlement and gold miners needed. In 1885, he bought the *NT Times and Gazette*, and owned and edited it until 1890. Some called him 'Black Solomon', after he blackened himself to resemble an Aboriginal person and walked naked through the town for a dare, and later 'Sudden Solomon', from the speed of his political promotions.* Other men called him 'Mr Everything' as his interests expanded into mining investment and the pearling industry – not always successfully, but by joining with a new partner, Walter Griffiths, in 1888, Solomon's influence increased. With a reputation as 'a ready and witty debater of more than average ability', Solomon called for economic development of the Territory. Despite this, he decried the presence of the Chinese community – advocating the total exclusion of Asians whilst championing the Adelaide to Palmerston railway, for which Chinese workers would have undoubtedly been necessary.

In 1893, Solomon was re-elected, and he was joined by his

---

member of the United Labour Party and Australasian National League (*The Register*, 22 August 1903).

* Apple, 2010.

friend and business partner, Walter Griffiths. The total polling in 1893 was Solomon 272, Griffiths 188, Stow 143, and Coward 11. The results of the election reflect the small population of the Territory and the fact that women, Aboriginal people, and Chinese people and other aliens were not entitled to vote. By the next election in 1896, 'in consequence of the woman's franchise'* South Australian women had won the right to vote. Nonetheless, the total number of votes changed little – Solomon with 239 and Griffiths with 199 votes prevailed again, against another old Territorian, Fred Finniss with 89 votes.†

Solomon remained in Adelaide for the rest of his career, continuing to be a staunch supporter of his electorate. With a forceful personality he was government whip for Playford's government in 1890-91 and again for Downer in 1893. By 1899, he was the leader of the conservative opposition, which brought down the Kingston administration in November that year, and he became Premier and Treasurer on 1 December – the only Territorian to achieve such high office in South Australia, and incidentally, the only Jew to ever have been a premier of an Australian state.

However, by 8 December Solomon's government was defeated. His term as premier (8 days) is still the shortest in the state's history‡ and, although he lived another eight years, he never again held a ministry.§ Solomon did not live an orthodox Jewish life, though as a member of the 1897 constitutional convention he objected to Saturday sittings on the grounds of religious conviction, despite his own office being open on a Saturday.

Solomon's ongoing legacy in Darwin includes the continued existence of a small porcellanitic stone building on Smith Street that

---

*   *NTTG*, 1 May 1896
†   Fred Finniss's father had been the government resident at the ill-planned Escape Cliffs settlement in 1864 (see Pugh 2018a).
‡   Donovan, 1990 (online 2022).
§   Incidentally, Solomon's death at 55 from cancer resulted in a by-election for the Northern Territory in 1908 and one of the candidates was a lawyer named Egbert Percy Graham Little, son of John Little, the superintendent of telegraphs.

currently houses the Brown's Mart Theatre. This building, designed by John Knight, was built by Solomon in 1885, using Chinese labour, and was across the road from the Town Hall, which was built of the same local stone:

> ... it is to be hoped that this example will be followed by others and permanent stone buildings soon replace most of the somewhat frail structures of wood and iron which have hitherto satisficed [sic] the ambitions of our local builders.*

In 1885, the *Times* editor hoped that the building would be 'an ornament to the street'.† It was 'the largest and finest stone store yet raised in Palmerston'‡ and for two years Solomon used it as a store, an auction house, and offices for his agency and mining interests. He sold out to V.V. Brown, H.H. Adcock and J.A.V. Brown in September 1887. The building is now known as Brown's Mart and is one of the few structures in Darwin to have survived from the 1800s. It is, indeed, an 'ornament to the street', just as Solomon had hoped.

Walter Griffiths

Walter Griffiths was Solomon's partner in a number of mining ventures in the Territory and Western Australia. He was the nephew of William 'Old Billy' Griffiths, a gold miner on numerous claims around the Union Goldfield and a storekeeper at Grove Hill until 1892.

Walter Griffiths was often the high scorer in cricket matches played in Palmerston, and he was an eager participant in the Debating and Literary Society. in 1893, he was elected to represent the NT and, at 25 years old, he was the youngest Member of Parliament. In his maiden speech, Griffiths showed a disdain for education, which was at odds with many of his senior colleagues:

> ... In the policy of economy and retrenchment the Government might have economised in the Education

---

* *NTTG*, 17 January 1885.
† *NTTG*, 21 February 1885.
‡ *NTTG*, 27 June 1885.

Department. The annual cost of £146,000 was far too exorbitant. The system was too comprehensive, and it was tending to give people an ambition above their own sphere and educating them to a height which they were physically incapable of attaining, and it was causing much of the present feeling of unrest.[*]

His battles in the house included: an attempt to establish a meat freezing works in Darwin; a demand that pearl shelling licences be reserved for Europeans, not given to Japanese; the sinking of wells throughout central Australia; support for the Territory mining industry; the construction of a transcontinental railway; the duplication of the Overland Telegraph Line; the Redwater fever tick problems in the pastoral industry and resultant embargoes from the states; and many other challenges of the day. Griffith's support for the mining industry was personal – he had, after all, grown up on the goldfields. It was he who bought the only diamond found in the Cullen River in 1894. Joe Johnstone, from the Telegraph Department, had taken charge of it, and it was sent to England to be cut. It returned a three-carat stone set in a ring that Griffiths paid £45 for in Adelaide.

Griffiths, like his peers, was vocally anti-Chinese, preferring to promote and subsidise European ventures before allowing Chinese workers to take them over. Conversely, in 1898, it was his motion that, in a vote against Vaiben Solomon, threw out the *Immigration Prohibition Bill* of that year.

Griffiths had great influence throughout the Territory because he travelled widely, twice overlanding from Marree to Palmerston by camel and horse. He visited Borroloola, Alice Springs and Tennant Creek several times to talk to constituents, because, he said:

> ... he considered that no man should allow himself to be put forward as a candidate for any constituency unless he had first gone to the trouble of gaining a knowledge of the wants of the whole of the district he proposed to represent.[†]

---

[*] SA Parliament, 6 July 1893.
[†] *NTTG*, 31 March 1893.

It was a shock to all in Palmerston when a telegram arrived from Vaiben Solomon in Adelaide during September 1900:

> My dear friend and colleague, Walter Griffiths, died last evening of typhoid fever at Miss Tibbitt's Private Hospital. All friends here deeply grieved. Kindly inform his friends at Port Darwin.

The *Times* lamented:

> ... Without indulging in any fulsome laudations, we think the opinion will be generally endorsed by electors throughout the Territory, that in the untimely death of Mr. Walter Griffiths, in the prime of life, this settlement has lost the services of a clever, shrewd and painstaking representative, who – whatever may have been his faults or weaknesses – always fairly and squarely did his best to carry out the duties he had undertaken to perform is his capacity as one of the members for the Northern Territory.*

---

* *NTTG*, 7 September 1900. Griffiths was 33 years old.

Darwin: Survival of a City

Gallery
Palmerston in the 1890s

Figure 21: The Residency 1895, now Government House (SLSA, B-24187/6).

Darwin: Survival of a City

Figure 22: The Commercial Bank and Victoria Hotel on Smith Street (SLSA, B 61457).

Figure 23: Palmerston Public School. It is possible that the small tree in the courtyard is a young boab tree that still grows in the grounds of Charles Darwin University, 1896 (LANT, B-61444).

Figure 24: Terminus Hotel c 1900 (Ted Ryko, SLSA, ph0413-0079).

Gallery

Figure 25: Alfred Edward Jolly's store on the corner of Smith and Bennett Street & Co (1890s, ph0352-0150).

Figure 26: Interior of P. R. Allen & Co.'s store, Christmas 1897 (Foelsche, December 1897, LANT, ph0560-0056).

Figure 27: Interior of Jolly's store (LANT ph0377-0329).

Gallery

Figure 28: Palmerston Town Hall, c 1893 (Foelsche, SLSA, B 24187/8).

Figure 29: Hotel Victoria (Foelsche, SLSA, B72713_15).

Figure 30: The steam ships Chingtu & Australind on Darwin jetty, 1899 (LANT, ph0560-0030).

Gallery

Figure 31: Ship repair (Bleeser, c 1890).

Figure 32: Unloading on Gulnare Jetty c 1895 (Florenz PIC-9981-147).

Darwin: Survival of a City

Chapter 3
The Larrakia

The Larrakia people are the traditional owners of the entire Darwin area. Despite being considered 'saltwater people' their lands extend some fifty kilometers south of Port Darwin, east to Gunn Point, and west across the Cox Peninsula and all of Darwin Harbour. As ancient shell middens and rock carvings attest, they have dwelled in this region for thousands of years.

When Goyder and the Second Northern Territory Survey Expedition arrived and set up their camp in the saddle between Fort Hill and the Palmerston Peninsular in 1869, the Larrakia living in the region may not have been surprised. Indeed, two of them canoed from the shore, climbed onto the *Moonta*, and welcomed the newcomers in the English they had learned at the failed settlement at Escape Cliffs, three years earlier.* The clans may also have heard stories of the settlements at Port Essington and Raffles Bay, decades before, and assumed that any settlers who came would stay a few years, bury their dead, then move on in a process that returned the lands to the local tribes.

The Larrakia were a friendly people, curious about the newcomers, and they were happy to guide them through their country – showing them sources of water and where to hunt game. Early on, it was clear to the new settlers that the Larrakia preferred to fight with neighbouring tribes, rather than their white invaders, and pitched

---

* See Pugh, 2018a

Figure 33: A studio photograph of Larrakia man Daly, and his family, from 1890 (Foelsche, SLSA, PH0001-0037).

battles on the beaches were watched by settlers sitting on the clifftops above. While battles were run along traditional lines, the Larrakia could see that the newcomers had technologies that might be of use to them in defending their country. Whatever the case, the Europeans were mostly welcomed in the beginning.

Figure 34: Larrakia men in 1890 (NLA2, Bleeser).

The Larrakia were survivors. During the 1860s an epidemic of smallpox had killed many hundreds, perhaps thousands, of Aboriginal people living on the coasts of northern Australia. So many had died that it was said that there were 'too many to bury.' Inspector Foelsche wrote that at least 30 of the survivors living near Port Darwin were scarred from smallpox.*

The Larrakia had, and still have, cultural obligations in the Darwin area. They had to address ancient traditions and visit and maintain culturally important sites, such as conception and birthing sites, cemeteries, men's and women's ceremonial 'business' sites, and landmarks that hold important Dreaming stories. The latter are often sacred, and they remind people of their ancestors or significant creation figures from the Dreaming. One of the most important sacred sites near Darwin is *Dariba Nanggalinya* or Old Man Rock, which is visible off the northern beaches at low tide. If Old Man Rock is angered or disturbed, he can bring storms – Cyclone Tracy is believed to have been summoned by *Dariba Nanggalinya*.†

---

* Kettle, 1981.
† Wells, 2002.

Cultural obligations continued for the Larrakia even while they negotiated their new role on their land in the first few decades after white settlement. Relationships with the new arrivals were not always good. In the first year, the lowest point followed the murder of John Bennett of the survey party, probably by men of the Wulna tribe, and a rumoured retribution by surveyors who are said to have killed several Larrakia people lured to the beach by a promise of food.

However, during the 1870s, relationships between the settlers and Larrakia improved. Aboriginal people, then referred to as 'Aborigines', 'natives', or 'blacks', bartered fish and crabs, brought sheets of roofing bark to the new village, and worked in return for food or tobacco. As the only potential labour force the new settlers could find, many Larrakia became crucial to the development of the settlement. Men and women were employed to find lost cattle and horses, build houses, cut, and cart firewood and carry water. They became police trackers, domestic servants, boat crew, stablemen, and workers in stores. They cleared weeds, broke stone for road repairs, unloaded ships, washed and ironed clothes, and became nannies for white children.

A Larrakia work gang cleared the land that became the Darwin Cricket Oval. Some joined the surveyors and explorers who travelled south of Port Darwin, as guides or guards and as liaison between the white men and other Indigenous groups. At least one Aboriginal man was employed by Robert Patterson when he was leading the construction of the northern end of the Overland Telegraph Line in 1871-2. In 1886, more than twenty Larrakia men joined the pearling fleet and travelled with them to Western Australia. Others are known to have visited the East Indies in the employ of the pastoral company, Goldsborough, Mort and Co.*

Payments for Aboriginal labour were initially woeful. The damaged flour, which was initially thought sufficient, gradually evolved into rations of flour, sugar, tea, meat, tobacco, pipes, and

---

* Wells, 2002.

clothing (paid at an employer's discretion). Proper wages were then more than sixty years away.

The Larrakia had little choice other than adapt to the new regime because the changes to their country were dramatic. Much of their land was cleared, their water sources were overtaken by cattlemen or market gardeners, and wells were dug where once there were springs. The bush and sea resources they relied upon for food were soon depleted because they hunted the wallabies, emus, possums, and other wildlife in the bush with spears, but their prey was now at the mercy of the white man's guns. On the beaches, fine-meshed nets took the small fish and prawns and dynamite brought in bigger fish from deeper waters. The changes to the environment meant that traditional life for the locals became impossible. If they were to stay on their land, they needed to change their lifestyle, and it is to the credit of many that they did so quickly. And it was just as well – stories abound of cruel and tragic 'dispersals' of Aboriginal people in remote areas that resulted in the deaths of many Aboriginal men, women, and children.*

Nevertheless, many Larrakia had great difficulty in adjusting to the new ways and they remained on the fringes of the community. They were refused the right to drink alcohol or smoke opium, and as those that broke this rule were visible to the white population,† they were considered a 'thorough nuisance and eyesore'‡ and were fined or

---

* Rose, 1991.
† It was illegal to supply alcohol and opium to Aboriginal people, and for them to use them, but this made little difference. Fanny Bay Gaol must have seemed like a second home to seasoned drunks in the 1880s and 1890s. The court reports are full of stories showing how often the law was broken. For example, in the Police Court, before A. Searcy and H. W. H. Stevens, Justices of the Peace: "William Chancellor was charged with supplying liquor to an aboriginal named Manders on September 21st. Pleaded not guilty but was convicted on the evidence of two blacks and Mounted-Constable Strath. Fined £5, in default to go to gaol for 14 days, with hard labour. The fine was not paid. Manders, an aboriginal, was charged with being drunk. Defendant admitted the indictment and was let off with a caution" (*NTTG*, 30 September 1891).
‡ *NTTG*, 17 November 1883.

Figure 35: A group of Larrakia men, women, and children in 1890 (Bleeser PIC-9981-207).

gaoled.

Many people built humpies in camps outside the town or on the beach, and raised their families in poverty, depending on what they might receive for a day's labour, petty thievery of food from gardens, or the scraps discarded by townsfolk. The Government's response was to impose greater regulations about where Aborigines could live and with whom, and control when they were allowed in the streets of town.

They also arranged rations and handouts. 'Blanket Day' became an annual event celebrating Queen Victoria's birthday, just before the cold season. Blankets were handed out, but never enough, and no doubt arguments and discord was the result for many:

> ... Tuesday last was Queen's Blanket Day, and the annual farce was gone through by the Protector of Aborigines. All the doctor could do was distribute Her Majesty's bounty over as wide an area of dusky humanity as it would go, and in this case, as it always is, it was a matter of 'devil take the hindmost.' It is about the meanest advertisement the Queen gets and is altogether a very fine burlesque of charity. The supply of blankets is not half what it should be, and if there's an object at all in giving out these warm coverings it is surely worth doing generously. But to give to the first callers and let

The Larrakia

Figure 36: Blanket Day in Palmerston, 1895 (Bleeser, SLSA, B 61446)

the remainder go begging is a species of economy that should make South Australia blush.*

Begging became a legitimate survival technique for some people across the Northern Territory, wherever settlements and pastoralism disturbed their hunting grounds and made traditional lives difficult. Wherever Europeans settled, local Aborigines would soon set up camp nearby. 'Ration days' became a part of the lives of any establishment in the bush, from cattle stations to telegraph stations.

Ironically, Aboriginal people in the remote regions became an integral part of the pastoral industry, without whose help the pastoralists would hardly have survived themselves. Aboriginal cattlemen and women, station hands and the infamous 'black boys' became synonymous with the Northern Territory cattle industry.†

Not everyone was blind to the plight of the Aborigines. Many Europeans of the nineteenth century thought that Aboriginal people were doomed to extinction within 50 years and, the best anyone could

---

* *NTTG*, 27 May 1892.

† 'Black boys' were young Aboriginal women who were abducted from their tribe, dressed as boys, and used by white pastoralists as wives, companions, horsewomen, camp managers and cooks. They were often particularly useful because they could track and catch the horses in the morning. As Searcy wrote, "it is impossible to enumerate the advantages of having a good gin 'outback'" … (1909).

do, they thought, was to 'sooth the dying pillow' of the black man.*

As the Northern Territory was divided up into cattle stations and towns, the *Times* suggested that Aboriginal people should be given parcels of their own land in reserves, so that they would stay put in their own country:

> ... As the country is being rapidly taken up for settlement... we ask, have any portions of the Northern Territory been set apart as aboriginal reserves? The colonial surgeon, their protector, should see to this.†

The call for reserves continued to grow. In 1886, George Bright, an erudite saddler from Southport, wrote extensively on the options. He said the Government needed to set aside large reserves of land where Aborigines could 'follow their natural instincts in hunting and fishing for a living' whilst providing a 'sufficient portion of the revenue to feed them... having taken by force the aboriginal's land, his game, his fish, his very birthright', it was, he said, 'simply an act of justice to keep him free from care for the rest of his days, in return for the wealth we make at his expense'.‡

One reserve was declared in the Top End during the 1880s for the Larrakia – a 435-hectare block about 50 kilometers from town, south of the current Manton Dam area.§ It was out of sight and out of mind, and little use to the Larrakia, or indeed, the settlers.

The *Northern Territory Crown Lands Act* of 1890 allowed the Governor to create further reserves, but most governments ignored their obligations under the Act for more than 20 years. An unsuccessful attempt to pass the *Aborigines Bill* in 1899 also stymied any of the changes it hoped to introduce. By then, most in the Government were concluding that the most effective way to protect Aboriginal

---

* This often-used quotation, used by a Chief Protector of Aborigines in Australia in 1860, comes from a traditional hymn from the early 1800s: *What if, in the final hour, / Round thee swell the gloomy follow, / He who saves thee has the power / Now to smooth the dying pillow?*

† *NTTG*, 24 June 1883.

‡ George H. Bright, *NTTG*, 16 March 1886

§ A second declared reserve was a large 233,000-hectare region west of Alice Springs

people was to control their freedom.* As the Government Medical Officer and Protector of Aborigines lamented in 1889:

> I... find we are powerless with regards to the actions of an Aboriginal as in all respects they are as free as the Europeans. To enable any action on our part as Protector, specialist legislation would be required...†

And so eventually, it happened. The early 1900s are littered with 'special legislations' that were designed to curtail the actions and movements of Aboriginal people, listed their children as state wards until the age of 18, and prohibited inter-racial relationships.

Stories of the illegal liaisons between white men and Aboriginal women shocked the establishment of the Victorian era. Indeed, many women were treated poorly, but they were not fools and the Territory's history would be quite different without them. Many played an unsung but vital role as 'ambassadors' for their people. They protected their families and taught Europeans about their culture and, no doubt, promoted the understanding of white culture to their families.

The liaisons, of course, were impossible to prevent, and children, then called 'half-castes,' were regularly the result. In 1899, Mounted Constable George Thompson was sent to make a survey of the children living in the camps and towns between Palmerston and Katherine. He found 50 half-caste children and made a list of their names and those of their parents, their mother's tribe, and a note on their apparent health. A few were Larrakia children. One, an unnamed 2-year-old boy, was living within a stone's throw of the Government Resident himself:

> ... This Half Cast is living with its mother, with the blacks who are camped at the Residency, does not appear to be well fed & has no clothes.‡

---

* Reid, 2022
† Letter: Dr Leonard O'Flahety to the Government Resident, 16 December 1889, NTAS 790 1612.
‡ Thompson, 1900.

Another, a 14-year-old girl named Lilly, was the daughter of George McKeddie J.P. and Minnie.* She may have been luckier than most:

> ... Half Cast Lilly is living with a Manila man named Antonio at the old icehouse on the beach, she appears to be well fed & clothed.

Government Medical Officer, and Protector of Aborigines (1897-1904), Dr Frederick Goldsmith, expressed his views in 1900:

> ... At the annual distribution of blankets in May over 300 natives attended, and it was a striking feature of this gathering that the proportion of children as compared to adults was very low. This points out, I think, to the fact that, as in other civilized parts of Australia, the aborigines here are on their way gradually to extinction.... Between Port Darwin and Katherine are over sixty half-caste children of various ages, and I would strongly urge that as soon as possible provision be made that they can be removed from their surroundings and educated to a certain extent, so that ultimately, they may be useful members of society and not–as too often happens when allowed to run wild in the blacks' camp–become a source of danger to the community.†

It was the supposed care for children like these that inevitably led to the tragedy of the 'stolen generations,' ramifications of which are still being played out.

---

* George McKeddie J.P. (1851-1927) was a long-term Territory resident. A businessman, he also served on the Palmerston District Council for many years. He was later a hotelier in Katherine with pastoral interests. He fathered two children (Lilly and Jack). He died in Melbourne in 1927.

† Fred Goldsmith, in Dashwood's *Government Resident's Report* for the year 1900.

Chapter 4
Asian Settlers

Chinese

In the 1890s, Palmerston was a Chinese settlement governed by a European minority, with Larrakia people living on the fringes. Chinese immigrants first came to the Territory as part of the gold rush in the 1870s. Some came under their own steam, but many were brought in groups as part of shiploads of cheap labourers, called 'coolies,' to work in the mines or to build the railway in the 1880s.

By the late 1880s, there were five times more Chinese than Europeans in Palmerston, but the Government remained steadfastly white and inherently racist. The Chinese, like the Larrakia, were excluded from the 'superior' society. They were not welcome in, so did not take part in 'white' sports or social clubs. This might not have worried them – they lived mostly separate lives anyway, and it was not until 1923 that Chinese citizens formed a club in a format that was recognizable to other residents.*

According to the 1888 census, the non-Aboriginal population of 7,236 people included 6,122 Chinese people living in Palmerston or on the goldfields. About two thousand men returned to China, died, or had otherwise left by 1890, but so too had many Europeans,

---

* Known as the Darwin Chinese Recreation Club, it promoted boxing, Australian Rules football, tennis, swimming, and soccer. They planned 'to place teams in the field in opposition to all comers in all those branches of sport' (*NTTG*, 28 December 1923).

and the Chinese were still more than 80 percent of the remaining population of 5,150. By the turn of the century there were only 3,931 non-Aboriginal people; 1,003 Europeans and 2,928 Chinese (74 percent). Over the next few decades, the population of Europeans slowly increased, and many Chinese left, but it was not until World War II that major and rapid growth occurred in the Territory and the non-Aboriginal population became substantially European.

Chinese men, and some women, remained at the forefront of mining, but they were also railway workers, shopkeepers, agriculturalists, and members of the service industry. Many Europeans, including those on cattle stations and in the telegraph stations for instance, had a Chinese cook. Government Resident Knight famously reported that his Chinese cook liked Palmerston so much he claimed that 'by and by, all China come, even the Emperor'.*

Of those Chinese people who came to the Territory to make money, once enriched (or bankrupted) most returned home to their families in China. These people were not politically active and were willing to work harder than anyone else for less pay. Importantly however, there were some Chinese folk who came to Palmerston or its surrounds for the long haul. They raised their families and built their homes and temples in Chinatown at the southern end of Cavenagh Street.

It is unlikely that a reader of Palmerston's nineteenth century newspapers would conclude that the town's population was mostly Chinese! The editors were European, and they wrote their editorials about the events other Europeans found interesting, and rarely mentioned the Chinese. When they did, it was usually to deride or denigrate, or report on Chinese criminals and court proceedings. Most of the white men and women living in Palmerston were arrogant and prejudiced products of their day. They gladly accepted cheap labour, but rarely mingled socially with their Chinese neighbours, and much of the anti-Chinese sentiment of the eastern states – especially from

---

* See Pugh 2021.

the gold fields in North Queensland, New South Wales, and Victoria – drifted north.

Despite this, it seems to have been better for Chinese immigrants in Palmerston than it was elsewhere. Chinese labour was so necessary to the Territory that the anti-Chinese sentiment was never as strong as it was 'down south'.* Plus, it helped that the Chinese mostly did not compete with Europeans – except as merchants and miners.

During the 1880s, the *Times* also recognised the value of Chinese labour and actively supported Chinese immigration, while at the same time, the South Australian Government was planning to restrict it.† In 1887, the Palmerston to Pine Creek Railway construction, led by the Millar brothers, chose to employ cheap Chinese 'coolie' labour. These men came mostly from Singapore and Hong Kong, and at one time there were 3,000 Chinese workers on the line.

There were other advantages too. Having Chinese workers allowed the upper echelon of Palmerston's society – the senior public servants and the cable company officers – to assume the airs and graces of gentlemen to an extent they would never have reached in southern cities.‡

About a third of the Territory's Chinese population lived and worked on the goldfields§ but few managed to attain the wealth of which they had dreamed. Some did: a gang of fifteen took 800 ounces from 35 tons of rock at Fountainhead in 1891; and Hang Gong found 50 ounces in a small rock at Brock's Creek.¶

As the railway construction ended, Inspector Foelsche was concerned about the potential influx of thousands of unemployed Chinese. What would they do? He knew the statistics:

... In Palmerston they have 39 stores and green grocer's shops, 3 carpenter's shops, 2 shoemaker's shops, 3 laundries,

---

* Donovan, 1981.
† *NTTG*, August 1881.
‡ Sowden, 1882.
§ Jones, 1990.
¶ Jones, 1987.

> 5 tailoring establishments, 4 eating houses, 3 fishing establishments, 32 fruit and vegetable gardens… 6 gambling houses, 7 Chinese brothels, occupied by 34 prostitutes…[*]

He need not have worried. Many of the railway workers joined the gold rush to become tribute miners – though by the 1890s their numbers were thinning. Some found work elsewhere. For instance, Nicholas Holtze employed 17 Chinese workers in the Experimental (Botanic) Gardens.[†] More than a few worked on the pearling luggers, but the vast majority went home to Singapore, Hong Kong, or mainland China.

The Chinese people who stayed rarely made the social pages in Palmerston. They were excluded from the sporting clubs that blossomed among the smaller white population and when they were employed by the Government, the white ruling class complained that they were taking their jobs.

In 1890, writers to the *Times* complained that Chinese contractors were being employed by John Little of the Telegraph Department to re-pole the Overland Telegraph Line south to Katherine. The arguments made sense to many: if the Government wanted European residents to remain in the Territory, they needed to provide employment.

> … Whether our public works cost five-and-twenty per cent more than they do at present, or even twice as much, is a matter of small importance when compared to the advantage of retaining a European population in the country and finding them profitable employment. In our opinion it is useless to trifle with this question any longer, it resolves itself into a simple choice between making an attempt to carry on a settlement with people of our own colour, or to at once admit, with men like Messrs. Warland, Bakewell, Leonard Browne, and others of that ilk, that the colony is only fit for occupation by Asiatic aliens…[‡]

---

[*] Foelsche, 1888.
[†] See-Kee, 1987.
[‡] *NTTG*, 25 April 1890.

Figure 37: Chinese procession, Mitchell Street (1893, W. Barnes LANT ph0112-0093).

There were also rumours of evil. It was said that several secret societies existed among the Chinese, but what these were, and how they operated, remained a secret. Nevertheless, Minister Solomon passed a bill in Parliament to limit the 'evil' effects of Chinese secret societies in 1891. His information was little more than the racist opinions of Inspector Foelsche and other Palmerston leaders. The Government Residents' reports only ever mentioned Chinese secret societies once, in 1889, after a new Joss House had been opened. Dashwood thought that the Chinese were rendezvousing there to settle disputes 'according to Chinese usages' which he claimed was 'all the same as Freemasonry.'*

The European community was treated to the best of Chinese culture during Chinese New Year and other festivals. Chinese New Year was the most important and work would stop for up to a week. The shops were full of fireworks, and this invariably led to house-fires, especially on the goldfields. And everywhere, wise housekeepers would lock up their fowls to keep them safe. Annual processions through the streets of the town brought out the crowds and celebrations continued

---

* Ironically, Foelsche would become the Master of the secretive Darwin Lodge of Freemasons in 1896 – and build the lodge using Chinese construction teams.

into the noisy night. One of the best was the 1893 celebration:

> ... Friday last was observed by the Chinese as a great day of rejoicing, and an immense demonstration was most successfully carried out. This was the best of its kind ever yet seen in the Territory and was not without its moral. The procession was a truly gorgeous display, in which not less than 200 Chinese took part. Banners and bannerets and flags, all of lively colours, contested for the acme of brilliancy and quaint taste with the bright garments of the bearers: gay colouring was everywhere visible. Bands, well-practised for the occasion, give out the soul-stirring strains which only a combination of Chinese performers could produce. There was the usual airing of joss-thrones, and roasted pigs, and fancy confectionery; the several clubs and guilds were placed in order in many distinguishing costumes, carrying emblems of office or other representative symbol. A posse of soldiers marched near the rear of the procession and contributed to the pervading din by periodically discharging their ancient muzzle-loaders.
>
> There were two disreputable dragons and a spanking new one just from China. This last was a big fellow, a perfect blaze of intermingled colours, and requiring the joint assistance of four artists to acquire the necessary grace and activity, to say nothing of the fifth help who danced at its head and irritated the fiery monster with a pliable pole. Sometimes its tail got out of joint, but that was a mere trifle.
>
> We also noticed our old friend William Tell seated importantly on a reverend looking charger, the said William being still in possession of his trusty bow and arrow. One of the prettiest sights of the show was the infant girl very daintily decked out and powdered and mounted on a horse led by attendants; and, indeed, all the juvenile members of the throng were attired in picturesque raiment; and were as pretty as pictures. Some of the men were masked, just as fancy suggested, giving the show a tincture of Guy Fawkesiness that helped to make one laugh.
>
> The procession formed in line at the new Joss-house and from there paraded the principal streets of the city, to the great enjoyment of the Caucasian element. It looked like a cross between an eight-hours demonstration and a circus arriving in town, but apart from all levity it was something well worth

seeing. In the evening there was the customary culminating exhibition of exercises in a bonfire lit ring, but this is always a sorry spectacle, and is about as amusing as watching a timid man killing a snake.*

Other festivals included the Dragon Boat, the Feast of the Hungry Ghosts, and the Moon Festival. The latter was barely mentioned by the press, though one paragraph from 1890, which seems to have been included under sufferance, clearly shows little interest or understanding of the event.

> ... the Chinese residents of the town waded through one of their annual festivities, the object of this regard in this instance having something to do with the full moon in Chinese held autumn, or some other Celestial lost time. For once the provoking little V crackers took but a small part in the 'show,' which was chiefly made up of feasting... and getting as drunk as circumstances and 'samshu' [sic: 'sam sui'] would permit.†

Chinese residents living in Palmerston were merchants, market gardeners or servants, and Chinatown stretched from the southern end of the Esplanade, north along Cavenagh Street, past Knuckey Street and as far as Edmund Street. Many Chinese private enterprises could be found here with customers coming from all parts of the town. The land mostly belonged to absentee property owners and there was little or no government control of its development, so most residents built their own houses, which were often businesses in themselves.

Yee Kee, for instance, took out a lease on lot number 303 on Cavenagh Street in 1886 for £50 per annum. He immediately built shanty-style accommodation shacks and rented them out to his compatriots. Trouble started in 1887 when his huts were decreed unfit for human habitation, and he was forced out of the lease in July 1891. It was then taken up by Geoy Choeng Loong at just £15 per annum for 10 years. The drop in rent reflects both the economic times, the decreasing population of Chinese men, and the quality of the buildings that had been erected there.

---

* *NTTG*, 10 March 1893.
† *NTTG*, 3 October 1890.

Unfortunately, behind several impressive two-story shopfronts, Cavenagh Street was soon an ever-widening slum with open sewers that easily contaminated a growing number of wells. Letters to the Times appeared at regular intervals complaining about the 'Asiatic quarter':

> … there are backyards in connection with the sweet-smelling frontages, backyards where living and sleeping rooms, kitchens, wells, and water closets are remarkably convenient to each other in fact, as the poem has it 'They grow in beauty side by side'*

Medical officers worried about typhoid and cholera, decried the conditions, and warned of the inherent danger of the constructions with good reason, Chinatown had already been destroyed by fire in June 1880. Then, 40 houses and two shops went up in flames. Despite this, Chinatown and its complex problems were mostly ignored:

> … Houses, or sections of houses, were rented out, subdivided further, and sublet until several levels of landlords let a few square metres to the poorest individuals. In this way overcrowding developed and with inadequate privies the whole area progressively became a major health risk. However, it was the stench from inadequate drains that tormented the sensitive noses of the European community…†

Almost all fresh produce for the settlement, locally grown fruits, and vegetables, came from the Chinese market gardeners. Some of the gardens were in the area next to Gardens Hill Road below Dashwood Crescent (now the Gardens Golf Course) as far as the Goyder Road Cemetery. Others were in McMinn Street (below the old Darwin Primary School and Frogs Hollow), in Police Paddock in Stuart Park, and on the land where the Parap and Fannie Bay Shopping Centres now exist. As See Kee said in 1987: 'wherever you see clusters of large mango trees, you can safely say they mark the site of early Chinese market gardens.'

The market gardeners also bred chickens – their meat being one

---

* Daniel Cohen. Letter to the Editor, *NTTG*, 7 July 1899.
† Kettle, 1981.

Figure 38: By the 1890s Chinese merchants were accepted as a vital part of Darwin's business community. L -R (rear): C. Hang Kim, P. Kelsey, Cheong Wo, J. M. Corr, Chin Pack Sue, W.C.P. Bell, Yuen Ng Kan, F.E. NIcholl, Ah San, Chin Toy. Front: George McKeddie, Wing Wah Loong, A. Cameron, Chin Yam Yan, V.V. Brown, Yet Loong, E. Luxton, Wing Chong Sing, P.R. Allen.

of the staples of the time. There were never enough, it seems, and night-time raids on the coops of white citizens in 1891 were blamed on the Chinese:

> ... The police have begun to lock up Chinese found wandering out late at night. This is a step in the right direction, and if not of the usual spasmodic order, should prove somewhat of a check to the operations of the fowl-stealers, who up to the present have had things pretty much their own way.*

In 1891, Governor Kintore was in favour of Asian workers immigrating to the Territory and the South Australian Government planned to bring in 100 families to work on suitable land. Delays occurred and nothing ever came of the plan because the idea was completely in opposition to the *Chinese Immigration Restriction Act* of 1888. Incidentally, in 1896 this Act was extended to include Afghans, Hindus, and Syrians and, by 1898, the Act barred *any* person thought to be unsuitable from entering South Australia.

Government Resident Charles Dashwood had to follow the

---

* *NTTG*, 21 August 1891

anti-Chinese policies of his government and in 1899 he let everyone know that helping Chinese people to enter Queensland through the Territory (to avoid Queensland's poll tax) would be a criminal offence:

> NOTICE TO ALL TO WHOM IT MAY CONCERN.
>
> NOTICE is hereby given that any Chinese who shall enter the Colony of Queensland from the province of South Australia contrary to the Statute or Statutes enforced restricting the immigration of Chinese into Queensland shall be guilty of an offence, and liable, on conviction, to fine and imprisonment. And further, that any debtor who shall quit or make preparations for quitting the said province with intent to defraud any creditor to whom such debtor shall be indebted to the amount of £10, or upwards, shall be guilty of a misdemeanour, and liable to imprisonment with or without hard labor for two years.
>
> CHS. DASHWOOD,
>
> Govt. Resident.
>
> Govt. Resident's Office,
>
> Palmerston, July 5th, 1898*

While most Chinese people lived in tiny ramshackle homes in Chinatown, raising their families and observing their religious and cultural duties, the records of those days are skewed towards the small European population. The peripatetic nature of the Chinese population, little self-promotion, poor information, and secrecy, means history of the white establishment in Palmerston is recorded – and therefore remembered – more prominently.

Chinatown, despite being 'steeped in oriental tradition,' remained a tin shanty town with fetid sewers until the land was compulsorily acquired and bulldozed in 1938. Modern Cavenagh Street, which ends at the Darwin Council offices, contains retail shops and businesses, hotels, and the NT Magistrate Courts. Only Kwong's 'Stone House' remains from the nineteenth century.

In 1891, an official government census of the Territory's population listed the name, age, occupation, country of origin, and

---

* *NTTG*, 22 Sept 1899.

Asian Settlers

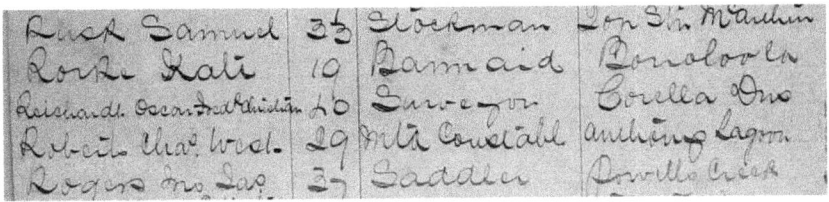

Figure 39: 1891 government census listed the name, age, occupation, country of origin, and religion of every white person in the Territory. A sample of the 1891 Census (NAA, F108, Vol 1).

religion of every white person in the Territory – page after page was handwritten in alphabetical order and tallied up in districts and towns across the land.

Non-European settlers were also counted, including Chinese people who accounted for most of the colony's population. However, census information about non-European people – Chinese, Japanese, Malays and 'others' – was limited to numbers, rather than names. The totals were reported by the Government Resident and the Gold Warden.*

Aboriginal people were included in census counts of the nineteenth century – but not in the same way as Europeans. A 'grand total' of 20,655 Indigenous Australians was declared in 1891, but the accuracy of these numbers is questionable. Each count is listed as a rounded number, so they are clearly estimates.

Timothy Jones studied the Territory population figures in detail and found discrepancies in the Government Residents' reports and records kept by other officials – or lack of them.† Jones noted that there were no records of the numbers of people coming or going overland and no death records for Aboriginal people, and quite often, none for Chinese people either. Much of the ongoing population monitoring happened through passenger lists provided by ships' captains.

Upon Federation in 1901, the Federal Government took over

---

* For example, in 1890 there were 4,141 Chinese people, 1,300 of whom were miners, as opposed to 1,009 Europeans. In 1891, the official census showed 4,898 non-Aboriginal people living in the Territory, of which 3,392 were Chinese men.
† Jones, 1987.

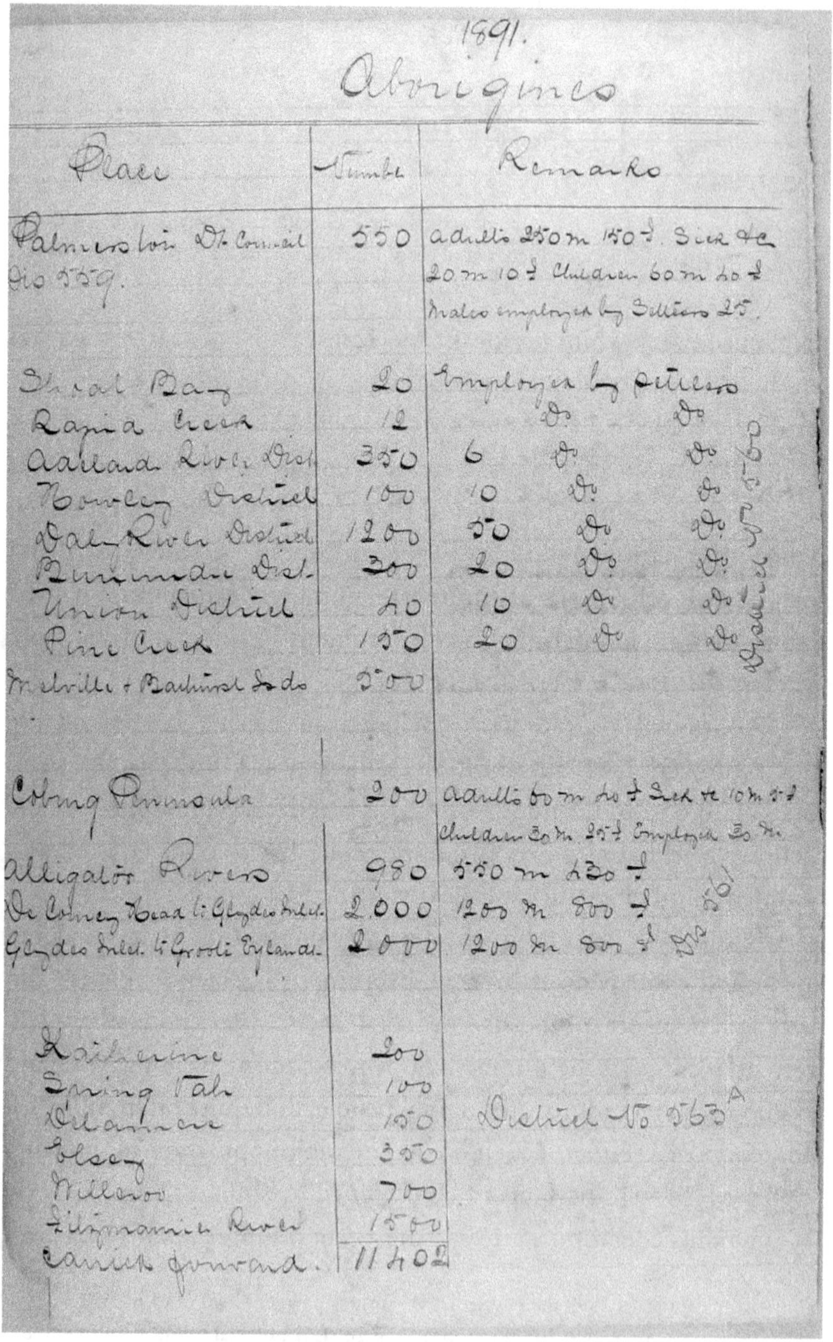
1891.

Aborigines

Place	Number	Remarks
Palmerston Dt. Council Dis 559.	550	adults 250 m 150 f. Sick &c 20 m 10 f Children 60 m 40 f Males employed by Settlers 25.
Shoal Bay	20	Employed by settlers
Rapid Creek	12	Do Do
Adelaide River Dist	350	6 Do Do
Howley District	100	10 Do Do
Daly River District	1200	50 Do Do
Burrundie Dist.	300	20 Do Do
Union District	40	10 Do Do
Pine Creek	150	20 Do Do
Melville & Bathurst Islds	500	
Coburg Peninsula	200	adults 60 m 40 f Sick &c 10 m 5 f Children 30 m 25 f Employed 30 m
Alligator Rivers	980	550 m 430 f
De Courcy Head to Glydes Inlet	2000	1200 m 800 f
Glydes Inlet to Groote Eylandt	2000	1200 m 800 f
Katherine	200	
Spring Vale	100	
Delamere	150	District No 563A
Elsey	350	
Willeroo	700	
Fitzmaurice River	1500	
Carried forward	11402	

Figure 40: The 1891 census counted Aboriginal people.

THE following returns, showing the population of the Northern Territory, are taken from official documents, and are true according to the last census, taken in 1891 :—

District Council of Palmerston—Bagot (portion of)	1176
Counties Disraeli, Malmesbury, Palmerston (portion of) and Rosebery, including Bathurst and Melville Islands	2893
Country east of Counties Disraeli and Rosebery	6
Country east of 134° east long. to the Gulf of Carpentaria and between 13° 58' and 15° 30' south latitude	21
Country east of 134° east long. to the Gulf of Carpentaria and between 15 deg. 30' and 17 deg. south lat., being portion of Daly Waters subdivision of Electoral District	126
Country west of 134 deg. east long. to the western boundary of the colony, and between 13 deg. 58' and 15 deg. 30' south lat	117
Country west of 134 deg. east long. to the western boundary of the colony, and between 15 deg. 30' and 17 deg. south latitude, being portion of Daly Waters subdivision of Electoral District	62
Powell's Creek subdivision of Electoral District	60
Tennant's Creek subdivision of Electoral District	87
Barrow's Creek subdivision of Electoral District	67
Alice Springs subdivision of Electoral District	230
Charlotte Waters subdivision of Electoral District	53
Total of Northern Territory	4898

NOTE—Of this population 3,392 are Chinese male adults.

———o———

Aborigines in Northern Territory—

Males, 12,819. Females, 7,806. Grand total, 20,655.

Figure 41: A summary of the results of the 1891 census (NAA, F108 Vol 1).

control of immigration. It soon developed the 'white Australia' policy that followed not only South Australia's racist legislation, but others coming from the previously separate colonies of Australia.

Descendants of the pioneering families from the nineteenth century are still living in Darwin and are famously proud of their heritage. Fortunately, this includes some of the Chinese who lived in Chinatown in the 1890s who never intended to go anywhere else. Their families became established and 150 years later family dynasties such as the Fongs and Ah Toys continue to play an important role in the history and development of the Territory.*

Others

Apart from the Chinese, seafarers, and people from other parts of Asia migrated to the Northern Territory. Nineteenth-century Palmerston was home to Malays, 'Manila-men' from the Philippines, and Japanese people who were either settlers or transients, adding to the melting pot that became twenty-first century Darwin. They were workers, crew members on ships, on the wharf, or in various service positions in the town, and they played a valuable role in the community.

Japanese men first arrived in Palmerston in about 1883 – most were actively recruited by companies looking for men to work in the pearl shell industry at Thursday Island, where Japanese divers had been active since 1878. A team of 12 'steady and industrious' Japanese divers arrived in Port Darwin during 1884 direct from Hong Kong, and others transferred on their luggers from Thursday Island. However, as the first rush of the pearl shell industry died down about 1888, things went quiet until the resurgence of the industry in 1892.

Some Japanese were attracted to the north for other reasons. According to C. Mann when interviewed by the Royal Commission in 1895, there were two Japanese ship's carpenters living in the town in 1890 and several more 'natty little chaps' who 'beat the Chinese into a cocked hat' who worked on the railway.† As Port Darwin was developed, lonely sailors and miners alike were happy to spend their money on wine, women, and song. Naturally, some women were attracted to work in brothels, or were trafficked there by unconscionable men. Twelve Japanese prostitutes worked in four Palmerston brothels in 1893.‡

---

* Today it seems that newcomers have to spend years in the Territory before they earn the title of 'Territorian.' The epithet 'Darwin Born' is used as a badge of honour. It gives a status to northerners that is unreachable by any Johnny-come-latelies from 'down south.'
† Sissons, 1977.
‡ Sissons, 1977: The prostitutes were recorded by K. Watanabe, who was contracted

In 1898, a report on the 'Moral Atmosphere of Darwin'* claimed that 'the Japanese women are almost all professional prostitutes, the Malay women are nurse-girls, the Chinese women are mostly patient grudging wives'.† V.L. Solomon objected to prostitution and mentioned a recent arrival of numerous Japanese women when debating Asian migration in 1898 – he wanted them to be in a specific category of prohibited immigrants.

In 1893, there were 21 Japanese men in Port Darwin and all but one of them were engaged in the pearling industry.‡ Three of them were masters of their luggers, rather than employees, and one of them, Charlie 'Japan' Hamaura (aka Hamarwa), became a successful businessman and a community leader in his own right.§

---

    by the Japanese Government to write a report on Australia and the Pacific in 1893. In 1888, Inspector Foelsche reported 23 Japanese prostitutes working in five brothels (Foelsche, 1888).

*   *Missionary Review*, 12 December 1898
†   *NTTG*, 20 January 1899.
‡   Again, recorded by Watanabe (Sissons 1977.)
§   Hamaura Street at East point is named after Charlie. Charlie's daughter, Cleo, married prominent businessman Felix Holmes in 1900.

Darwin: Survival of a City

Chapter 5
Communication

Palmerston lay 3,000 kilometres north of the seat of Government and the Northern Territory was a huge tract of sparsely populated land. It still is.

When Goyder first surveyed the Palmerston peninsula in 1869, the fastest transport available to get messages to and from the Government in Adelaide took about six weeks. Port Darwin and Port Adelaide were separated by 3,939 nautical miles. As steam ships improved the transit time shrunk to about two weeks – but it still meant over a month for any replies to mail to arrive – but only if a ship was available. Very soon, however, the connection of the electric telegram between Adelaide and Palmerston cut this time to an hour or two.

The importance of the Overland Telegraph Line cannot be understated. It opened to great fanfare on 22 August 1872 with Robert Patterson's final twist of the wire near Frew's Ironstone Ponds, 650 kilometres south of the coast. A public holiday was declared for all South Australians. International communication, to London and beyond, took a few more months to come 'on line', but that meant Adelaide was in communication with the Imperial Government in England. Telegrams took less than seven hours to cross the globe! Palmerston, then just a few years old, was an important link in the chain.

Unfortunately, telegrams were not for everyone – they were

prohibitively expensive. In 1894, one British pound (the currency used in Australia until Federation) equated to over £150 by today's standards, and a 10-word telegram from Adelaide to Darwin in 1894 cost the equivalent of about £50:

> ... From any point in South Australia proper telegrams may be sent to Adelaide for the uniform charge of 1s. for ten words, but directly the Territory is entered the charge runs on a sliding scale upwards until it eventually stops at the theft of six shillings. Thus, to Strangways Springs the charge is 2s. for ten words to the Peake, 2s to Charlotte Waters 3s to Alice Springs, 3s Barrow Creek, 4s; Tennant's Creek, 5s; and the same to Powell's Creek and Daly Waters. All further northern stations pay the 6s.*

Most of the telegraph traffic, as a result, was business or mining orientated, with the Government the major customer. The general public benefited most from telegraph through the newspapers – from 7 November 1872 the Palmerston newspapers published any news from across the world that was sent via the Overland Telegraph Line.

Of course, not every Territorian lived in Palmerston, and newspapers would take an inordinately long time to travel out bush. There were weekly mail services by train to Burrundie and Pine Creek, but residents in Borroloola only received mail from Palmerston four times per year (although they did have a monthly service from Queensland) and Roper River twice. There were no regular mail services at all to the Victoria and Daly rivers region. Many complaints were made to the newspapers about these issues.

Telegraphed news was printed under the heading 'Latest Telegrams' in the *Northern Territory Times and Gazette* with items were divided into 'Colonial and Intercolonial' and 'British and Foreign' news. The following (truncated) example shows how well-informed North Australian readers were of the news – they had the headlines at least:

Colonial and Intercolonial

---

* *NTTG*, 23 Feb 1894.

Adelaide, January 26.

The following telegram was received at this office on Wednesday after noon:

Tom Coward* is coming out for Parliament. He has issued his address to the electors of the Northern Territory, announcing an excellent programme, including completion of Transcontinental Railway from Oodnadatta to Pine Creek on land grant system. The construction, as soon as possible, of cheap branch lines to MacDonnell Ranges or any good gold diggings or other good mineral country; also, to Queensland border.

Putting down bores for water and constructing reservoirs. Doing everything possible to secure the development of the mineral, agricultural, and pastoral resources of the Northern Territory. Tom Coward is well known as a first-class bushman, well acquainted with the country. He is receiving a large amount of encouragement.

February 1st.

Mr. V. L. Solomon left for Sydney to-day to catch the steamer Chingtu. A number of members of Parliament and old Northern Territory identities assembled at the railway station to see him off.

… Mr. Walter Griffiths leaves for Alice Springs, on an electioneering trip on Monday.

The Federal Bank has suspended payment. A general meeting of shareholders will be held in a fortnight's time. The assets show a surplus, and the Bank's notes are being cashed by the other Banks.

The Government, in pursuance of the resolution recently carried by Mr. V. L. Solomon in the Assembly, has paid the claims of owners of opium stolen at Port Darwin.

The death is announced of William Voules Brown†, aged 84, a

---

* Tom Coward came a poor fourth in the general election of 1893. The results, declared by Returning Officer J.J. Symes, were Solomon 272 votes; Griffith 188 votes; Stow 142; Coward 11 (*NTTG*, 26 May 1893).

† W.V. Brown was the father of prominent Darwin citizens Victor Voules Brown, and John Alexander Voules Brown. John was town clerk at the time of his father's

well-known old colonist.

Parliament is prorogued till the 21st of March. The date of dissolution is still undecided.

The Treasurer has definitely declined the offer of a London syndicate to subscribe the balance of the last loan and has decided to call tenders locally for Treasury bills for a quarter of a million sterling, payable in five years, and bearing interest at the rate of four per cent. per annum.

The thirty-fourth anniversary of the birth of the German Emperor has been celebrated by a large and patriotic gathering at the Adelaide German Club.

Camels are coming largely into use in outlying country for packing purposes, and over five hundred have recently been imported.

A Chinese resident here has murdered his European wife through jealousy.

Melbourne, February 1. H.E. the Governor's term of office expires in November next year, but it is generally understood that he intends resigning and returning to England in March next.

New South Wales.

February 1.

The annual cricket match Victoria versus New South Wales has resulted in an easy victory for the former team, the scores standing as follows: Sydney in first and second innings scored 263 and 91 and the Victorians, 331 came 261.

British & Foreign.

London, February 1.

News has been received of the total wreck of the Messageries-Maritimes steamer Niemen whilst on the voyage to Colombo. The crew and passengers were saved, but all the mails were lost.

A terrible catastrophe has occurred in a colliery at Teplitz,

---

death. One wonders if the brothers heard the news via these telegrams (see obituary: *Adelaide Observer*, 11 February 1893).

in Austro-Hungary through an explosion of firedamp. One hundred and thirty miners were killed.

The new Imperial coinage is to be issued in a fortnight's time. The superscription describes the Queen as the Empress of India.

The Bank of England authorities are amazed at the sudden stoppage of the Federal Bank, and a feeling is prevalent in financial circles that the Associated Banks, should lists prevented such a disaster. It is feared that Scotch depositors will withdraw from other Australian concerns.

The death is announced of Sir Jas. McCulloch, formerly Premier of Victoria, aged 71.

The death is also announced of James Gillespie Blaine, the eminent American politician. He was born in 1830.

The excitement at Cairo, arising out of recent political occurrences, continues.

Secret meetings among the native population, with the object of fomenting rebellion, are of daily occurrence. The English military force is being strengthened.

The marriage of the Princess Margaret of Prussia with Prince Frederick Charles of Hesse was celebrated at Berlin, with great pomp, on Thursday last.

Ten, £93. Copper (Chili), £45 10s.

The Earl of Elgin is mentioned as the probable successor of Earl Jersey in New South Wales.

Kruger has been re-elected President of the Transvaal Republic for the fourth time in succession, by a one thousand majority.

The principal market in Berlin has been destroyed by fire, the damage being estimated at £50,000.[*]

---

[*] *NTTG*, 3 February 1893.

Darwin: Survival of a City

Chapter 6
Daily Life in Palmerston: Clubs and Societies

The D.M.S., Entertainments and Fancy Dress

Desperate to ensure that their 'souls did not waste away', talented musicians and thespians provided entertainment on Palmerston stages from the very first months of settlement. From the Theatre Royal days of the survey party in 1869, men, and later women, came together to sing, dance, recite and act for their fellows.

The Dramatic and Musical Society had its genesis in March 1883, with the opening of Palmerston Town Hall. Six members signed up at an annual subscription if £1 1s and their first entertainment hit the stage on 3 April 1883. In October, Palmerston's Chief Clerk, F.C. Ward, imported a Vogel 'upright grand' piano that was at first much admired as a piece of furniture, rather than for its sound – for no one could play it until a Mrs. Reichardt joined the society. The £92 piano was:

> … a full tri-chord, cross-strung, and of six seven-eighths octaves compass. It has a full, rich, and mellow tone, sounding splendidly in the large hall, as different from the jangling, discordant boxes strummed on by uneducated fingers, which are here and there made to discourse excruciating torments as can possibly be imagined.*

Perhaps inspired by the quality of the sound, the society

---

*   *NTTG*, 23 October 1883.

prospered. At the turn of the next decade, it was the D.M.S. who brought in the new year in style for the white citizens of Palmerston – although not without criticism. The songs, declared the *Times*, were delivered by amateurs and the chorus tended to sing too loudly. Nevertheless:

> ... Mr. G. H Sims* came in for a hearty round of applause for his rendering of a song entitled 'The Fisherman and his Child,' and Mr. K. L. Glyde's song 'Call me back again,' and Mr. T. H. Harwood's 'Madeline,' equally well deserved the similar mark of appreciation which was unstintingly accorded... and... the farce 'Paddy Miles' Boy' was a great success'.

The paper saved its scorn for the comedians:

> ... we would like to remind those who do the alleged funny business... With reference to the jokes, they were the most utterly feeble attempts a Palmerston audience has yet been treated to, and to make matters still worse, both 'Corner Men' seemed to have forgotten that simple personality is neither witty, nor amusing.†

Then, like revellers everywhere on New Year's Eve, the Palmerstonians partied the night away:

> ... After the conclusion of the performance, the members of the Club and a few of their friends had a merry dance until the Post-office bell announced the advent of January 1st, 1890.‡

The decade rolled on with the society presenting various entertainments to the community. Fred Finniss could report in 1896, for example, that they 'had during the year... one entertainment, six socials, two dance practices and one fancy dress ball.'§

The fancy dress balls were very popular and, of course, the children were involved as well – an 1894 photograph of shows a group of them dressed in their finery. The balls were the 'event of the

---

* George Henry Sims J.P. was an accountant for the Commercial Bank in Palmerston and from 1895 the visiting justice for Fannie Bay.
† *NTTG*, 3 January 1890.
‡ *NTTG*, 3 January 1890.
§ *NTTG*, 12 March 1897.

Daily Life in Palmerston: Clubs and Societies

Figure 42: The children's fancy dress ball, 1894 (Barnes, LANT, 19085).

season' and were often held during 'race week' to attract the out-of-town miners and cattlemen in town for the horse races.

The fancy dress ball of 1891 was particularly memorable. It was honestly recorded as '*THE* success of the 'social' season, and the best thing of its kind ever held in Palmerston.'*

The *Times* was impressed at the trouble people were willing to go for their costumes. Despite the tyranny of distance and their 'remoteness from the fountain of supply for drapery and haberdashery and the like', which meant that fancy dressing in Palmerston was 'a decidedly aggravating and wearisome labour', the success of the costuming for the night showed that when Palmerston people made up their 'usually uncertain minds to accomplish an object [they] go straight ahead, through or over the obstacles, and generally come out of the task with credit'. About 80 men and women attended the ball that year, dancing until the small hours.

As for the women:

> ... some of the costumes worn bordered on the plain, but there were many delightfully artistic ones, suiting the gentle

---

* *NTTG*, 16 October 1891.

Figure 43: Theatrics 1894 (Foelsche, LANT, PH0111-0126).

wearers to perfection. Miss Pickford as a 'Dancing Girl,' and Miss Callaghan in the guise of a 'Spanish Dancing Girl,' were perhaps the most conspicuous characters in the room, though many other representations were just as complete in detail if not quite as striking in appearance. Mrs Johnston made a true picture of a *vivandière*: the costume of 'Esmeralda' formed a graceful habit for Mrs Adcock; 'Music' found a friend in Mrs Harwood, whose ability in that accomplishment made the character all the more complete…

And of the gentlemen:

… The Government Resident as 'King of Diamonds', Mr Ward as a Spanish bullfighter, Mr. Harwood as a 'Guard Française,' and Percy Freer counterfeiting the redoubtable Earl of Leicester, were perhaps the pick of the lot for style, although Mr. Black in the appropriate garb 'Black and White,' and Dr. O'Flaherty in all scarlet representing Mephistopheles up to Date, were novelties quite up to A1 standard…*

The Palmerston Dramatic and Musical Society continued well into the twentieth century. Its annual general meeting report in 1915 shows it still going well, though with a name change to the *Darwin*

---

* *NTTG*, 16 October 1891.

Dramatic and Musical Society in 1911. Sadly, the society seems to have struggled during the Great War and by 1917 it was being called the 'old Dramatic and Musical Society', and it soon disappeared from the records. It was a force to reckon with, as far as entertainment goes, for more than 30 years.

The Palmerston Brass Band

Fred Finniss, who was a member of the First Northern Territory Expedition in 1864, had been in the Northern Territory for longer than most other settlers. He was a keen member of the Dramatic and Musical Society and one of his legacies in the mid-1890s was the establishment of the Palmerston Brass Band:

> … The brass band question was a subject for debate at a meeting of the committee of the Dramatic and Musical Society on Monday night. Mr. F. I. H. Finniss, who has been especially active in the matter, reported that an order had been sent to England for a dozen instruments, comprising cornets (3), saxhorns (2), euphonium, clarinet, piccolo, bass, and big and side drums and triangle. A band committee consisting of Messrs. H. J. B. Carbery, F. I. H. Finniss, F. Becker, and W. J. Barnes was elected, and Mr. Mayhew was formally appointed bandmaster.
>
> Arrangements are to be made to secure a suitable room for practice*, but as the instruments cannot arrive until about the end of September citizens need feel no immediate alarm.†

Bandmaster George Washington Mayhew played the cornet, and, as the owner of the *Times* newspaper, ensured they received good publicity. He gave fair-warning to those who had donated money for the instruments – they might have got more than they bargained for:

> … many who have thoughtlessly contributed towards the funds may possibly feel somewhat repentant of their liberality when the initial practices commence. A full brass band in its

---

* The Brass Band were allowed to use the Town Hall free of charge on Thursday nights, as long as the hall was not needed for other purposes (Palmerston District Council meeting 5 October 1897).
† *NTTG*, 12 July 1895.

Figure 44: Palmerston Brass Band, formed in 1895. V. V. Brown seated centre with a hat, and W. J. Barnes kneels front. Bandmaster George Mayhew played the cornet, so he may be the seated man on Brown's left. Fred Finniss, who was a driving force behind the band, may well be one of the other players. (LANT ph0560-038).

infancy is not what can be termed a soothing affair…

But not to worry, he consoled his readers:

… when it has once got past the rudimentary stage our band will doubtless pleasantly assist in greasing the wheels at many a social gathering.*

Like the Dramatic and Musical Society, the Brass Band continued for many years, and often worked in concert with the dramatists. The Band appeared at every official function from the opening of the railway line to the farewells and welcomes of the new administrators. In 1893, the best vocalists in the band were keen recruits in a new society – the Dingo Glee Club.

The Palmerston Dingo Glee Club

The Dingo Glee Club was formed at a meeting in the Town Hall in February 1895. It was a gathering of men who wanted 'instruction and practice in part singing', including members such as Beckwith (the musical director), Green (honorary secretary), G.H. Sims, Andrews, Harvey, Knight, Barnes, Lawrie, Williamson, Woollcombe, Dobinson, and Price.

* *NTTG*, 21 June 1895.

Figure 45: The Dingo Glee Club in the 1890s (SLSA B-24243).

These men had full social calendars. Their names also appear in the lists and activities of other active clubs and in the guest lists at Government House. Some were Freemasons, four were Justices of the Peace, and most were occasionally seen on jury benches. Many were listed in the results of the athletics, billiards, and cricket clubs, as well as sailors in regattas, and as owners of racehorses. Some were eloquent speakers in the Palmerston Literary and Debating Society – seven were committee members. Their community involvement was admirable.

The Dingoes performed nine times during their first year of operation – the best year of the 10 they enjoyed – usually sharing the bill with individual singers and duets, musicians, and other acts.* The Dingo's first concert was a part of a farewell 'smoke social' for Charles Dashwood, who was going away for a few months. They made a good impression – the *Times* thought the club to be 'sufficiently advanced to render some fine part songs.'†

Literary and Debating Society and the Pickwick Club

Across the colonies, Literary and Debating Societies were a common form of entertainment in many towns and cities, and Palmerston was no different. The Palmerston Society had its genesis in 1879 when there was a lack of options for entertainment and relaxation in the colony. The *Times* liked the idea:

> … Many a long evening may be pleasantly passed, in a comfortably appointed room, discussing the topics of the day, special and general, to each one's mutual advantage.‡

By the 1890s, the Society was in full swing, and many a long evening was indeed enjoyed by its members. They met fortnightly at the Town Hall, and each event was faithfully reported in the newspapers, providing a 'who's who' of one level of Palmerston society – even the Government Resident performed. For example, the meeting at the end of January 1895:

> … may be safely characterised as being about one of the most successful gatherings of the kind that has taken place since the inauguration of this association, and the hearty applause with which the various items on the programme were received must

---

* See Fabrice and Farram for an excellent rundown of the Dingo Glee Club that includes biographies of its members (Fabris and Farram, 2022).
† *NTTG* 15 March 1895.
‡ *NTTG*, 30 August 1879.

have been gratifying alike to the President (who arranged the programme) and to those members who assisted.

The entertainment opened with a charmingly rendered musical selection by Mrs. Harwood, entitled 'The Dying Poet,' and was followed by a song, 'Pretty Pond Lilies' by Miss Maggie Byrne; reading 'The Battle of Ivry' Mr. Kirkland; song 'No my Courage' Mr. Beckwith; recitation 'Mark Antony's Oration' Mr. C. J. Dashwood; song 'Call me back' Mr. Dobinson; duet (piano) 'Selections from La Mascotte' Mrs. Lawrie and Miss Maude Little; recitation 'Hamlet's Soliloquy on Death' Mr. Freer…

… The entertainment was brought to a happy conclusion with two inimitable humorous recitations by the Hon. Sec. (Mr. Macdonald), viz., 'Jehosophat,' and, in response to an encore, 'Courting under Difficulties'. During the evening Mrs. Lawrie, Mrs. Harwood, Miss M. Little and Miss Birkett very kindly and ably assisted at the piano.*

Not all the songs or recitations were entertainment. One man was famous for showing off his skills of memory. John Dolan, a ganger on the railway, had an extraordinary ability:

… the strange subject chosen by Dolan for the display of his elocutionary powers was some of two columns of a statistical article from the Sydney Bulletin, fairly bristling with dates and figures. This he poured forth in a monotonous stream with scarcely a pause, and with (if we remember rightly) only one error. As a recitation it was not entrancing, but as an effort of memory… the exhibition was a unique one.†

The Society continued successfully for about 20 years. In June 1895, it had 71 paying members and a 'handsome cash balance at hand'‡ but it slowly died a natural death, perhaps suffering like so many other organisations by the transient nature of the population. By 1900, the meetings were monthly and attended by less than 20 people and many of the men transferred to a newly formed men-only debating and social club, known as the Pickwick Club. The Literary

---

* *NTTG*, 1 February 1895.
† *NTTG*, 26 June 1908.
‡ *NTTG*, 21 June 1895.

Figure 46: The Pickwick Club, c1900. L-R Standing: W. J. Barnes, W. Holtze, C. H. Davis, F. A. Price, Williamson, Tulley, W. C. P. Bell, P. R. Allen, R. Peak, H. H. Adcock. L-R Seated: Kelsey, Kilgour, Bert Little, J. E. Mercer, N. Stephenson, D. C. Witherden, Dr. F. Goldsmith, W. Wurm, F.S Burgoine (LANT, PH1238/2040)

and Debating Society stopped meeting altogether soon after. There was a brief revival in 1910 with His Honour, Mr Justice Mitchell, reading Dickens to about 50 people (including 'some ladies'), but at the start of the first world war, the Society's vestigial funds were transferred to the Red Cross, and the Debating Society was no more.

Cricket

Cricket was the first field sport played in Palmerston. It was played as early as 1873 on the Esplanade where today the cenotaph and memorial gardens sit. A match between the Banana and Cocoanut Clubs was described by Adelaide's *Evening Journal*: 'Bananas showed very indifferent form and fell easy victims to the superior play of the Cocoanuts.'*

The Cricket Oval was cleared and developed further for cricket in 1874, and it was soon well established.† It was fenced, and a windmill was installed to pump water for the purpose-built pavilions that were provided for the cricket and archery clubs. The Athletic Association and the cyclists also had pavilions built during the 1890s,

---

* *Evening Journal*, 18 July 1873.
† Wilson and James, 2002.

but cricket remained the Oval's main purpose.

The cricket clubs in Palmerston, as similar clubs were in the rest of Australia, were an important marker of the development of British society. It was mostly a European men's pastime, although occasionally Aboriginal players would get a game – such as Charlie, a storekeeper's assistant, in 1882.*

Several clubs existed during the 1890s: Port Darwin Cricket Club, Palmerston Cricket Club, the B.A.T. (British and Australian Telegraph) and OT (Telegraph Co), the Wanderers, the Country Eleven, the Outcasts, the Electrics, and the Railway Cricket Club. In 1897, the Palmerston Cricket Club had enough players to form teams for a married verses single men's game.†

There were also intercolonial cricket matches, following the first game in 1889 between the West Kimberley team and the Port Darwin Cricket Club. The latter were victorious after J.C. Hendry scored the first century in Palmerston. Competitions between schoolboys occasionally entertained the crowd as well, with games between the private school and the public school during 1898 and 1899.

Newspaper readers were usually treated with a blow-by-blow description of the important games. A single example may be enough for anyone. This from 1897:

> … Price and Tracey resumed the batting for the Electric, and the former knocked up 13 ere he was disposed of, his wicket falling to the credit of Deane, who was bowling in great form. Tracey made two and was fairly beaten by a ball from Deane, it was very evident that Pitcher was not at home with the bowling, and after scoring two singles he was bowled by Deane. Bryant was not out man with eight to his credit, which were made in good style. The innings closed for 51. The Outcasts had to make 47 runs to win, a task which should have been easily accomplished, but which proved to be a more

---

* Historian Matthew Stephen points out that Aboriginal players are often only recognisable in the newspapers because they were called by a single name (Stephen, 2010).
† *NTTG*, 18 September 1897.

Figure 47: By the end of the decade there were interschool cricket matches, Private School v Public. In this 1899 photo, the only identified player is Willie Allen. He is standing holding a cricket bat at the end of the back row cricket (1899, LANT ph0238-2081).

difficult one than was expected. Cleland and Morton were the first to face the bowling, but the dissolution of partnership was affected by Price, bowling Cleland with his first ball; and Morton, from whom a good score was expected, had only made two when he shared the same fate…*

Some matches would be related ball by ball. The game between Palmerston and Country in February 1898, went for three days and the *Times* used more than 3000 words to describe it.†

Northern Territory Racing Club

Horseracing was another integral part of British culture transported to Palmerston and the mining camps and telegraph station communities of the Territory in the nineteenth century. This is not surprising – bushmen who made their living on horseback often had tremendous pride in their horses and their skill in the saddle.

As an industry, it began at the Easter race meeting of 1873,

---

* *NTTG*, 16 April 1897.
† *NTTG*, 29 February 1898.

when Palmerston's population was about 500 people. Darcy Uhr, a horseman, drover, and gold miner of prominence, organised a race at Fannie Bay, just outside of town. There were seven races on the card, with two of them won by Government Resident Douglas's horse, Bowerlee. The first event, the Maiden Plate, had five horses competing over one mile. Only three made it to the post:

> … Capt. Douglas's chesnut [sic] gelding Bowerlee was the favourite, but many pinned their faith to the little chesnut cob Palmerston. Their hopes, however, were soon floored, as Palmerston, when going well with Bowerlee, bolted, and threw his rider in the sea, Bowerlee winning in a canter.*

Bowerlee won £15 for that race, and later the £20 Ladies Purse.† From then on, the *Times* and the *North Australian* regularly reported the results of horseraces from across the colony and even from England as the news arrived by telegram.

By 1890, the sport was controlled in the colony by the N.T. Racing Club, chaired by V.V. Brown. The Fannie Bay Racecourse was firmly established but horse owners continued to race their horses wherever there were people to bet on them. Most white communities in the Northern Territory had races, from Tennant Creek Telegraph Station to Timber Creek and, of course, the goldfields. The Palmerston to Pine Creek Railway, fully operational from 1889, was used by racegoers intent on reaching the meetings on the goldfields at Burrundie, Pine Creek and others, and special trains were laid on for the punters.

There were also special trains for the local meets. In August 1895, a first-class ticket to 2½ Mile, Parap, cost two shillings or three for a return trip. The punters rode the train from Palmerston station, alighted at 2½ Mile, walked to the Fannie Bay Racecourse, and returned immediately after the last race.

Like most sports, horse racing was dominated by the European

---

* *Evening Journal*, 18 July 1873.
† Incidentally, 'Bowerlee' was jockeyed by Griffith Todd, a nephew of Sir Charles Todd, who built the Overland Telegraph Line in 1871-72 (*The Advertiser*, 28 October 1938).

members of the population, but Chinese horse owners also had a look in. Races for horses with Chinese owners were run separately and advertised as such. The following can be found in a 3000-word *Times* article on the European races at the 1892 Annual Goldfields Race Meeting, near Pine Creek:

> ... CHINESE RACE of 5 sovs. For all horses owned by Chinese. Entrance, 10s. Distance 1 mile. Start at 12.30 pm.[*]

The race was won by 'Bones', owned by Mr A. Hang Gong.

In 1891, Patrick 'Paddy' Cahill arrived in town leading a string of racehorses and quickly became a stalwart of the racing industry.[†] He was to have a positive effect on nearly every aspect of white society in the Territory and was later described as the most popular man in Palmerston.

Paddy arrived at the age of 29. He was a short and stocky horseman of great skill and charm from Queensland,[‡] and his racehorses, Hard Times, and Treasurer, were a cut above the average for Palmerston at the time. He brought them overland, racing at country meets along the way. At the Katherine races he pocketed £60 and then more at Pine Creek. As owner, trainer, and jockey of the winners, he had fewer expenses than most other owners. He arrived in Palmerston in time for the ninth meeting of the N.T. Racing Club, and soon pocketed 70 sovereigns in three events.[§] In 1892, Hard Times took out the Palmerston Cup at a meeting where Cahill's horses won six races and took placings in four others. One of the champions was St Lawrence, a horse who became so famous that he warranted an obituary after his death 16 years later.[¶] St Lawrence, as we shall see, was just as famous for his exploits as a 'buffalo horse'.

---

[*] *NTTG*, 24 June 1892.
[†] Paddy's two brothers, Tom and Matt Cahill were also horsemen in the Northern Territory. Tom was a boss drover for Nat Buchannan, and Matt a drover, when they brought 20,000 head to the Daly River in 1881. Paddy joined them in 1883 for a drove to the Victoria River (see Mulvaney, 2004).
[‡] Mulvaney 2004.
[§] Sovereigns were the first coins minted in Australia. One gold sovereign equalled £1.
[¶] *NTTG*, 23 October 1908.

Palmerston Athletics Association

Athletics events occurred sporadically in Palmerston from the very earliest days of the colony, and records of numerous events both in the town and the goldfields camps are easy to find. All the public holidays, but especially Easter, New Year's Day and the Queen's birthday were community event days.

New Year's Day in 1890 was no different. George Washington Mayhew, owner of the *Times*, gathered a committee together and eleven events were organised for the afternoon program with total prizes amounting to £30 and 'three handsome trophies.'* The most entertaining event was the obstacle course:

> ... under a tightly stretched cricket net, under a heavy cricket matting, over a stiff 4ft. hurdle, and then under a barrel, and finishing the last ten yards in cornsacks which they had to pick up from the ground. Five competitors started, and after a dispute over the conditions, a second heat had to be run to decide upon the winner, the final result being E. Coughlan 1, W. H. Adcock 2, J. J. Cooper 3.†

An official Athletics Club was formed in January 1891, under the patronage of the Government Resident‡ and the ubiquitous V.V. Brown as president. Annual membership was set at 10s. 6p and it was resolved to run at least two meetings every year with perpetual trophies. At most subsequent events the sports and games offered were of 'such a variety of contests that one would have had to be tremendously hard to please not to extract a bit of fun from the sport'.§ Athletics days usually included running (for example, the Sheffield Handicap over 135 yards and the Maiden Plate over 100 yards), hurdles, cycling,

---

* *NTTG*, 20 December 1889.
† *NTTG*, 3 January 1890
‡ Patron: J. G. Knight, Esq., S.M., Government Resident; President: V. V. Brown, Esq., Committee: Messrs. J. C. Hillson, J. C. Hendry, G. Sabine, J. J. Lawrie, R. M. Stow, G. H. Sims, H. F. Holt, R. D. Beresford, W. Rundle, G. W. Mayhew, G. McKeddie, and Dr. L. S. O'Flaherty. Hon. Sec. Mr. G. W. Mayhew (*NTTG*, 9 January 1891).
§ *NTTG*, 31 May 1895.

'tilting at a ring' from horseback, shot put, hammer throw, pole vault, cricket ball throw, catching a greased pig and others.

The winners were listed in the newspapers and the names must have been familiar – Kelsey, Williamson, Becker, and Bryant, for example, were regular winners. However, readers could be forgiven for believing that Chinese and Aboriginal community members did not participate. The only mention of a Chinese sportsman in May 1895, for example, was a note about the greased pig chase – the *Times* reported that the pigs 'refused to strike out when released, and both Europeans and Chinese had to scramble for their trophies'. The winner of 'Greased Pig: European' was Robinson. Presumably there was also a 'Greased Pig: Chinese', but neither the event, nor the winner, was named by the newspaper.

In its early meetings in 1891, the N.T. Athletics Association committee decided on their rules and prepared for their first official event the following Easter. During Goyder's 1869 survey, and the early settlement of the 1870s and 1880s, the local Larrakia people were encouraged to participate in sports days[*] – usually running and spear throwing events – but the Athletics Association 'resolved that no aboriginals be allowed to compete for any of the events advertised in the programme'.[†] The attitude towards Aboriginal participation can perhaps best be exemplified by the following, which comes from a report on a Burrundie Sports Day in 1890, when Aboriginal men *were* allowed to participate. Despite all the non-Aboriginal winners being listed:

> … About a dozen blacks had the next event all to themselves, and one of them won it.[‡]

However, the exclusion rule in Palmerston immediately came under pressure. Soon, there were races for Aboriginal people tacked on at the end of the program, such as running and spear throwing

---

[*] Stephen, 2012.
[†] *NTTG*, 6 February 1891.
[‡] *North Australian*, 21 March 1890.

Figure 48: New Year's Sports, 1897 (W. Holtze, LANT, ph1139-0003).

competitions, and in January 1893, they included hurdles:

> ... sprints were arranged for... the blacks. A better finish to a good day's sport could not be had even in Chicago. The darkies were sent over the hurdles and different distances on the flat. In one event about 70 started. They were set out in 'layers' first the men, then a squad of women, and away ahead of them a battalion of boys. The finish of this race was something to remember.*

Good cash prizes and trophies were presented to the European winners. Businesses such as P.R. Allen and Co and Rundle Bros were sponsors, and many pounds could be pocketed by the athletes. For example, first prize in the Champions Cup, a 150 yards race in 1893, was £7 7s. This was a time when a good wage was £3 per week, so it was a prize worth winning. At that meeting, even the 'Siamese Race' paid £2, and only two pairs paid the one shilling entry fee:

> ... Only two couples started, and as the other pair hadn't the remotest idea how to get along, Price and Beckwith had an easy task.†

At the same meet, a race between all the members of the club over the age of 30 was hotly contested. George Mayhew managed to hold off the faster men behind him with his 8-yard handicap. His prize was a case of whiskey, donated by P.R. Allan and Co.

The social value of the organised sports days for the white men

---

* *NTTG*, 20 January 1893.
† *NTTG*, 20 January 1893.

of society cannot be understated. A fun time was clearly had, for example, after an event in 1897:

> The settling up took place in the No 1 dining-room of the Club Hotel, in the presence of goodly number of Competitors and others. Mr Stretton, the club's starter, occupied the chair. The cash prizes won at the sports were paid over, Mr. S. Lewis, the winner of the double, taking the largest slice of money. The secretary informed those who had won medals that their prizes had been sent south so that the necessary inscription might be inscribed upon them. A very large list of toasts were proposed, and it is quite unnecessary to state, duly honoured. From the speeches made during the evening it could be seen that everybody was satisfied with the handicapping, judging, and starting, and also with themselves, the visitors from south particularly expressing themselves as to the very enjoyable afternoon's sport they had had, and one and all complimented the committee upon the creditable programme they had presented to the public.*

The 'settling up' turned into a party that was 'tassels up with conviviality, songs and recitations following one another in quick succession'.† It is unlikely that Mayhew's case of whiskey made it home.

Cycling

Bicycles and tricycles had developed a strong following in Sydney and Melbourne during the 1880s. Southern papers were full of stories about them and cycling clubs, races, speed records and tales of heroic long-distance travelling abounded.

The first bicycles arrived in Port Darwin in June 1894. Two telegraph workers, Albert MacDonald and Herbert Bryant, ordered them by telegram in March, and their arrival on the S.S. *Airlie* was a cause for celebration. They were before their time – the local roads were not always ready for cyclists:

> ... A smash up of bicycles occurred out along the railway line

---

* *NTTG*, 14 April 1897.
† *NTTG*, 14 April 1897.

last week. Two wheelmen, Messrs. MacDonald and Bryant were cycling merrily along about 15 miles from town when the latter suddenly began to perform some artistic evolutions not set out in the programme of amusements for the day, and before MacDonald could realise the situation, he found himself assisting the acrobatic display and forming part of a tangle of men and machinery. It was a brilliant performance, we are assured, and the principal actor was an insignificant little stump that was mistaken for a tuft of grass. It afforded a splendid opportunity for high-class stump oratory. One machine was so badly damaged that the rider was glad to take the train home.*

Bicycle races were initially run by the N.T. Athletics Association. The earliest was in May 1895, with only three entries: MacDonald, Herbert Bryant† and his brother Peter G. Bryant. It was a handicapped race over one mile, with a prize of £2 (entry cost 2s 6d).‡ It was not as exciting as the spectators had hoped:

> ... The race for bicyclists was not so interesting as was desired. H. Bryant, with 90 yards start in the mile, was soon put out of it, while his brother... was in no condition to tackle so worthy a foeman as Macdonald, who won by any distance. The time, 3m. 18sec. is not fast for a mile on an asphalt track, but it is not slow for an up and down rough course like the Oval.§

Bicycles and bicycle racing became more popular in Palmerston over the next few years. The North Australian Cycling Club was formed in 1898¶ and it shared the pavilion on the oval with the

---

* *NTTG*, 26 October 1894.

† Herbert H Bryant (1867-1938) was an athletic man – he captained the cricket team in 1897-98 as well as cycled. Bryant appears in Jeanie Gunn's *We of the Never Never* as 'The Dandy'. A South Australian, he and his brother Peter arrived in Palmerston in 1896. He worked for Rundle Bros store until the 1897 Cyclone and in 1998 went bush, sinking wells and fencing. He continued to compete in sport – he won the running race at Brocks Creek on Boxing Day in 1898. On Elsey Station he cut timber to build the homestead and soon became joint manager with Dave Suttic. After droving for several seasons, he returned to Angaston, S.A. and died there on 17 November 1938, aged 69.

‡ *NTTG*, 24 May 1895.

§ *NTTG*, 31 May 1895.

¶ *NTTG*, 11 February 1898.

Figure 49: Jerome J Murif, wearing his riding gear: pyjamas and high boots. The hole in the wall beside him is an embrasure with what may be a rifle barrel visible (several telegraph stations had embrasures in case of attack (SLSA B61438, Murif Collection).

cricket club.*

In 1897, the Athletics Association members were happy to welcome a visitor who arrived overland. Jerome J. Murif had come from New South Wales by bicycle. He was alone – unsuccessful in finding anyone to join him in his travels because everyone thought that such a trip would be impossible. He became the first person to ride a bicycle from the south coast to the north coast.

Murif rode on the 'pads' made by horses and cattle and followed the Overland Telegraph Line. He relied on the hospitality of the white men he met on the way for food and shelter, as he carried few supplies, and mostly avoided interacting with Aboriginal people and Chinese travellers (although at one point he camped with some Chinese goldminers who were heading overland to Queensland to avoid the government poll tax in the ports). Carrying an autograph journal, he collected signatures from people he met along the way, to

---

* The Palmerston oval was situated on the Esplanade where the cenotaph now stands. Its maintenance was the responsibility of the clubs that used it, particularly the Cricket Club, Archery Club, and the Athletics Association and others, and several times during the 1890s the Council refused to fund repairs.

prove the route he had ridden.

When Murif pulled up in Palmerston on the afternoon of 21 May 1897, the town was still recovering from the destruction caused by the Great Hurricane the previous January. Damage was still clearly visible:

> ... 'cyclone' was writ large and in unmistakable characters everywhere – in uprooted trees and other features.*

As Murif travelled by himself and was not sponsored (except by those whose hospitality he drew upon), he made interesting observations of the country and people along the way without obligation to anyone. His book, *From Ocean to Ocean: across a continent on a bicycle*, describes his journey. Of his hosts, he wrote that 'white people seem to live there as much for the purpose of making strangers welcome as to amass money in a leisurely fashion'.†

Of course, the members of the Athletics Association were thrilled to host the novel traveller, and so too were the other residents of Palmerston. He was joined by everyone with a bicycle for a ride around town. They cheered as Murif dipped his bicycle in the sea, as he had at the beginning of his ride in Glenelg, and the site was renamed *Bicycle Point* in commemoration of the event. Murif made no attempt at setting a record, so at 74 days his journey seems rather leisurely compared with those who came later.

On 12 August the same year, Tom Coleman and Alfred W.B. Mather left Palmerston to cross the continent as fast as they could, hoping to set a record. Of course, bicycle companies took full advantage of the publicity generated, and sales of their machines soared. One English company advertised their machines for £7

---

* Murif, 1897. The book was available for sale in Palmerston by 1898: price 3 shillings.

† Murif's little book about his expedition (available easily online) is well worth reading. Unfortunately, he did not name any of the people he met along the way, although Francis Gillen in Alice Springs, who took photographs of Murif, and Essington Lewis, then a teenager near Dalhousie, are both recognisable (Murif, 1897). His journey took 75 days, and as a first was the record to beat.

17s 6d delivered worldwide in the port from where it was ordered. Another, the Dunlop Tyre Co, earned huge publicity when Mather and Coleman's ride became known as the 'Dunlop Transcontinental Ride'.

Mather, who was a last-minute replacement on the ride, took much of the glory because it was he who sent the telegrams from each Overland Telegraph Station they passed. The telegrams were published across the country. Coleman was unhappy – he was one of the original pair of riders and not just 'the man who took part with Mather'.*

Unfortunately, Coleman broke the front fork of his bike by riding into a hole, fell sick with dysentery near Barrow Creek and, at one point, cut the Overland Telegraph Line to secure help from a relief party. The riders took 65 days because Coleman's illness slowed them down. Mather blamed the water at Ti Tree Well, which was 'thoroughly rotten, myriads of birds floating on the surface', although others on the Line said Coleman had eaten a breakfast of 'tinned potted tongue' which had gone so bad it was poison.

The pair carried their machines to Oodnadatta on horseback and eventually made it back to Melbourne. Mather continued to garner most of the media's praise, and Coleman remained Alf Mather's 'companion on the transcontinental bicycle ride'. He also paid a heavy price for cutting the telegraph line – in March 1898 he was served with a claim for £49 9s 23d for repairs to the line. Worse, by then he was in Melbourne Hospital suffering from a spinal disease 'brought on by his long and hard ride'.†

The next rider was Albert 'Mac' MacDonald, who rode a Swift No 1 Light Roadster. MacDonald had been a Powells Creek Telegraph Station operator for several years, so knew the interior well. Inspired by Murif's ride, MacDonald thought to go one better, and ride from Port Darwin to Melbourne. He left on August 23,

---

* *Bunyip*, Gawler 1 April 1898.
† *Border Watch*, 2 March 1898.

Daily Life in Palmerston: Clubs and Societies

Figure 50: Albert MacDonald and his Swift No 1 Light Roadster, at the start of his record-breaking ride to Adelaide on Kitchener Drive in 1898 (LANT, ph0238-2069).

accompanied for the first section by friends from the North Australian Cycling Club, who dropped back as MacDonald rode further south.[*] His progress was tracked by the telegraph stations and reported by the *Times* in each issue. He took less than five weeks, leaving Port Darwin at 6.15am Monday 22 August 1898 and arriving in Victoria Square, Adelaide at 9.45 PM on 19 September. He then rode on to Melbourne, arriving on the 24th. The North Australian Cycling Club were ecstatic and celebrated their 'Mac's' achievement in true Territory style.[†] MacDonald's record was unbroken until Ted 'Ryko' Reichenbach crossed the continent more quickly in 1914.[‡]

---

[*] Including John Dolan, E. Cleland and others who appear at other times in this book.

[†] For cycling enthusiasts: there were other overlanding cyclists not included here. Men like A. Richardson, who rode around Australia from Perth to Perth. He arrived in Palmerston in September 1899 (*NTTG*, 22 September 1899).

[‡] FYI: the current record for a bicycle ride from Darwin to Adelaide sits at 5 days 19 hours and 12 minutes by Gerry Tatrai in 1996, set 99 years after Murif's ride (https://ultracycling.com/).

Daily Life in Palmerston: Clubs and Societies

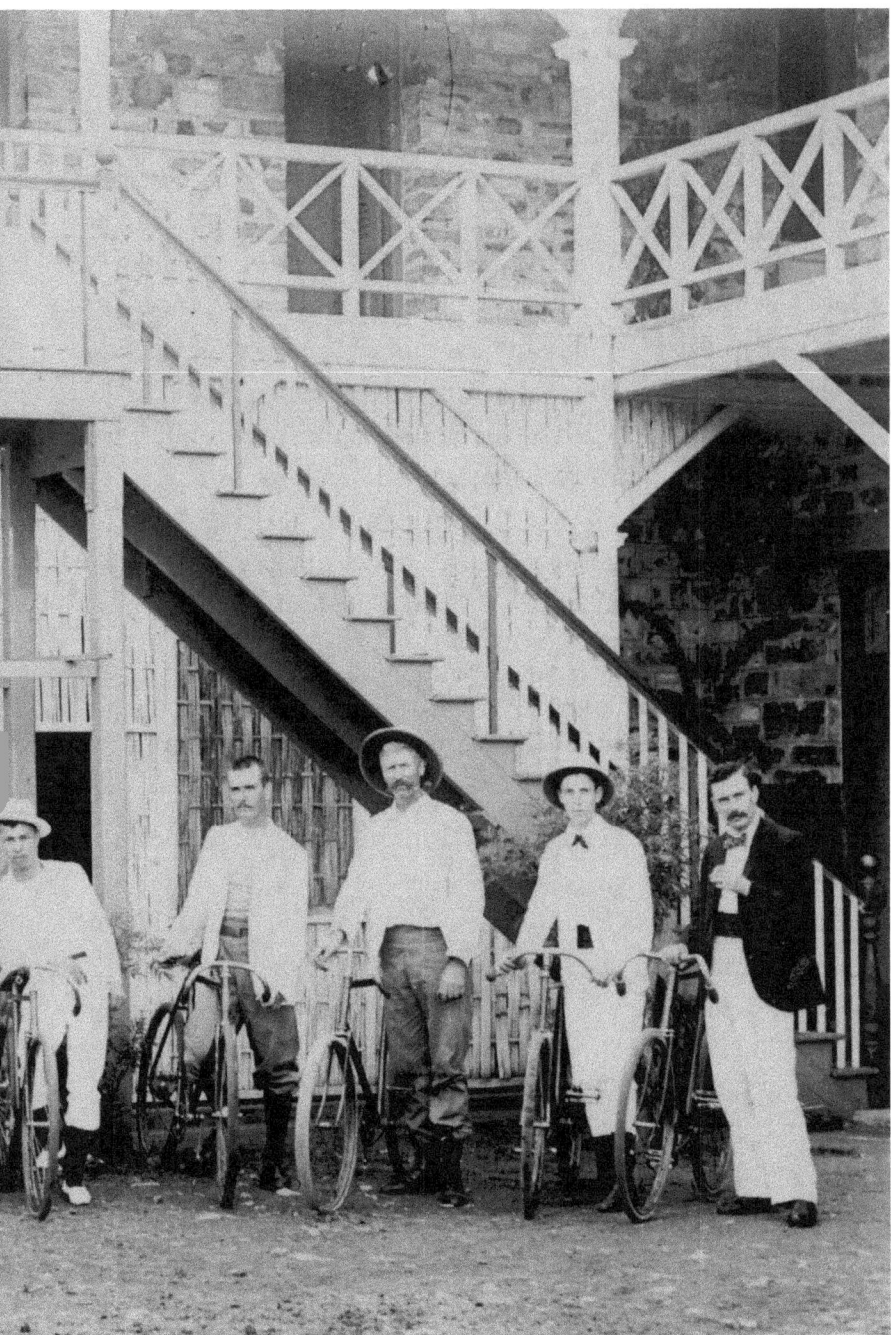

Figure 51: Cyclists at the rear of the Victoria Hotel c 1898 (LANT, ph0238-0650)

Palmerston and Port Darwin Rifle Clubs

Competitive rifle shooting has been a sport since the invention of rifles, so it comes as no surprise to see that clubs sprang up across the Territory as fast as settlements did. Rifle clubs existed in most of the camps in the gold fields during the 1870s. The Union Rifle Club was so successful it could afford to donate over £2 to the Miner's hospital at Yam Creek in 1874.

The Port Darwin Rifle Club was formed in 1887 in competition to Palmerston Rifle Club, which had been operating since October 1881. It then dominated the sport during the 1890s in Darwin, although both clubs used the same range.*

The Rifle Clubs enjoyed competition with the states and their members didn't even have to leave the Territory to join in:

> ... A friendly match between Cooktown and the local club took place last Saturday, each team firing on its own range. The conditions were: seven men a side, with seven shots and one sighter at 200, 300, and 600 yds. Mr. J. C. Hendry was appointed to watch the firing here on behalf of the Cooktown team. The match, as will be seen by the totals, was of a very close nature, the P.D.R.C. winning by ten points only. The following are the scores made by the local team, the average exceeding that of any previous match:
>
> N. Waters. 80
>
> J. J. Lawrie. 70
>
> F. C. Ward. 72
>
> F. E. Becker. 71
>
> W. W. Andrews. 68
>
> S. Pye. 62
>
> J. A. G. Little. 60
>
>   489
>
> At the conclusion of the match a wire was despatched to the

---

* The rifle range is marked on early maps as being a strip of land which today is parallel to Garramilla Boulevard at the north end of McLachlan Street (see Dept. of Works Map: *Town of Darwin: Hundred of Bagot*, 1939).

Secretary of the Cooktown Club, giving the above result, and at half-past eight the Cooktown message came through, giving their total score as 479.*

Port Darwin won, this time, by 10 points.

A similar match was held between the Port Darwin Rifle Club and B Company, 1st Regiment, based in Port Adelaide, in August 1895. The Port Darwin club were victorious by 93 points, despite the top sharp-shooter coming from the company – the ironically named Sergeant Sharp scored 96.

The Port Darwin Rifle Club persisted until 1940, and the members progress can be tracked throughout successive issues of the local newspapers. The Club was particularly active in the first decade of the twentieth century.

Port Darwin Sailing Club

The first regatta in Darwin Harbour brought in the new year on 1 January 1874.† Every sailing vessel in the harbour was involved, including the government cutters *Larrakeeyah* and *Flying Cloud*. While sailing matches were underway, those on shore engaged in sports on the beach with cash prizes – W. Manson won £1 by walking the greasy pole and £4 in the 'duck hunt' where he was the 'duck' and won by evading capture. His brother M. Manson won £2 in a swimming match and two more in the tub race. The £2 prize in the diving match was won by two unnamed Aboriginal men.‡

Further regattas were occasionally held over the next few years. The 1876 regatta was worth over £60 in prizes, and fierce competition between men from Southport and Palmerston ensured an interesting series of races. In 1884, the Palmerston Regatta Club held its first event to celebrate Queen Victoria's birthday with yacht races worth £10 each.

---

* *NTTG*, 3 July 1891.
† There were also regattas held in Port Essington during the time of Fort Victoria (1838-49).
‡ *NTTG*, 9 January 1874.

But that was it for at least seven years. By 1891, the *Times* was asking why there were no more regattas in Port Darwin and its editor encouraged a return to the days of water fun:

> … with a programme comprising sailing and rowing events, swimming, sports for blacks, whites, and Chinese respectively, duck hunts, greasy pole, and the many other customary items of regatta… it should be no difficult matter to make up a day's enjoyment on the water.*

Finally, in 1896, there was sufficient interest and support to begin an annual regatta program, led by businessman Hildebrand Stevens. By this time Darwin Harbour was home to numerous schooners and pearling luggers and seven or more entrants could line up and race for the prizes and the glory. Large and small luggers, dinghies and rowing boats all competed. Although it was a spectacular sight, it was:

> … impossible to describe the different races, as half an hour after starting, the yachts and small and large luggers were mixed up beautifully, absolutely precluding any one from picking out the boats engaged in the different races…†

In the 1898 regatta, Hildebrand Stevens unwittingly caused much amusement by collecting the turn-around buoy and bringing it in before the final race was run:

> … The most amusing feature of the day was the sampan race. Previous to the starting of this event Mr. Stevens went out in the launch and towed the Pioneer Reef buoy into the bay. All four sampans were sent away to a good start, and all the way across the harbor kept well together, until they started to look for the buoy, which of course was not there. Then they spread out in all directions and commenced a vigorous search for the much-coveted flag. After cruising about for some time, and finding that all their efforts were fruitless, one of the Chinamen turned his head for home. He was followed shortly afterwards by the others, and a desperate race to the flagship ensued, but the first boat to start for home secured such an advantage that the others could not pick it up, and he

---

* *NTTG*, 31 July 1891.
† *NTTG*, 31 July 1891.

Figure 52: Third annual regatta day at Port Darwin (January 1898, LANT ph0560-0035).

consequently won easily.*

Each regatta, of course, was accompanied by much partying. In 1896, Stevens catered for 'the comforts of that invisible person the *inner man*' as he 'stood free refreshments and free lunch for all who chose to partake of them, stinting neither meat nor drink...'.† The prize monies, once again, probably never made it home:

> ... the settling up, which was attended with much conviviality, took place at Mrs. Ryan's Club Hotel, and the intervals between the songs were filled with the popping of fizz corks and honouring of toasts. Thanks to the liberality of the winners of the lugger races 'the trough was never dry.

The Asian population were well represented in the regattas. Japanese, Filipino, and Malay sailors on the luggers, and the high-profile contributions of Charlie 'Japan' Hamaura in his lugger *Cleopatra*, ensured the presence of his countrymen. The Chinese were surprise participants. It was said in the 1890s that if 'you say *Japanese* you mean *diver* just as if you say *Chinese* you mean *miner*'.‡ Nonetheless, it appears that even Chinese miners enjoyed a day by the sea.

---

* *NTTG*, 1 September 1897.
† *NTTG*, 18 September 1896.
‡ Sissons, 1977.

Figure 53: A pearl Luggers' race c 1895 (SLSA B-53803).

Port Darwin's annual regattas did not last long. The men who were the main drivers of the events during the years of 1896-1900 appear to have moved on, and there were no more grand regatta days in the first decade of the new century – a loss which was long mourned by old Darwin residents like Bessie Drysdale, who still felt that regattas 'were missing from the modern scene' more than fifty years later.*

---

* *Northern Standard*, 1 August 1952.

Australian Natives Association: Palmerston Branch

A branch of the Australian Natives Association (A.N.A.) opened in Palmerston in February 1890. It was not, as the name suggests, an association of Aboriginal people. Rather, membership was limited to white males who were born in Australia. A 'Benefit Society' formed in Melbourne in 1871, its aim was to 'raise funds by subscription, donations ... for the purpose of relieving sick members, and defraying funeral expenses of members and their wives, relieving distressed widows and orphans and for the necessary expenses of the general management of the Society.'

At its first meeting in Palmerston, V.L. Solomon complained that 'there were large numbers of desirable members who had arrived in Australia as mere children, who would be shut out'.* That remained the case, because the Territory Branch was only small part of the Association.

The A.N.A. became a strong lobby group for federation. Its Australian-born male members demanded the political union of Australia's colonies, helped train politicians and looked after their fellow members, particularly in sickness, medical and funeral cover.†

Tennis

A tennis court was built in the early 1870s behind the British and Australian Telegraph (B.A.T.) offices and it became home to the B.A.T. Tennis Club. In 1885, another court was constructed on the edge of the cricket ground, near the archery club – it was a concrete slab laid down by 'Chinamen...for the sum of £12'.

Soon after, the Palmerston Tennis Club (P.T.C.) was formed and its seven initial members' subscriptions totalled £14 14s. The equipment cost £17 4s 6d, which meant the Club started at a deficit

---

*   *NTTG*, 26 February 1890.
†   The last branch of the ANA closed in Perth in 2007. Incidentally, it was the ANA that first promoted January 26 as a public holiday, originally calling it 'ANA Day.' It was renamed 'Australia Day' in 1935.

of £2 10s 6d. This was solved during the first meeting by the Secretary being permitted to sell the four rackets, and the Club began playing.

Soon tournaments between the B.A.T. Club and the P.T.C. were regularly reported on by the newspapers, and interest in the games was high. The members were even allowed to invite lady players.

The Palmerston Archery Club

The Palmerston Archery Club formed in April 1886 after securing agreement from the cricket club for permission to use a strip of land '¾ of a chain wide, and running north along the eastern fence, starting from the well, and running to the northern fence'.* It was an active club that held regular matches, and popular with the ladies of Palmerston society. Inspector Foelsche's daughter Mary Jane, and Telegraph Master General John Little's daughter, Edith, were regular trophy winners.

Freemasonry

Freemasons held regular meetings in the Victoria Hotel lounge from 6 May 1896 on the Thursdays nearest the full moon. In the same year they secured land on the south-eastern end of Mitchell Street next to the Hotel Darwin upon which they built a lodge. The trustees of the new lodge were solicitor, Charles Edward Herbert, storekeeper, George McKeddie, and Inspector Paul Foelsche, of the Police. The latter was installed as the first Master of the Port Darwin Lodge after the consecration ceremony on 6 May with G.H. James as Treasurer, and P.M. Liddell as Secretary.

The Temple was built by Chinese builders. There was a lodge room and a festive hall with a formal entrance built of timber and corrugated iron. The interior was lined with 'small' corrugated iron.

The Port Darwin Lodge, as it was called, survived for decades. In 1939 a large hall was added, and the original lodge and festive hall were combined to make a single lodge room.

---

* *NTTG*, 17 April 1886. This site is just to the east of the Darwin Cenotaph.

Figure 54: The Masonic Lodge c 1896 (SLSA B-25064).

Darwin: Survival of a City

Chapter 7
Alcohol and Opium

Having a drink with a mate is an age-old tradition in Australia, and particularly in the Territory. Given the number of hotels and sly grog shanties in Palmerston, it was not surprising that daily life involved the regular consumption of a wide range of spirits, wine, and beer. Residents also used drugs such as opium, sold in Chinese opium dens.

Alcohol was a scourge of the Territory that caused much trouble in the nineteenth century (as it still does today) but its importance as the glue that held some communities together cannot be underestimated. Pubs were important meeting places where men and women let their hair down, made friends, found opportunities for work, and kept up with the gossip. More than a few people took drinking too far and ended up in court after some unfortunate turn of events. Some ended up dead.

Banjo Paterson summed up the problems associated with alcohol in Palmerston:

... Palmerston is the city of booze, blow and blasphemy,
and the people have a curious delusion that they are a very
energetic and reckless sort of people. The inhabitants of
Palmerston start drinking square gin immediately after
breakfast and keep it up till after midnight.*

Being drunk in a public place was illegal, and every magistrate's court in the Territory was run ragged convicting offenders and cautioning or fining them five shillings or a pound. Often the guilty

---
* Paterson, 1898.

would be fined a little extra for using foul language, which was also illegal.

Alcohol was used by most people at all levels of society and there were many places to procure it. Hotels such as the Club, the Family and the Victoria were busy places and were advertised in every edition of the newspapers.

Recreational use of opium by the Chinese had been encouraged by the British since their settlement in Hong Kong, but media right across the empire howled that opium dens were 'vile places.' Nonetheless, members of the white population, and even luminaries such as Charles Dickens and Samuel Taylor Coleridge, used the drug through a popular over-the-counter painkiller known as laudanum. Governments had been happy to charge a duty on the importation of opium, as it was mostly used by Chinese. However, towards the end of the nineteenth century there were increasing calls to curb its importation and use in Australia.

As early as 1891, Victoria recommended its banning, except for medicinal purposes, and shocking stories of 'depravity' made the papers in every state for most of the 1890s. For example, Florence (aged 15) and Edith Bennett (13) were rescued from a grubby mattress on the first floor of an opium den in 1896: 'the latter was lying on a bed in a state of nudity and intoxicated…'*

The opium dens in Palmerston were mostly concentrated around Chinatown, for obvious reasons, but there were also others further afield. One of the most prominent Chinese merchants importing opium to Port Darwin in the 1890s was Kwong Sue Tak.† Kwong and his five wives started business in 1888 in premises now known as the Stone House in Cavenagh Street. The Stone House remains as one of the oldest buildings in Darwin and the fortified shop house on its southern end, now a wine-bar with barred windows and extra thick walls, is a reminder of the security needed in the opium trade.

---

* *Maitland Mercury*, 1 August 1896.
† aka Kwong Sue Duk or Sun Mow Loong.

Figure 55: Kwong Sue Duk (also known as Kwong Sue Tak and Sun Mow Loong) who built the stone houses in Cavenagh Street, with two of his wives (LANT, ph0238-0478).

Kwong and his wives also sold *sam sui*, a rice wine imported from Singapore and Hong Kong without any trouble from the Australian customs officers. Sam sui was available from most of the Chinese merchants in town and, as few Europeans were interested in drinking it, it remained a Chinese product. It found its way through the goldfields as a comfort to the diggers who were a long way from home.

Smoking opium was a vice that was tolerated among the Chinese, but Aboriginal people were discouraged from joining in. Sometimes, concerned for their welfare, dens were raided to seek out Aboriginal drug users:

> … On Wednesday the police raided some Chinese dens in Cavenagh street and discovered three aboriginal women all more or less the worse of opium. The trio of fallen sisters were

taken to the lockup and retained for treatment as seemed most desirable.*

The anti-opium movement spread across Australia, as more states brought in legislation controlling its distribution and use. Finally, in 1896, Aboriginal people were refused the right to smoke it:

> ... Aboriginals in South Australia must not be supplied with intoxicating liquors, and the penalty for offending against the law in this respect is a fairly heavy one. Last session Parliament in its wisdom extended the prohibition to opium, and assuming that there is a real danger that a craving for the narcotic drug may seize upon the Australian natives, the step thus taken was unquestionably a wise and beneficent one.†

Thus, supplying alcohol and opium to Aboriginal people became a crime, and the Palmerston Court reports and Fannie Bay Gaol cells were suddenly full of offenders – some serving the maximum 12 months. It took another 10 years before states began passing legislation prohibiting the sale, manufacture, possession, and use of opium and the dens were closed – or at least driven into hiding.

Government Resident Dashwood's concern about drugs increased towards the end of the century. His report in 1899 saw his strongest views to date, and he called for legislation to allow harsher measures:

> ... I have arrived at the conclusion that the penalties for infringing the opium laws do not operate as a sufficient deterrent... the Chinese who supply this drug to the natives are of the lowest class, and imprisonment in the Palmerston Gaol is no punishment to them. I think if, in addition to imprisonment, power were given on commission of second offence to administer a whipping to the offender, it would have a salutary effect.‡

One of the issues for the Government was the duty opium attracted – a state in recession could hardly ignore the income. In 1895, John Richards explained the problem in verse:

---

* *NTTG*, 6 October 1893.
† *South Australian Register*, 22 July 1896.
‡ Dashwood, 1899.

Alcohol and Opium

There was a bold Premier in Adelaide did dwell,
He had a good Treasurer, and him he loved well.
A mighty smart man, neither young nor too old,
But he always was wanting more silver and gold.

This Premier, so bold, had admirers galore,
Some craved for his billet and some for his score.
But one fair admirer to him there did come,
And implored him so sweetly re vile opium.

'Tis sapping the virtue, said she, of Li Fat,
Who while he smokes opium will always eat rat.
'Tis corrupting the morals of cunning Ki Lee,
Who grabs all the gold in the tropic N.T.

There's gentle King Billy, he's going to the bad,
He's smoking of opium. Oh! isn't it sad?
His nerves are all shattered, 'as shocking, said she,
He no longer can flourish his deadly waddie.

Then there's Billy's poor lubra, who dresses with taste,
in the style of Horn's Venus, so charmingly chaste.
She no longer, I hear, drinks good whisky or rum,
But she goes in big licks for that bad opium.

Then the Treasurer screwed up his classical face,
Said he, Madam, already I'm in a very tight place,
But if you've your way, my good woman, why zounds,
I'll be short in my cash nearly nine thousand pounds.

On the Premier, so bold the fair lady she smiled
(This made the good Treasurer feel a bit rated),
And she said, my dear Premier, you'll do as I bid,

And not mind the loss of a few thousand quid.

The loss to the State is eight thousand a year,
In that paltry sum there is nothing to fear.
You can increase the land tax, or, well let me see,
You can clap on more duty on sugar and tea.

Said the Premier, so bold to the lady, so fair,
We'll not mind the Treasurer tearing his hair,
True reformers we'll be, and we'll roam through the slums,
Where they do the skirt dance to the banjo's tom-toms.

Through the sweet-smelling slums we will trot hand in hand,
Where ladies they blush and where burglars look bland,
Where the heathen Chinee smoke that vile opium:
Then how blest we shall be in the bright kingdom come.*

---

* *NTTG*, 27 December 1895.

Chapter 8
Industry

The three industries that had dominated the Northern Territory since settlement – mining, pastoralism, and agriculture – were in trouble during the 1890s. Their success had waxed and waned over the years, but with South Australia in drought and recession, and with politicians antagonistic towards the debt-ridden north, they were all 'hard rows to hoe'. Their full stories are beyond the scope of this book, but this chapter visits each of them and adds a couple of stories on the pearl shell industry to round off.

In 1887, after several very dry years, European miners had left the Territory in droves, chasing the new finds in the Kimberly alluvial goldfields. More left in 1892, when gold was discovered in Coolgardie, and in 1893 when Kalgoorlie's rush started. This left Chinese diggers to play an increasingly important role in the Territory goldfields, despite the Government's stated intention to limit their influence. In 1886, Reverend Tenison-Woods, a geologist, reported on the industry and one of his major recommendations was that the 'Chinese should be entirely excluded from the goldfields except as hired servants'.* This was easier said than done.

In 1892, the Millar brothers (who had built the railway) pulled out of mining on their Union Property, near Pine Creek, and sold their five claims and all their machinery to a syndicate of Chinese miners for £1,000 cash. Another company was bought out by

---
* South Australian Parliamentary Papers, 122/1886

English investors 'for a large sum', and renamed the Cosmopolitan Mining Company, but after a year of losing money, they suspended their operation and allowed Chinese miners to work it on a tribute system. Another, the Eureka mine, made a clear profit of £6,000 in 18 months, but when the owners decided to sell in 1892, there were no buyers. It was then tributed to Chinese miners, joining a whole host of other mines across the region that were similarly left to the Chinese.

The European miners, of course, were unhappy about this but there were not enough of them to make a difference. By 1895, 16 of the 19 batteries were either owned by Chinese or tributed by them, so they had a near-monopoly in the Territory. Despite this, Government Resident Dashwood tried to limit their influence by keeping newly discovered goldfields for Europeans, exclusively. European miners were outnumbered sixteen to one, but they still felt that it was their right to have first go at recovering the gold. In 1886, Dashwood banned the Chinese from working any new fields for two years after they were discovered. They were, however, allowed to work the alluvial fields and older areas not wanted by the white men and they were often successful anyway.

The exclusion time on new fields could be extended if the fields were proving productive, such as happened on the Ferguson River goldfields in 1898:

> NOTICE is hereby given that Asiatic aliens are prohibited from working on the above-named goldfield for a further term of twelve months from the 30th inst, and that no Miner's Rights issued to Asiatic aliens are available for the said Goldfield.
>
> CHS. DASHWOOD*

As with mining, all was not well in the Northern Territory's agricultural industry. Charles Dashwood was succinct in his annual report in 1892: 'This industry is practically at a standstill...' and four

---

* *NTTG*, 29 October 1898.

years later: 'it is with regret that I have to report that no progress is being made in this industry' and again the next year: 'There are no operations to report under this heading'.*

It was not from want of trying. In earlier decades, sugar, coffee, rice, and other crops were trialed in the north, but most farmers were bright-eyed investors from the south who returned home poorer, but wiser, for the experience. It was not because the Territory's soils were leeched of their nutrients, nor that the 'desert climate' of the dry season and the inundation of the wet season were too much to cope with – because the Chinese market gardeners did well. They, like Nicholas Holtze in the Palmerston Experimental Gardens, grew excellent produce. Their secret was plant husbandry – each plant was fertilized, watered, and cared for as can only be done in small plantations. VIPs would visit the gardens and wonder at the abundance growing in the warm tropical climate.

In contrast, the sugar plantations of Cox Peninsula and Adelaide River produced a fraction of the sugar that came from the Queensland cane fields, and the thousands of coffee bushes planted by Poett at Rum Jungle hardly fruited, and his tobacco plants barely grew at all. Only one sugar plantation remained in 1891 – Otto Brandt's plantation at Shoal Bay. But it suffered from rising salt as soon as cultivation started and was abandoned later that year. Then Brandt and his manager, Mr Jaentsche, began looking in the one area that still held out hope, Daly River.

The Daly was, as one writer called it, 'the only agricultural trump card we hold in our hands.' It already had some agricultural history – the plant and equipment from the Delissaville Sugar Plantation had been moved there in 1884 when the Daly River Plantation Company took them over at a bargain price. However, that particular plantation effort ended when the manager, Wright Wainwright Heath, shot and killed his cuckold, Donald MacKinnon.†

---

*   Dashwood, *Government Resident's Reports for 1892, 1896 and 1897.*
†   For this extraordinary tale, see *Darwin: Growth of a City: The 1880s.*

The pastoral industry also found itself in the doldrums during the 1890s. It suffered from dark beginnings: the establishment of cattle stations in the Northern Territory was, without doubt, an invasion of populated lands that had disastrous consequences for the local Aboriginal peoples. Even Government Resident Parsons considered that 'the intrusion of the white man is a declaration of war, and the result is simply survival of the fittest'.*

The pastoralists' war against the traditional owners of the lands they procured came with Government and police support, and no one was ever brought to trial for most of the violent crimes committed.† It was a one-sided battle – Terry and Snider breech-loading carbines or Martini-Henry rifles, plus six-shot revolvers, and unlimited resources, were used against spears and boomerangs.

There were more than 50 massacres on pastoral stations before 1910.‡ At the same time, as traditional lands became ecologically degraded by cattle, Aboriginal people became increasingly dependent on station owners for their survival, and station owners became reliant on Aboriginal stockmen and stockwomen to work with the cattle.§

During the 1880s land-rush, people and companies had fought over parts of the country they had never seen. Some became the proud lessees of hundreds of thousands of hectares that they soon found was unsuitable for both agriculture and pastoralism, or too far from markets. More than a few of these 'stations' collapsed, and pastoral leases were forfeited and surrendered at an increasing rate. In 1898, this meant about 100,000 of the 460,000 square kilometres of land previously under lease was released. As Dashwood explained:

... These lands were not taken up for pastoral settlement,

---

* Parsons, *Government Resident's Report for 1889*.
† The crimes committed by pastoralists in the 'frontier war', are so 'forgotten' that some of the worst protagonists are revered pioneers with streets named after them in Darwin and Alice Springs.
‡ The Australian Museum defines massacre as 'the deliberate killing of six or more defenceless people in one operation'.
§ See Lewis, 2004.

but for speculative purposes and in order to acquire mineral concessions under the Act of 1896. These concessions were granted with the object of inducing the holders to expend moneys in prospecting operations or other works of development, but, I regret to say that, except in two instances, nothing has been done by the lessees in this direction.*

The stations had another problem, one that took a few years to understand and solve. Hundreds of their cattle fell sick and died of Redwater fever, so named because the disease causes an animal's urine to be as red as blood.† Throughout the 1880s and 1890s, it infected cattle from eastern Queensland through to the Kimberley, with disastrous consequences:

> … The tick trouble bids fair to dwarf the rabbit-plague into insignificance. From the Archer to the Bloomfield (N.Q.) are now only remnants of herds which once numbered thousands. A thousand bullocks were put into a paddock on the Lower Burdekin, and in a few weeks 400 survivors were marched off to be boiled down. If driven the cattle die; if left in the infected paddocks they die also. The sweat-glands seem to be completely destroyed, and the cattle are often afflicted with panting like a dog. Horses have been affected of date, and even human beings are not exempt from the attacks of the latest of Australia's blessings.‡

Redwater fever first appeared in Territory cattle when infected ticks arrived with cattle drives from Queensland in 1882. Thousands of Territory cattle died, but rather than being caused by 'miasmatic vapours,' as the Chief Inspector of Sheep claimed in 1887, its source was a blood parasite transmitted by the ticks.§ In 1894, a director of the Queensland Stock Institute and 'government bacteriologist' identified the source¶ and began working on a cure by inoculating calves with the blood of other calves who had recovered naturally

---

* Dashwood, *Government Resident's Report 1899*.
† Redwater fever (aka 'tick fever', or bovine babesiosis) is a cattle disease caused by blood parasites transmitted by the cattle tick, *Boophilus microplus*.
‡ *NTTG*, 26 June 1896.
§ *NTTG*, 10 May 1887.
¶ *NTTG*, 28 December 1894.

from the disease.*

In 1896, Redwater fever was proclaimed an infectious disease under the *Stock Diseases Act* of 1888 by the South Australian Governor,† which gave the Government more control over the movement of cattle. It was serious indeed – many stations went broke because of it, and others suffered when the Territory live export market to Java and Singapore closed in 1896 for seven years.

The live cattle export business had begun well. In the early 1890s, thousands of cattle were shipped alive to Singapore. Goldsbrough, Mort and Co received the cattle at their railway yards at Fountain Head (near Grove Hill) or sent company drovers out to stations to bring in the cattle. The income the cattlemen received depended on where they sold their cattle, but, as Alfred Giles went on to comment when promoting Goldsbrough, Mort and Co, it did not matter to the cattlemen if their beasts went to local butcher shops or to Singapore, the income would be the same.

However, the income still needed to cover the costs of droving and provide a reasonable profit, which became major issue when cattle prices dropped. The 1891 economic depression decimated cattle prices, and worse, surrounding states introduced protection for their own industries. Western Australia imposed a tax of 30 shillings on N.T. cattle crossing the border in 1892, and they were banned in 1893 as Redwater fever spread. Queensland cattle were already suffering badly from the fever, and South Australia banned cattle from Queensland and the Territory for most of the decade.

The droughts of 1895 and 1900-03 added to their woes, with cattlemen unable to afford staff or build infrastructure, and many stations closed. At the end of the decade, the pastoral industry was almost bankrupt, and the agricultural industry was moribund. Fortunately, the cattle continued to breed and run wild, so all was not lost, and the industry picked up again with better prices from about

---

* *Brisbane Courier*, 6 November 1897.
† *NTTG*, 20 March 1896.

1903.*

Being the Northern Territory, the plight of pastoral industry does not mean a lack of stories. A few tales of the industry's struggles are worth repeating here.

Arnhem Land

Arnhem Land is the region east of the East Alligator River and north of the Wilton and Roper Rivers. It contains about 80,000 square kilometres of coastal floodplains, forests, and the great stone escarpment – a nearly impenetrable area up to 100 metres high. There are huge forests of stringybark, woollybutt, and ironbark trees, mangrove swamps, flood plains and wetlands. The country is so rich with food and natural resources that the traditional owners never had to go far for a meal. Tribal lands are therefore compact, compared to the huge rangelands Aboriginal people relied on in the desert.

The British tried to settle on Arnhem Land shores twice – Fort Wellington in Raffles Bay in 1827 and Fort Victoria in Port Essington in 1838. They brought guns, diseases like influenza, weeds, and animals such as ponies, cattle, rats, pigs, and cats. Sailors left goats on remote islands to breed and provide fresh meat for the next time they passed. As the settlements failed and the British left, they released their buffaloes, Timor ponies and banteng cattle. Free to roam the bush, these feral animals thrived.

After the failure of the settlement in Port Essington in 1849, few Europeans visited Arnhem Land for many years.† Then, in 1883, Government Surveyor David Lindsay explored the area in a five-month journey that began and ended in Katherine.‡ His reports encouraged the pastoralists but warned of troubles with the 'blacks'. Ignoring the warnings, cattlemen soon followed. In 1885, an 8,000 square kilometre lease near the Glyde Inlet in Castlereagh Bay (east

---

* See Lewis, 2012.
† Francis Cadell visited in 1867 on the *Eagle*.
‡ See Pugh, 2021.

of Milingimbi Island) was called Florida Station. It was 'magnificent, either for grazing or agriculture, and unsurpassed in the Northern Territory, these magnificent plains extend for 40 miles.'*

The lessee, John Arthur Macartney, and his manager Mr Randall, drove a mob of cattle in from Waverley Station with the help of some Chinese 'coolie' labour. They built a cypress pine homestead on Horseshoe Billabong and three others joined them – an English stockman named Epworth, a French cook named Louis Fayre and Charley Araby, an African ex-slave.†

Everything started off well – cattle remained healthy and calved regularly. They planted food plants which grew at astonishing speed and Macartney thought he could farm sugar cane with at least two harvests each year.‡ Florida Station 'might without exaggeration be styled as *A Squatter's Paradise*,' wrote Alfred Gore after a visit. There was 'nothing finer than Florida' he claimed. But there was a cloud on the horizon:

> … The pioneers of Arnhem Land may at first experience some little trouble with the natives, but that will be easily overcome. A few well applied judicious lessons may be necessary, after which I think it will be found that the natives will prove of considerable value in working the stations.

One of the 'judicious lessons' soon arrived as a cart load of poisoned horse meat. After it was presented to the tribe, it killed many of the men, woman and children who ate it.§

The local tribesmen saw Randall and his staff as invaders and unsurprisingly, speared his cattle, both for food and as a mark of their resistance. They were in a war that quickly escalated when two Malay workers, Ali and Salim, were speared in 1888. Their bodies were never found but the white men quickly responded with punitive

---

* Edgar, 1986, Lindsay 1888 (Lindsay, 1888). Lindsay does not say how many of the 300 warriors had been hurt or killed.

† Charley Araby was one of the Territory's great characters. He died in Darwin in the 1950s.

‡ Alfred Dewhurst Gore, 1887.

§ Trudgen, 2000.

expeditions carrying Martini-Henry rifles. Stories are still told in Milingimbi of white men shooting children from the trees they had climbed for shelter.* They didn't even have to get off their horses:

> ... And they all just went falling down onto the ground. Every one of them, just lying there, and not only a few, lots of them.†

In 1892, Macartney gave up, dismantled his house, and sent anything valuable back to Darwin on the steamer *Adelaide*. A Queensland cattleman named John 'Jack' Watson, who was rumoured to have been killed by natives, surprised everyone by turning up in Palmerston in good health in March 1893.‡ Macartney employed him to round up what was left of the cattle and drive them west to Auvergne Station, near the Western Australia border.

Watson was a man who would 'charge hell with a bucket of water' and a merciless slayer of Aboriginal people. It was said that Watson found 'the blacks of Blue Mud and Caledon Bays good hombres, but he had to wipe out a lot to make them so' and when Watson 'threw the lead at them' he 'threw it to kill'.§ Emily Creagh visited Watson in Queensland in 1883, and wrote that he had on his shed:

> ... 40 pairs of blacks' ears nailed around the walls collected during raiding parties after the loss of many cattle, speared by the blacks.¶

Buffalo

Originally introduced through the failed British settlements at Melville Island (1824-29) and Cobourg Peninsula (1827-29, and 1838-49), by the end of the century there were thousands of buffalo roaming the wetlands. They grew wild and dangerous and had a devastating environmental impact. It wasn't long after settlement that newcomers started to see their economic potential.

---

* Personal discussions, 1994.
† University of Newcastle 2022, Read and Read 1991.
‡ *NTTG*, 3 March 1893.
§ Gaunt, 1934.
¶ Creaghe, 1883.

Figure 56: Slain buffalo in the Northern Territory (SLSA, B-72713-6).

There was money to be made by harvesting the hides of feral buffaloes. It was a cruel and bloody industry that was dominated by several larger-than-life characters throughout the 1890s.* Men like Paddy Cahill, who hunted in West Arnhem Land, and Robert Joel 'Joe' Cooper and his brother Harry Cooper on Melville Island, were household names in Palmerston. So too was Edward Oswin 'E.O.' Robinson, who first hunted buffaloes on Cobourg Peninsula after his partner in trepang fishing, Howard Wingfield, was murdered by Wandi Wandi in 1878 (see Chapter 12).

By 1897, Robinson claimed to have exported 20,000 hides from Cobourg and the Alligator Rivers region, and another 6,600 from Melville Island.† The 1890s produced about £32,000 worth of

---

* Buffalo hide harvesting was first conducted by John Lewis and others in Port Essington during the 1870s.

† When the leasing of Melville Island was being planned, debate raged on who should be allowed to buy the leases. White Territorians were favoured of course, and the island was 'sold' as if it was uninhabited. For example, in the *Times* 28 August 1891: 'it is absurdly unjust to expect local bidders to have to buy up leases through expensive metropolitan agents, when the land under offer is purely Northern Territory and theirs by right more than anyone else's. No doubt when it is sold Melville Island will be sold with all its wild cattle.'

hides and horns.*

There was an occasional public outcry regarding what people saw as 'waste':

> ... What tons of meat have been wasted in the 20,000 buffalo which have been killed for their hides and horns alone in the Port Essington district since the slaughter begins, and what tons will be added to the waste before buffalo hunting is a dead industry?†

Buffalo hunters usually lived in Palmerston during the wet-seasons and spent the dry seasons hunting and shooting as many buffaloes as they could. It was a dangerous occupation that required great skill and daring.

The affable horseracing personality, Paddy Cahill, and his remarkable horse, St Lawrence, worked in the Oenpelli region of Arnhem Land and took up to 15,000 hides during his decade of operation. Larry, as the horse was known, would gallop alongside a fleeing buffalo, which Paddy would shoot in the spine. The horse would then immediately change direction, firstly to avoid a collision with the falling beast, and secondly to pick up the chase of the next. In the tropics without refrigeration, there was limited time for skinning an animal before decay set in, so killing them outright risked losing the hides. Crippled buffaloes, by contrast, could wait for hours, even overnight, for the skinners to arrive to finish them off.

The danger of the hunt thrilled the readers of hunters' exploits in the press. In one issue of the *NT Times*, two near-death occurrences were reported. Paddy Cahill had been 'brought to earth by a calf running between his horse's legs while chasing a mob of buffaloes, but with no more serious result than a few bruises', and Harry Cooper had:

---

* Coincidentally, this is also about the size of the trepang industry for that decade. Both were small industries compared with pearl shell (about £111,000) and all were dwarfed by the value of mining (£964,000) (Mulvaney 2004). The buffalo industry's importance comes more from its status in Territory lore than as a financial bonanza.

† *NTTG*, 13 April 1894.

Figure 57: Paddy Cahill (c 1898 LANT ph0238-0707).

Figure 58: Paddy Cahill and his wife Mariah (nee Pickford) with unnamed buffalo workers (c 1900, LANT ph0412-0093).

... an exceeding narrow escape... He badly wounded an old buffalo bull, who thereupon took refuge in a thick bit of scrub. Cooper, following up his quarry with more zeal than caution, inadvertently passed the spot where the buffalo was standing. The latter at once took up the chase in his turn, and overtaking his would-be slayer with a rush, knocked him down and proceeded with great satisfaction to convert his foe into pulp. Fortunately, some blacks came up and succeeded in driving the brute off, but not before Cooper had received several very nasty injuries.*

Cahill's skinners and hide salters were Aboriginal men and women paid with sticks of tobacco and other luxuries from distant lands – a system that seems to have satisfied both parties at the time. Cahill developed a love and respect for the local people that eventually morphed into the establishment of a community for their welfare at Oenpelli.

Joe Cooper, who was to have an equally profound effect on the Tiwi people, visited Melville Island in 1893 with E.O. Robinson. The latter was interested in taking the pastoral lease over the whole island to harvest the buffaloes. These were descendants of buffaloes brought by the British to Fort Dundas after 1824. The British had hoped the fort would become a 'new Singapore' but were sorely disappointed as no traders ever came. Disease ridden and harassed by the Tiwi, the soldiers and convict volunteers transferred to Raffles Bay on Cobourg Peninsula, to be closer to the areas visited annually by Macassan trepang fishermen. The buffaloes either escaped or were released when that fort was abandoned and seventy years later, thousands of them roamed almost unmolested over the island.

E.O. Robinson, with Cooper as his manager, returned in 1895 with a party of about 20 Iwaidja workers. They were well-armed and wary, particularly because Muckaluggee, a crewmember of the *Zaleika*, had been speared when collecting firewood. A large spear had been driven almost through him:

---

* *NTTG*, 7 July 1893.

Figure 59: E.O. Robinson and Harry and Joe Cooper (SLSA, B72713_36).

… When this boy [sic] was struck he made a flying leap about four feet from the ground and falling backwards broke the point of the spear in his body. We fired into the bush, but could neither see nor hear anything, for everything was as still as death.*

Muckaluggee died a few days later in Palmerston hospital. As it was a murder of an Aborigine by another, it was not further

---

* *NTTG*, 21 December 1894.

investigated, and nothing of Muckaluggee's background was recorded, but his death certainly added to the Tiwi's reputation as fearsome in their defence of their island:

> ... The spear was... a terrible looking thing, 9ft long, made of white mangrove wood and barbed on one side of the point only. On every possible occasion the islanders keep up their reputation for ferocity and cunning...

Robinson's party shot and salted the hides of more than 300 buffaloes in the weeks after their arrival, without at first experiencing similar problems:

> ... The buffalo hunters on Melville Island appear to be in a fair way to realise their most sanguine anticipations as to the number of skins and scalps (our playful term for horns) obtainable on the island. Mr. E. O. Robinson, the lessee of the place, came into port a few days ago with 359 hides in the 'Essington,' and these are stated to be the produce of less than a fortnight's shooting. Moreover, the whole of the hides were got within five miles of the party's camp; reasoning from which Mr. Robinson jubilantly considers he has struck oil.[*]

However, trouble started six months later:

> ... The buffalo hunters who recently settled on Melville Island are being troubled by the blacks on the island. On Monday Mr. R. J. Cooper, who was on horseback, accompanied, by several mainland blacks, started from a camp near the seaboard with the object of buffalo-hunting. Cooper, who was in advance of his native employees, was surprised by a spear thrown by a Melville Island black[†]. The weapon entered his shoulder. Cooper dismounted and managed to fire his rifle to attract the attention of his assistants, and this led to the disappearance of his assailants. Returning to Palmerston, the spearhead was extracted, and Cooper is now progressing satisfactorily.[‡]

The hunters managed to get to their boat and return to Port Darwin, but were back on the island within three weeks, despite the

---

[*] *NTTG*, 7 June 1895.
[†] Morris (2000) says that Cooper was actually stabbed by the spear around a tree, as he was holding his 'assailant' by the wrist and trying to pacify him.
[‡] *Evening News*, 27 June 1895.

Tiwi's resistance. Cooper's off-sider, Barney Flynn, who has long been blamed for the shooting death of six Tiwi men and women*, also had a narrow escape when a spear grazed his shoulder.

No one was surprised:

> ... The attack made by the Melville Island blacks on Cooper and Flynn's camp only proves what many have thought all along, namely, that, it was only a question of time. It was alleged a few weeks back that the blacks had forsaken Melville Island and removed bag and baggage to Bathurst Island. If that were so, it is evident that they did not give up hope of getting their native island back. More than this, the very boldness displayed by them shows that they fear the white man and his rifle but very little, notwithstanding the way Cooper and Flynn have been bowling over the buffalo. Melville Islanders are hard subjects to subdue, and it has been proved repeatedly that when in their country you require to be always on the *qui vive* for spears.†

Despite this, some Tiwi welcomed the hunters, particularly several families of the Mandimbula clan, who began camping near the hunters' camp. At least one of their women settled down with a new Iwaidja husband and more than a few people offered their labour and worked for Cooper as skinners and salt bearers, in return for coveted goods, such as sticks of tobacco and flour.

It was a dangerous business, but few, if any, paid the ultimate price. Robinson said in 1899 that he had never seen any fatalities among the hunters:

> ... although some of the natives have had narrow shaves through being a bit too slow at shinning up a tree. They have to move smartly if a buffalo is charging, although the animals cannot gore like a bullock, as their horns are turned too far back. They can do a great deal of damage, though, with both horns and hoofs.‡

During the next two years, 7,000 buffalo hides were harvested

---

* Morris, 2000.
† *Evening News*, 27 June 1895.
‡ *NTTG*, 15 September 1899.

Industry

Figure 60: Joe Cooper in 1912 (Campbell, LANT, PH 0100-0132).

before Robinson withdrew his men to allow the herds to replenish. On Cooper's departure at least 12 Tiwi women, several babies, and two men, left with him on his lugger. They settled in West Arnhem Land and worked in the buffalo industry with the Iwaidja for years. One was a man named Samuel Ingeruintamirri, an impressive Tiwi man who helped Cooper learn the Tiwi language.

Eventually, it was Ingeruintamirri who was sent back to the island with presents and trade goods, to negotiate on behalf of Joe Cooper and his brother Harry, who wanted to land unmolested and recommence hunting on the Tiwi Islands. Two Tiwi women also landed on the beach and called out, 'pongki, pongki! peace, peace, this man quiet'. What stories Ingeruintamirri and the others would have told their clan, the Mandimbula, for they had long been thought to have been lost forever.

With such help, the Coopers were nervously welcomed and, over the next 10 years until 1916, Cooper exported about 10,000 hides to Port Darwin, as well as cypress pine timber and trepang. Naturally, difficulties arose between Cooper's workforce of Iwaidja men and the Tiwi because there were no Iwaidja women among them, so demands were made of Tiwi women instead. The Iwaidja, armed with rifles, made several deadly incursions into the island's interior to steal women. The names of at least 24 women stolen in this fashion could still be recalled by elders in the 1960s.* Joe Cooper was never called to account for the behaviour of the Iwaidja men he employed.

Cooper lived and worked as 'the king of Melville Island' until 1916,† when he returned to Cobourg Peninsula and continued trepang fishing east of the peninsula, living at Port Bremer with his family.‡ By 1933, he had retired in Darwin and died there, aged 76, on 7 August 1936.

A Meat Extract Industry

It was a pity, many thought, that nothing could be done with low priced cattle, and the carcases of the buffalos that were killed for their skins. In the days before refrigeration, any value adding process that could improve the return on the cattle or buffalo industry and avoid the huge waste inherent in the buffalo skin industry, was welcome. One idea, from John Henry (Harry) Niemann, seemed to provide a solution:

> ... Mr. Niemann has invented a process, which be claims will take both extract and fat from the beef at one operation, and do it very cheaply, too. The machinery is simple, and Mr. Niemann has offered to put up an establishment on Melville Island to deal with the bullocks there if the process proves a success at Victoria River, where Mr. Bradshaw has offered to provide a number of ordinary cattle for an experiment.§

---

* Morris, 2000.

† Joe's brother Harry died of syphilis on the island in 1907 (Entry 132, Archives of Registrar of Births, Deaths, and Marriages).

‡ Joe Cooper had several children with his Iwaidja wife, Alice Rose Marla-oldain. Their son Reuben (1898-1941) is credited to have been one of the founders of Australian Rules football in Darwin. Many think of him as the Territory's finest player before the Second World War. Reuben drowned in the Alligator River in 1941.

§ *NTTG*, 15 September 1899.

E.O. Robinson was keen to experiment with the meat extract, as he thought the darker buffalo meat would be superior to beef, and he was keen to know the results of the experiments on the Victoria River. However, Niemann's journey was delayed by what became an epic tale of survival, followed closely by the community of the day.

Niemann, his wife Mary (nee Nicolson), their two young daughters, Alice, and Kitty (Catherine), and a partner/engineer named Nicholson boarded the pearling lugger, *Midge*, for the journey to Bradshaw's station on the Victoria River. A sailing lugger was a difficult ship to manoeuvre through strong currents, particularly when its anchors were useless in the fastmoving sand:

> ... they were carried by the resistless tidal currents on to a tenacious series of sandbanks that held them fast prisoners for many weeks. Their supply of food and fresh water-taken in quantity only sufficient to meet the requirements of a brief voyage became exhausted, and they were compelled to subsist on catfish and young sharks caught over the side, whilst one ingenious member of the party contrived, from the scanty materials at command, an apparatus to convert salt water into fresh. Eventually the boat succeeded in breaking free from her dangerous environment and returned to Darwin, where the whole party [were] welcomed as people risen from the dead, a search party having failed to find any indication of their whereabouts, and the conclusion having been arrived at that the boat and all on board had been lost.*

The family were safe, but Niemann decided against both the Victoria River and Melville Island. Instead, the Niemanns and Nicholson moved into the Daly River mission buildings, recently abandoned by the Jesuit missionaries.

By December 1899, all was looking good. A visitor reported:

> ... the process... appears to be very perfect, and... Messrs. Niemann and Nicholson claim great improvements on any [system] now in use elsewhere, and judging by the satisfaction

---

* *NTTG*, 11 November 1913. The full story, written by Mrs. Niemann, can be found at *NTTG* 4 August 1899 in: *The Mystery of the 'Midge': A Schooner Lost in The Bush. Passengers Existing For A Month On Catfish.*

they express at the way it works there should be money in the business...*

But their optimism was misplaced. After a decade of doldrums in the cattle market, there was a sudden and sustained upswing in the price of live cattle and the potential profits from the meat extract plummeted. Niemann and his family abandoned their machines, but stayed on to make a living in a different way:

> ... Being compelled to submit to the inevitable, Mr. Niemann has for some months past been devoting his energies to collecting and preparing the skins and plumage of the numerous beautiful birds to be found in this district... In collecting these birds and also skins of alligators, snakes, etc. the blacks about the station are found very useful and think themselves handsomely rewarded for a day's tramp in search of specimens by half a stick or so of the much-coveted black stick tobacco. On the same terms and supplied with a shot gun and two or three cartridges, the table is kept well supplied with every variety of game.
>
> The system adopted is to give the darkie who has been elected as hunter for the day, say three cartridges one for himself and two for the house – the understanding being that all he shoots with his own cartridge he may take to camp, whilst that which falls to the other two is to be brought to the house.†

Pearling

The possibility of a pearling industry in the seas off the Northern Territory occasionally rippled into waves of excitement during the 1870s and 1880s. The industry was first suggested by the French consul, Monsieur Edouard Durand, in 1874. He was a licenced storekeeper with shops in Palmerston, Southport, and The Shackle. Intent on expanding his empire, he employed Captain Black of the *Northern Light*, a pearling lugger with a crew of Malay divers, to collect pearl shells in Darwin Harbour.

The Government was at first confused – the *Northern Territory*

---

* F.D. Holland, *NTTG*, 8 December 1899.
† *NTTG*, 29 June 1900.

Industry

Land Act of 1872 made no mention of pearling, so no one knew whether pearl divers needed licences. Captain Black didn't wait to find out and collected pearl shell in Darwin Harbour and later moved to Port Essington, where calm waters were ideal for seeking pearl shells. From time to time, the *Northern Light* returned to Port Darwin to restock – and to deliver the bodies of some of his crew. There were four: Suntah died of the bends on 9 August, writhing in agony on the deck; Batch Bonlong, died spitting blood three weeks later; Conba, was killed by 'congestion of the lungs'; and Heman succumbed to dysentery on 24 January 1875.*

Durand never recorded his emotions at the loss of his crew, but he was continually frustrated by the Government's lack of interest in the industry. Unfortunately, his plans and the industry died with him when he sailed on the final journey of the *Gothenburg* in February 1875. He drowned when she sank in the waters off Bowen during a cyclone, clutching a heavy black bag that was said to contain £3,000 in sovereigns.†

Several pearl shell prospectors made occasional discoveries in the harbour over the next five years, but it wasn't until 1883 that commercial amounts of pearl shell were found. Then, on 10 February 1884, Acting-Government Resident Gilbert McMinn welcomed the *Sree Pas Sair*, a 112-ton vessel that carried eight boats and sixty-four divers, to Port Darwin. As soon as customs formalities were completed, the divers went over the side and had considerable success, and everyone was soon talking about a bright future for the pearling industry.

Unfortunately, the Territory's pearl shell beds were never as extensive as those in Western Australia or Thursday Island, and the shells never grew as large. In addition, the water in Darwin Harbour was so murky the divers usually had to work blind.

For a while, many Aboriginal, Malay, 'Manillamen', South Sea

---

* LANT, Palmerston Register of Deaths, 1870s
† McInnis, 1952.

Islanders, and Japanese men were employed as divers,[*] but by 1890 the pearl shell industry in Darwin Harbour had run out of steam. Most of the luggers moved on to the clear waters of Thursday Island or the Kimberley where 750 shells weighed a ton compared with 1000 shells in Darwin.

Then in 1892, pearlers from Japan tried to resurrect the industry. They exported 10 tons of 'fair to medium' shell valued at £1,705 from Darwin Harbour that year, and during 1893, six Hong Kong-built luggers took 45 tons of shell worth £5,995. In 1897, there were 29 luggers in Darwin Harbour when the Great Hurricane hit. At least 18 of them were sunk or run ashore and about 16 crew members died.

Figure 61: A diver on Port Darwin Jetty (c 1896, nla.obj-150843779-1).

Average prices neared £140 per ton and a successful lugger was said to have an income of about £566 for the season.[†] By 1899, the pearl shells brought nearly £30,000 into the Territory revenue,[‡] but then the industry began struggling and the leading men in the

---

[*] Unsurprisingly, the influx of foreign men caused tensions in the small community of Palmerston. In 1884, several Larrakia women moved in with some Malay crew and even went to sea in their boats (Reid, 1990). All sorts of trouble arose, as the *North Australian* reported: 'Mary Ann and several of her sisters, cousins, &c, have become attached to certain Malays in Palmerston, by whom they are fed, clothed, and housed, and looked upon as wives. As a compensation, the male relatives of these girls receive gifts of flour, tea, sugar, &c., from the Malays, and if these are not forthcoming at the proper time the blacks take the women away.' But Mary Ann had a mind of her own, and when she had trouble with Charley, her brother, forcefully trying to remove her, she took him to court. 'What for Malay keep 'em that girl?' Charley said, 'that not right' (*NTTG*, 15 February 1884).

[†] Bach, 1955

[‡] Mulvaney, 2004.

industry moved their operations elsewhere.

One lugger captain who left was Charlie 'Japan' Hamaura who, having been brought to Palmerston in 1892 by the North Australian Pearl Shell Company, fished for pearl shell in Darwin Harbour and its surrounds for most of the 1890s.[*] His luggers were called *Cleopatra* and *Esau*, both of whom appeared regularly as winners in the annual lugger races in the Port Darwin Regattas. According to the *Times*, he was sadly missed:

> … It is now some years since Hamaura made his first appearance in the Territory. He may be regarded as one of the pioneers of the local pearling industry, and although he be an 'alien' we think we shall be voicing the general opinion when we state that throughout his career here he has uniformly shown that he possesses most, if not all, those qualities universally conceded as going to the making of a good public-spirited citizen. His hearty generous assistance has always been readily forthcoming on all occasions of public interest – from the promoting of a regatta or other sports to the alleviation of distress, and his open-handed generosity has become proverbial… he was always one of the first to join in any movement in the direction of prospecting for new grounds, or in other ways to throw in his lot with the European boat owners in forwarding the general interests of the industry.[†]

The remaining pearlers struggled on. A new pearling ground was found near Bathurst Island, but the local industry remained only marginally viable for decades. There was a revival during the 1930s, but World War II, and the invention of plastic buttons, soon brought it to its knees.[‡]

---

[*] Sissons, 1977. (Sissons, 1977)

[†] *NTTG*, 26 October 1900.

[‡] It was not until the cultivation of pearls took off in the 1950s and 60s that pearling again became a major Territory industry. Interestingly, it may have been a small industry for *centuries*: Yolngu people of Eastern Arnhem Land are now thought to have actively farmed pearls to trade with annual 'Malay' or Chinese visitors (Dobson, 2021).

Figure 62: Pearl fleet 1895 (SLSA, B-24187-25).

Figure 63: *Petrel*, a pearling lugger in Darwin Harbour (1897, Bleeser, nla. obj-150841035-1).

Chapter 9

The Railway

South Australian Governor Richard Graves MacDonnell mooted the idea of a transcontinental railway soon after the Northern Territory was annexed to his state, and many calls for it quickly followed John McDouall Stuart's successful exploration in 1862. It was an idea before its time and MacDonnell was laughed at – it was 'preposterous' they said.

But the idea persisted. California was being settled in part by a successful land-grant system where railway companies were granted half the land through which their rails would pass. Some thought the same system would work in Australia too, but no one came forward during a five-year search for companies who could do it. The Outback was less attractive in the 1860s than the golden hills of the American West.

Nevertheless, the idea didn't die, and it was a recurring theme during the time the Territory was a South Australian entity. With a 'build-it-and-they-will-come' philosophy, the railway's proponents saw it as being the saviour – and population and industry in the Territory would automatically follow.

In 1872, the Overland Telegraph Line connected Adelaide with London, right through the heart of the continent. Surely, it was just a matter of time for roads and railways to follow. Rumours were rife – an English company became interested in constructing the line in 1872, and someone from Ballarat thought he could raise £20 million and find 100,000 immigrants.* Government support waxed and waned, depending on the party in power at the time. There were prospectuses printed and plans made, but nothing happened until John Langdon Parsons became interested in the Territory in 1882.

As a minister, Parsons passed the *Palmerston to Pine Creek Railway Act* in a time of great confidence. The Territory budget in surplus in the early 1880s, so finance for a railway was easy to find at four percent interest. Parsons became Government Resident in 1884, and by 1886 the Millar brothers had been contracted to build the railway south to Pine Creek. At the same time, a narrow-gauged railway snaked forward from Farina to Oodnadatta in South Australia, and it was assumed that these lines would eventually meet somewhere in central Australia.

The Palmerston to Pine Creek Railway was handed over to the Government by the Millar Brothers construction company in September 1889. Despite being built with huge optimism, the railway attracted such little traffic that the daily service was almost at once cut to three trains a week, then two. Its immediate effect was to blow-out the Territory's debt.

Throughout the 1890s the receipts for both passenger and freight movements could not cover the interest on the loans. The South Australian Government decided that the interest and operating costs would be paid out of the Northern Territory budget – without any increase in funding. The result was a near paralysis. Government money was so tight that normal development stagnated for decades, and no funds meant no new infrastructure.

Writing in 1915, Masson concluded the abandonment of the railway was a sign of the South Australian Government's disillusionment in their northern venture:

> … The making of the railway was the last decisive action on the part of South Australia; its abandonment was a sign that

---

* Surprisingly, V. E. Fletcher, in his history of the railway, thought that this might actually have been achievable (2013, page 5).

The Railway

Figure 64: Palmerston Railway Station yards (c 1889, Foelsche, LANT, ph0297-0033).

she had thrown up the sponge, realising that not only time and continuous effort but also the expenditure of more money than she could afford, would be necessary to subdue the obdurate north.*

The population of the Territory was too small to afford such a luxury, but the railway extension was seen as necessary for the future of the country. Many people remained enthusiastic, causing Governor Kintore to report during his travels that 'in every speech, every address I received [the railway] was made the leading topic'.†

Petitions to extend the railway as far as Katherine began as soon as the Pine Creek line was opened – but they were quickly knocked back:

> … The Government have carefully considered the petition of the residents in the Territory that the railway should be extended from Pine Creek to the Katherine. Mr. Stewart's estimate of the cost of a line from Pine Creek to the Katherine is £503,000. The Government feel that they must not increase the indebtedness of the Territory to that extent, at least for the

---

* Masson, 1915
† Kintore, 1891 (Fletcher, 2013).

present. They are anxious also to see if the construction of the line to Pine Creek will result in the benefit to the Territory and the development of the mineral country around Pine Creek to the extent many anticipated.

I have. &c.

F. C. WARD*

The Royal Commission held in 1895 into Territory affairs opened a 'Pandora's box' of complaints laid against South Australia and its management of the north. The railway debt was foremost among them. Vaiben Solomon claimed that if the railway was indeed a 'transcontinental' rather than a local line, then the cost should have been born by the entire colony. Solomon wrote: 'Let the railway account be taken away, the Northern Territory debt would almost disappear.'†

But the transcontinental railway idea persisted. Dreams were free, and the optimistic could only see a brighter future after its construction:

> What extraordinary benefits will accrue to the province in connection with the scheme need no recapitulating here, but there is no question of doubt that with the passing of a bill permitting the construction of the through railway all the Territory's disabilities will disappear as if by magic before a new era of certain and permanent prosperity.‡

Territorians were to be disappointed for generations. The line did eventually extend to Katherine, and then to Birdum Creek (just south of Larrimah) but that, like the extension of The Ghan from Oodnadatta to Alice Springs, was not until 1929. The railway was handy for the mining and cattle industries, and particularly useful for the military during World War II, but it never extended further south than Birdum and it was finally closed in 1976. The metal lines were pulled up and recycled and thousands of wooden sleepers were recycled into garden walls and picnic tables, or just left to rot.

---

*   F.C. Ward's letter published in the *Times* of 7 March 1890.
†   Solomon, 1895 Royal Commission Report p5, (SAPD HA 17/12/1895, p2912).
‡   *NTTG*, 18 September 1896.

Many decades later the transcontinental railway was finally built. It opened in January 2004 and the first freight train reached Darwin on the January 17. The first passenger train, called The Ghan like its predecessor, soon followed, arriving in Darwin from Adelaide on 4 February 2004 with its carriages bursting with politicians and other VIPs sipping the best Clare Valley wines. It took 47 hours to travel the 2,979 kilometres on a line that had cost $1.2 billion.*

---

* ABC, *The World Today*, 10 June 2010.

Chapter 10
The Charles Point Lighthouse

Despite its huge size, the opening to Darwin Harbour could be missed by ships searching the coast at night. A beacon was needed to guide mariners, preferably something better than the temporary construction announced in 1882:

> Notice to Mariners,
>
> Clarence Straits, Point Charles, Northern Territory.
>
> NOTICE is hereby given, that a wooden XV pyramidal beacon has been erected on Point Charles for the guidance of mariners. It is Forty-one feet high, Twenty feet at the base, and Eight feet Six inches at the apex, having twenty feet from apex downwards covered with galvanized iron, and painted white.
>
> K. H. FERGUSON,
>
> President Marine Board.
>
> Marine Board Offices, Port Adelaide,
>
> January 16th, 1882.

Ten years later, in October 1892, a traveller claimed that a visit to Point Charles was 'one of the most interesting outings a person can take'.* It was not an easy journey generally, but the steamer provided to him by the superintending engineer working on the construction of a new lighthouse, Mr. M. Warton, meant the day spent crossing the harbour to the western coast was simple enough.

The traveller (unnamed, but most likely one of the editors of the *Northern Territory Times and Gazette*) was treated to a visit to the

---

* *NTTG*, 21 Oct 1892.

construction site out of which was a rapidly growing and 'imposing mass of ironwork… nothing more nor less than an immense iron tube'. It was:

> … securely braced from bottom to top and supported, on all sides by iron stanchions set at an angle and raised, from firm concrete blocks. Inside this tube there is a spiral stairway which leads up to the platform which is to receive the lantern at an altitude of 74 ft from the ground. The ascent of this stairway is not the most enjoyable undertaking on a hot day, but the view from the platform is truly grand.

V.L. Solomon, on the campaign trail for his second election, made an official visit – and assured his voters that Chinese men were to be kept away for the construction. He gave a promise that only Europeans should be employed in the construction of the Charles Point lighthouse because it was:

> … the thin end of the wedge, and if there had been a difficulty in obtaining the necessary labour locally, that was the fault of the policy of the past, which had driven every white mechanic out of the country.*

The 20-ton lantern and the clockwork apparatus to drive it was ready to be installed and the visiting party was most impressed. On completion, the centre of the light was about 40 metres above sea level, and it was:

> … a sight well worth seeing. Its design is new and novel, and it will be one of the best and most substantial things of the kind in South Australia, or in fact in the whole of Australia.

Four buildings went with the lighthouse, three of which were the cottages of the staff and their families – each with an underground water tank.

As demanded for significant infrastructure developments during the 1890s, the lighthouse was given an official opening to be remembered, and a large party went with the Government Resident to the site on a steamy February morning, in 1893:

> … The time fixed for starting was 2 p.m. sharp but owing to

---

* *NTTG*, 24 March 1893.

the delayed arrival of the steamship *Adelaide* from Wyndham it was fully an hour after that time before the party found themselves fairly under weigh for their destination. The nasty swell left by the rough weather of the preceding 24 hours soon had its effect on several of the passengers, and by the time the steamer dropped anchor off the lighthouse all interest in the proceedings on the part of these unfortunate ones had sunk to zero.

Owing to the lateness of the hour and the rough nature of the landing place it was deemed inadvisable at the last moment to carry out the original plan of conveying the ladies on shore and the Government Resident, accompanied by about a dozen gentlemen, landed, and were duly welcomed by the head keeper (Mr. Christie) and his wife.

After a few necessary preliminaries the all-important lucifer was duly applied by Mr. Dashwood, the clockwork machinery started, and the Charles Point revolving light of the first order, visible from a vessel's deck in ordinary weather a distance of eighteen miles, emerged into the realms of reality.

The inauguration was greeted with three hearty cheers, followed up by a like compliment to the Government Resident and to the keepers of the lighthouse. On returning on board a start was immediately made for Palmerston, which was reached shortly after 11 p.m., bright moonlight and comparatively smooth water making the homeward run a most enjoyable one for everybody. All who felt inclined that way had an opportunity of partaking of a capital cold collation and following this the toast of 'Success to the Charles Point Lighthouse' was proposed by Mr. Dashwood in an appropriate little speech and drunk in bumpers.

Unfortunately, within days there were problems:

… There would seem to be already an unfortunate irregularity with the Point Charles lighthouse. From all we can gather the light is strangely erratic, sometimes flaring up badly, at other times threatening to go out entirely, and the keepers are not able to leave it for a moment during the night. Glasses are said to be breaking with expensive frequency, and wicks that should last two months under ordinary conditions now run out in as many nights. Various theories are being urged to account for this unenjoyable state of things. Defective oil and some disarrangements of the air drafts are generally regarded as being at the bottom of the mischief. It is just possible, also, that unless the keepers have had previous experience with a light of the kind, they may not understand its mechanism exactly. The matter has been officially reported and steps will be taken at once to set the defects right.*

The lighthouse looked like it might be a lemon, so the Government Resident sailed across the harbour to see it for himself:

... In regard to the mishap at the Point Charles lighthouse, it is satisfactory to know that the responsible authorities lost no time in getting the matter under consideration. On Saturday last the Government Resident, accompanied by Captain Marsh and Mr. Warton, proceeded to Point Charles and investigated the irregularity, but with what result we are not at present in a position to say.†

By the next week there was some improvement. The *Advertiser* reported:

... The light is not at present working so satisfactorily as could be wished, but it is hoped that it will be in thorough working order shortly.‡

Indeed, the problems were ironed out and the light was a pleasure to see on the horizon. Because the light burned kerosine, Dashwood advertised regularly for tenderers who could supply '2,500 gallons of Kerosine Oil of a fire test of not less than 1,500'.

The first lighthouse keeper, Henry Christie, was assisted by his brother Hugh. Together they remained in charge of the lighthouse for most of the next 21 years, assisted by others who came and went over the years, men like Alfred Patt who was there in 1896, and an ex-trooper named Larry Benison, who worked at the lighthouse for about two years around 1897.

Benison lived at Point Charles with his wife, Rose Isabel (nee Lane), and their daughters, Mary and Blanche. Mrs Benison was

---

* *NTTG*, 17 February 1893.
† *NTTG*, 24 February 1893.
‡ *The Advertiser*, 6 March 1893.

The Charles Point Lighthouse

Figure 65: Point Charles Lighthouse, 1895 (Foelsche, LANT, ph0754-0034).

complimented by several visitors for her fine cooking and generous hospitality and their garden produce:

> … On arrival at the lighthouse, we were very cordially invited by Mrs. Benison to a nice supper, to which full justice was done. The inner man being satisfied, a visit was made to the light.
>
> Some of the party had already viewed this wonderful reflector on previous occasions, but to those who had not done so, or been inside a light before, the sight was truly amazing. Everything was so bright and clean, reflecting great credit on the keepers, who thus show that their heart must be in their work.
>
> After a peep into every nook and cranny, and a visit into the light proper, a descent was made to the quarters of the Christie Bros.
>
> Here we were shown some of their handiwork in the way of beautiful sets of carvers, mounted with buffalo horn and inlaid with mother-o'-pearl. These are wrought from files, shear-blades, bayonet, or sword blades, etc., which seem all the more

astonishing as the Christie Bros, have very few tools and no machinery at their disposal.

They also turn their hands to the manufacture of walking sticks from native wood, such as rose-wood, yellow lancewood, bloodwood, bannon ball mangrove, red mangrove, etc. With such woods at the disposal of the people of this district it is astonishing there is no industry of any kind started to put them to a practical and profitable use; one branch of their utility being very clearly demonstrated by the Christie Bros, with their excellent walking sticks.[*]

Despite living remotely, the Christie brothers were well known in Palmerston. Hugh Christie had a reputation as a naturalist. He collected zoological specimens – particularly seashells, fossils, and corals. In 1904, he showed his collection that included 95 named species of shells and 30 corals, at the first Palmerston Agricultural, Horticultural and Industrial Society Show.[†]

The lighthouse rapidly became a tourist attraction and selling items to visitors gave the keepers and their families extra income. Turtle shells were a profitable item and polishing them gave the lonely keepers something to 'beguile the long silent vigils of the watchers on the tower'.[‡]

---

[*] *NTTG*, 24 September 1897.
[†] *NTTG*, 4 November 1904.
[‡] *NTTG*, 6 August 1914.

Figure 66: Point Charles Head Lighthouse Keeper Henry Samuel Christie (left) with Alfred Patt and Hugh Watson Christie (right) before the Great Hurricane of 1897 (SLSA, B-54508).

Chapter 11
Territory Women

Many of the women who pioneered life in South Australia's northern colony were business owners and community leaders in their own right. During 1895, 82 Territory women who had joined the suffrage movement in 1894 enrolled to vote in the South Australian House of Assembly and the Legislative Council.* Many of them voted for Vaiben Solomon, who polled 272 votes – 84 more than the runner-up – even though Solomon had opposed the bill to allow women the vote.† The *Times* confirmed that voting was 'much heavier' than in the 1893 poll, because of the 'woman's franchise'.‡ In fact, in some South Australian electorates, there were more women voters than men.§

These women believed that it was 'the foundation of all political liberty that those who obey the law should have a voice in choosing those who make the law'. Territory women, perhaps because of the Territory's isolation and their low numbers in a male dominated society, were more able to take advantage of the legislative and social reforms than women in more settled areas of Australia.¶ Many women

---

* South Australian women earned the right to vote on 18 December 1894, when the South Australian Parliament passed the *Constitutional Amendment (Adult Suffrage) Act*. This granted women in the colony the right to vote and allowed them to stand for parliament – thus South Australia was the first electorate in the world to give equal political rights to both men and women.
† Paynter, 2013. (Paynter, 2013)
‡ *NTTG*, 1 May 1896.
§ Barbara James, 1995
¶ Barbara James, 1989.

were demanding more independence and were looking at alternative ways of living rather than relying on their husbands:

> … A woman who is earning her own living has, other things being equal, a greater range of choice, or perhaps it would be more correct to say of refusal, than the woman who must either marry or remain dependent on her parents or her friends for the rest of her days.[*]

In Palmerston, there was debate among the men that white women would never be suited to living in the tropics: Government Resident Dashwood, a bachelor, and Vaiben Solomon MP, a widower, publicly stated that women were never healthy in Palmerston. Nicholas and Annie Holtze, in charge of the botanic gardens, said this was nonsense. Their family had been in the Territory for 17 years without any ill effects.

Whilst debate over the 'woman question' raged, Darwin was destroyed by the Great Hurricane of 1897. After four months, the town was mostly rebuilt, and businesses were again running – particularly the hotels and boarding houses – and many were managed by women. Through the adversity of the storm, Territory women had proved their metal as they picked up the pieces and went on to make, as Barbara James says, 'major contributions to the Territory's physical and social development'.[†]

Some of the 82 women enrolled in the electorate have names that may be familiar to Territory residents[‡]. For example: Annie Holtze (schoolteacher); Carolyn Cleland[§], Eliza Ryland (of Rum Jungle Hotel), Mary Lindsay, Sarah Ann Beasley (licensee of Grove Hill Hotel from 1877), Mary McLaughlin (Pioneer Eating House, The Union), Anna Giles (Springvale Station Katherine), Anna Maria

---

[*] *NTTG*, 14 June 1895.
[†] Barbara James, 1989.
[‡] The husbands of many of these women have streets named after them.
[§] Carolyn's husband Jack Cleland was a survivor of the *Gothenburg* disaster in 1875. He rescued several people and was awarded a medal for his bravery (see Pugh 2018).

Woide Waters (artist)* and Marion Pinder (pianist)†.

From the very early days of settlement, women held their own alongside male pioneers. A few of their stories are related here.

Eliza Tuckwell

Eliza Tuckwell arrived in Port Darwin on the *Kohinoor* in February 1870. On board were the first wives and children who came to join husbands and fathers who had stayed behind in Palmerston after George Goyder's successful survey of the Top End. Eliza's husband was a carpenter, named Ned Tuckwell, who had joined both the Northern Territory Survey Expeditions.‡ A man of many skills, Ned successfully built a punt out of bush timber and horse hides that saved 16 men during McKinlay's explorations to the east of Escape Cliffs.

In the 1870s Tuckwell was a primary builder of The Residency for Government Resident Douglas so, with ongoing work that paid well, he was keen to remain in the north. This lasted until December 1872, when he was sacked by Douglas because he was 'incorrigible', 'drunk at times', and 'really doing nothing' to earn his pay of 56 shillings per week.§ From the most respected carpenter in town, his downfall to a town drunk was unstoppable and, although Eliza stoically stood by him, she distanced herself by advertising in the *Times* that she was not responsible for her husband's debts. When Ned died in 1882 at the age of 52, Eliza was left with four children to raise – one of whom, George, who was 'long in failing health' died in 1891 at the age of 27.¶

Ned's death left Eliza free to become one of the most successful

---

* Mrs. Waters died in 1939. Her water colour paintings of butterflies and N.T. wildflowers were famously realistic and "persons often made the mistake of attempting to flick painted insects off the stems of the flowers" (*Northern Standard* 11 July 1939).
† Barbara James, 1995.
‡ The Northern Territory Survey Expeditions were to Escape Cliffs (1864-66), and Port Darwin (1869). See Pugh 2018 and 2019.
§ Douglas, 1872
¶ *NTTG*, 16 January 1891.

businesspeople in the Territory's early history. She registered as a taxpayer when the South Australian Government started to levy taxes during 1884 and was among the first of the 82 South Australian women to registered to vote in 1894. Her daughter Eleanor also joined in the vote.

Eliza worked as a midwife and nurse to the Palmerston Community and built a boarding house she called the Resolution Villa in Smith Street, advertising space for 'four steady, respectable young men'. As we'll see in Chapter 17, when her villa was destroyed by the Great Hurricane in 1897, she was helped to recover by her soon to be son-in-law, Victor Voules 'Daddy' Brown,* and was quickly back in business.†

Eliza Tuckwell became a well-respected elder, known to everyone as 'Granny' Tuckwell. She died in August 1921 at the age of 85, after 43 years in the Territory. At the time of her death, she had nine great-grandchildren.‡

Marie Allwright/Elliot

Marie Agnes Allwright arrived in the northern colony in 1873 with her husband, Henry.§ In the early years, Marie became known for her nursing skills but eventually she and Henry became hoteliers and miners. The record of the publican's licences they held shows that the Allwrights were happy to move their premises to follow the goldfield populations and the changing fortunes of the diggings. In 1881, they traded in Port Darwin Camp and ran the Margaret Crossing Hotel

---

* The Tuckwell's eldest daughter, Eleanor, married Tom Styles, manager of Zapopan Mine near Pine Creek and Eliza Sarah Tuckwell married V.V. Brown in 1901. Eliza was tragically killed in a horse cart accident in 1925 when 'the horse bolted… and the vehicle came into violent contact with the last of a number of iron standards supporting the verandah of the Darwin butchery and bakery in Knuckey Street. Mrs. Brown had her neck broken, her arms were fractured in four places, and there were other injuries' (*Northern Standard*, 3 November 1925).

† Carment et al, 1990.

‡ *Northern Standard*, 9 August 1921.

§ nee Marie or Mary Agnes Durant.

until Mrs Ellen Ryan took it over in 1885.* It is likely that Marie ran the hotel and bar whilst Henry mined – and he seems to have been successful! He also owned racehorses, such as Glencoe, who won £30 against D'Arcy Uhr's Pioneer in 1885. Throughout the 1880s, Henry was the benefactor of the Allwright Cup, valued at £25.

Marie gave birth to a son† on the Union Goldfield in 1885 and they soon moved on to run the hotel at Burrundie, by then the largest town on the goldfields. It was here Marie was fined £10 for selling alcohol to Aboriginal people.

In 1887, Henry was quickly onto the newly discovered Maude Creek reefs and had:

> … a grand show of gold upon the reef he is working now, and is, I hear, sinking on it. The reef is four feet wide and is getting wider as he goes down.‡

But Henry died in Palmerston in 1888. Widowed, Marie took over the reins of their businesses. She remained the proprietor of the Playford Club Hotel in Pine Creek, advertising 'good accommodation for travellers' from 1888 through to 1890. She also inherited Henry's gold mining leases but is listed as owing rents on them in the *Times*, so it seems she was not an active miner. Marie married gold miner Henry Elliot J.P. in August 1890.§ Thereafter known as Mrs Elliot, she stayed in the Territory for the rest of her life, involved in both her new husband's mining interests and the horse-racing industry. The marriage produced a daughter, Ellen Marie and by the time Marie died in 1932, aged 83, she had nine grandchildren and a great grandchild.¶

---

* Port Darwin Camp was a mining camp on the goldfields, some 200 kilometers from Port Darwin.

† Allan Durrant 'Jack' Allwright was the first white child to be born in the Pine Creek area and many of his descendants still live in the Northern Territory. He became a miner, blacksmith, and wheelwright in Pine Creek.

‡ *NTTG* 8 October 1887.

§ The marriage ceremony took place in Pine Creek, performed by the Reverend Father Strele in August 1890.

¶ Ellen Marie Elliot became a schoolteacher at Parap, Pine Creek and she was the first

Ellen Ryan

Ellen Ryan and her husband William arrived in the Territory from Adelaide in 1873, initially chasing gold in the Territory's rush. Soon realising that there was more money to be made by serving the miners, the pair leased the Miner's Arms Hotel at Yam Creek. Unfortunately, William Ryan was a violent drunk

Figure 67: Ellen Ryan's advertisement *NT Times*, 21 August, 1891.

and, when he began to drink the profits, Ellen took out a protection order against him and divorced him 'owing to his threats, cruelty, and drunkenness'. William Ryan left Palmerston in 1877, saying he had 'had quite enough of the Territory and the people in it'.

Ellen kept working. She took over the Margaret Crossing Hotel in 1885 and began buying land in Palmerston as well as several mining leases. In 1888, she employed the architecture firm of Beresford, Bowen, and Black in Adelaide to draw plans for a two-storey hotel she wanted to build in Smith Street and found herself in court when Beresford sued her for unpaid fees. She fought the charges, but a four-man jury found that Beresford was owed £80.[*]

A single tender to build the hotel came in from H.M. Debross at £4,260, and the *Times* announced commencement of the build

---

schoolteacher at Emungalan (Katherine) in 1932. In 1921 she had a breakdown, and her father Henry Elliot was ordered to manage her property on her behalf under the 1864 Lunacy Act (*Northern Standard*, 6 December 1921). She recovered under medical treatment in New South Wales and returned to teach in the Territory. Elliot Street in Katherine is named after her.

[*] *North Australian*, 13 Dec 1889.

in September 1889. Just 12 months later, Mrs Ryan opened the North Australian Hotel. It was the first two-storey hotel in Palmerston.

During the 1890s, Mrs Ryan was a rare visionary for the future of Palmerston:

> ... It has been commonly asserted that Mrs. Ryan exhibited more pluck than wisdom in entering upon such an expensive undertaking. Be that as it may, the fact remains that she has departed from the old weatherworn system of wood and iron houses and has now placed at the convenience of the public a hotel which is a credit to her enterprise and an estimable token of city improvement. And the least we can do is to wish that she may find, as time goes on, that her confidence in the residents of Palmerston was not misplaced. The outlook at present is not particularly cheering for any branch of business, but the North Australian Hotel is bound to secure its share of what trade is doing in its peculiar line.*

Figure 68: Ellen Ryan's advertisement *NT Times*, 30 October, 1896.

The North Australian quickly became the premier hotel in Palmerston, and the most prestigious. It was here that Premier Thomas Playford stayed during his visit in 1892, the annual athletics and sports day was run, and meetings of community organisations, such as the Palmerston Dramatic and Musical Society were regularly held.

Mrs Ryan was not finished. Six years later she relinquished the

---
* *NTTG*, 12 Sept 1890.

North Australian Hotel to George Henry James, manager for A.E. Jolly, who renamed it the *Victoria Hotel*. It was well built of stone, so it survived three major cyclones and the ravages of time, and it still stands on Smith Street.

Ellen took over the lease of an established hotel that was built in 1883 by Edward and Margaret Hopewell, called the Palmerston Club Hotel. There she introduced several new technologies that proved very successful – particularly the ice machine, an electric bell system for ordering beer, and one of Palmerston's first telephones. Her reputation for care and quality followed her.

It was at the Club Hotel that Ellen ran afoul of the law, albeit in a minor way. Miss Scott, one of the barmaids gave, or sold, an Aboriginal woman a glass of liquor, which was illegal. The barmaid just finished her day's work and Mounted Constable Thompson waited in plain clothes, watching from the shadows. The barmaid was arrested, and Ellen as the proprietor was fined £2. M.C. Thompson believed the fine was too lenient and he started a campaign against Ellen and the Club Hotel, saying that 'Mrs Ryan had now trodden on his corns, and he would be on her like a scorpion'.* The squabble between Mrs Ryan and Thompson lasted for years. In letters to the papers, Ellen pleaded with Inspector Foelsche to pull his man into line.

Then, on the night of 7 January 1897, the Great Hurricane destroyed the town. The Club Hotel was badly damaged and the Victoria lost its roof. Ellen organised extensive repairs and, as they were done, took the opportunity for a trip to Adelaide. She successfully started the business again on her return.

Life was mostly good for Ellen. She was a generous benefactor to any fundraising activity, she ran a stable of racehorses and was very involved in the turf club, she ran tattersalls and catered for the fancy dress balls of the community, joining in whole-heartedly.

Nevertheless, there were a few dark episodes that affected her

---

* *NTTG*, 18 Sept 1896.

badly. In August 1897 a man named Harry Harvey died in one of her rooms and Ellen was required to report to the coroner's inquest. Then, in 1899, she fell so sick she needed to travel south for medical help.

When she returned, she was a fit and healthy 50-year-old, ready to get back to work. She took back control of the Victoria Hotel in 1901 and managed it until the Gilruth government took over the sale of liquor in the Territory in 1915. This destroyed her business, but Ellen was eventually compensated £1,500 for her loss, although by then she was elderly and living with her sister, Mary Kelsey, in Adelaide. She died in May 1920 at 78 years old. Forty of those years were lived in the Territory.*

Many years later, during a renovation, a curious inscription was discovered on two stones in the walls of the Victoria Hotel. The words of a love poem were inscribed in pencil in the cavity of the wall, with a sketch of Mrs Ryan. The poem, that was to be 'read at some far distant time' included the following:

> She promised she would seek me here
> If death was as she thought
> Sometimes, less drunk, I think I see
> Her lovely ghost form beckons me
> Or could it be that liquor has me caught.
>
> At the Vic Hotel in Darwin Town,
> They'll all be drinking still,
> Not knowing that her face lies hid,
> May it haunt them as for me it did
> Oh God! This life's a bitter pill!

The poem serves to carry the legend of a great Territory pioneer forward and, despite the building being 'mothballed' for a decade or more at the time of writing, the much-loved Victoria Hotel building is still her lasting legacy.

---

* James, 1990.

Anna Elizabeth Dolan

Another successful woman who registered on the electoral roll in 1895 was Mrs Anna Elizabeth Dolan. Described by Alfred Searcy as a 'tall, handsome, well-made woman, and a splendid equestrienne', Anna arrived in the Territory overland from Queensland, in the mid-1880s with her husband, Thomas John Dolan, and their son Dudley. John, according to Searcy was a 'thin little fellow with a marvellous memory'.[*] He could recite reams of text, and with skills in saddlery and harness repair, he found work in Borroloola and Anthony's Lagoon in the gulf district. Anna lived there with him, but their relationship was feisty. However, Anna was clearly an independent and strong personality:

> … Annie Elizabeth Dolan was charged with that she did on the 29th September [1888] feloniously, unlawfully, and maliciously shoot at one Thomas John Dolan, with intent to kill and murder.[†]

The couple had been quarrelling for several days. The day before the shooting, they were both at Matthew Hart's Royal Hotel in Borroloola, and Anna was heard to declare that 'she would not go with her husband, and that she would pay her board whilst living in the hotel' and 'if I cannot get protection I will protect myself'.

She got hold of a revolver from somewhere and on the morning of 29 September, fired it twice at her husband from about 30 meters away. She then locked herself in the hotel room, and remained there, threatening to shoot the brains out of anyone who came through the door. Eventually, Mounted Constable Donnegan used an axe to break the door and arrested Anna.

Donnegan's testimony in the Borroloola Police Report told more of the events that led to the shooting:

> … Prisoner came to the station on the 28th September, and complained of bad treatment on the part of her husband and

---

[*] Barter and James, 1990. (Barter & James, 1990)
[†] *North Australian*, 3 November 1888.

wanted to know if she could get away from him; she said then 'If I can get no protection from him I will shoot him – rather than live with him again'.

On her arrest Anna said that she had not meant to shoot her husband but wanted to frighten him. This she clearly did, and the local police court, concluding that there was a case to answer, granted bail and sent the whole party to Palmerston for trial. They travelled from the MacArthur River on the S.S. *Adelaide* at the end of October, and the trial was set for mid-December. In the meantime, because John was forced to stay several weeks in Palmerston at Pickford's Hotel, advertising that he was available to repair any saddles and harnesses that needed his services.

Justice Pater clearly saw the issue as a domestic problem, and released Anna, but importantly, went further:

> ... His Honor reprimanded John Dolan for his conduct to his wife, and cautioned him that if he misbehaved in future, he would certainty have him punished.*

John was incensed. He wrote to the newspaper editor:

> ... Mr. T. J. Dolan has written to us in reference to the reprimand that was administered to him last week by His Honor Judge Pater from the Bench, and denies the charge in toto, and complains that he did not have an opportunity of explaining the matter there and then. He states that Mrs. Dolan herself, when she heard of the matter, wished to appear in the Court and tell His Honor that he had been misinformed. In confirmation of his statement that he had uniformly treated his wife with kindness and consideration, he refers to Mr C. Wurmbrand, who knew them at Anthony's Lagoon, and to Mr. Pickford, with whom they lived while in Palmerston.†

Whatever the truth was, the Dolans remained together for the next decade or so. During 1889, John worked as a railway ganger out of Burrundie, and Anna had a second son, Richard. Anna managed the tea rooms on Adelaide River Railway Station for a few months,

---

* *NTTG*, 22 Dec 1888.
† *NTTG*, 29 December 1888.

but by 1893 she and her sons were back in Palmerston, with John mostly working away on the railway.

Anna successfully applied for an agricultural lease of 400 acres in Nightcliff and in July 1896, took over lease No 14 for a rent of £10 per annum. This was a property recently relinquished by the Rapid Creek Jesuit Mission, so some of the groundwork in clearing and planting had already been done.* Anna cleared more land and planted coconuts, bananas, and pineapples, and by 1902 had a good reputation for her produce.

Unfortunately, Anna died of peritonitis on 14 April 1903, aged just 40. She had three surviving children, Dudley, Richard, and a daughter named Daisy, who was only eleven. John, now a sole parent, took over the management of the farm. He was a sportsman of note and with his son Dudley, played cricket and enjoyed cycling. His ability to recite also brought him attention, and he was an active member of the Palmerston Literary and Debating Society.

Six years later, John also died – although in a more unusual way. In 1908, it was John's job, as a ganger, to ensure the railway line from six to 16 mile was clear. On 20 June, S. J. Weedon, the fireman of a four-carriage train, saw a man lying across the tracks ahead, and called out for the train to stop. He then leapt off the engine to run ahead and pull him aside, but landed badly, fell, and cut his knee, so was too slow. The train hit the sleeping John Dolan and dragged him for many yards and, although the body 'would not go past the cowcatcher':

> ...there were a few minor injuries and cuts about his head, but the immediate cause of death was division of his spine. Body was also disembowelled. Injuries could be caused by train accident and death would be instantaneous...There were only a few rags of stomach left. Impossible to say whether the man

---

* The land runs along Rapid Creek north from MacMillan's Road in the current suburb of Millner. In 1913 it was sold to Felix Holmes by auction as Section No. 842, and it changed hands several times, but was resumed by the government in 1946 to become suburbs.

had been drinking.*

Dolan was known to be a 'man of drunken habits,' and Coroner Stretton concluded that he had passed out drunk on the rails. His death, said the coroner, had been his own fault. Dolan was 53 years old.

---

* *NTTG*, 26 June 1908.

Chapter 12
Capital Crimes

In the Territory's early days, crimes were usually sorted out by a Magistrate's Court, sometimes with the Government Resident presiding, although just as often a Justice of the Peace, such as Inspector Foelsche, would sit on the bench. The only judge to visit in the 1870s, Justice Wearing, came on a short visit to hear a handful of cases, and then drowned on his return to Adelaide in the *Gothenburg* disaster.*

During the 1880s, Palmerston hosted its very own judge, Justice Thomas Pater. Pater ran the court for John Parsons who, despite being the Government Resident, had no legal training. After a few years, however, the pair were declared to be too expensive by the South Australian Government, and they were withdrawn to save money. Parson's successors would, they hoped, be lawyers as well, but the plan immediately went array. Parsons was replaced by John George Knight, albeit temporarily at first, but after a few months Knight was confirmed in the role despite his lack of legal training.

When Knight died in office he was replaced, at last, by an experienced lawyer, Charles Dashwood, who fulfilled the Government's requirements. The most serious crime Knight had to deal with was a murder of an Aboriginal man by a buffalo catcher named Rodney Spencer, who worked in Port Essington for E.O. Robinson.† During

---
* See Pugh 2021.
† Searcy calls Spencer 'Sticklegs' and Manulocum 'Manialucum' in *By Flood and Field* (1912).

1889, Spencer shot and killed a man named Manulocum. Witnesses told how he 'caught hold of Manulocum by the hair of the head with one hand and shot him in the forehead with the revolver'. When Manulocum fell down on his face and lying on the ground Spencer shot him in the back. Apparently, the victim had stolen some rice.*

Spencer was found guilty 'of the most wanton and cowardly [crime] ever perpetrated in the colony'. He was sentenced to death, though this was later commuted to imprisonment, and he was released in 1901. Four years later he was himself murdered near Cadell Straits. Woken by his killer late one night, he tried to reach his revolver but was too slow. He was 'brained with the blow of a tomahawk'.†

Another murder brought retribution on a grand scale. Alfred Giles, who managed Springvale Station near Katherine, was famous for his bushmanship, worked well with Aboriginal employees and for decades was a community leader in the small white community. He was a hard man to disagree with and his anger and willingness to join a retribution party to hunt down the murderers of a cattleman named Sid Scott in 1892, spoke volumes about interracial relationships at the time.

Giles wrote long letters about the party's activities and the reasons for them. He stoked the fear that unless the white men's reaction was severe enough, matters would only get worse:

> ... unless a swift and terrible example is made of them no one will be safe in travelling about as before... the safety of travellers will depend on united and decisive action being taken at once that they will remember for some time to come...‡

Indeed, a 'swift and terrible example' was made when, it was said, Lindsay Crawford, a local station owner, avenged Scott's death 'in a terrible manner':

> ... he and his half-caste dealt out white man's justice

---

* *NTTG*, 14 March 1890.
† *NTTG*, 27 January 1905.
‡ The Willeroo Tragedy, *NTTG*, 11 November 1892.

with their Winchesters, and when the police arrived from Pine Creek, a couple of days later, they found plenty of employment burying the sons of darkness.*

The massacre was forgiven by the white establishment without ever being brought before a court of law. The killings were seen as a legitimate response to the murder of a white man, and a lesson to the black man.

With an uncounted tally of massacres in the Territory during those years, it seems surprising that anyone was ever tried at all, but Government Resident Charles Dashwood was required to preside over a number of capital crimes. Soon after his appointment there were 10 murderers on death row – Charlie Flannigan for a murder at Auvergne Station he admitted to, and a group of nine killers of six ship-wrecked Malay fishermen, led by an Aboriginal man and recidivist named Wandi Wandi.†

There was much public interest and debate about capital punishment, but there was no doubt about the guilt of these men. In fact, they were 'as guilty of the crime of murder as it is possible for an Australian law court to make them'.‡ However, no one had ever been legally executed in the Northern Territory and despite the clear appetite for execution among some of the population, the Government and people of South Australia were not so sure:

> … South Australia is evidently not a too firm believer in the good moral effects to be derived from a gallows and a public hangman. Numerous murders have from time to time been committed in the Northern Territory, but up to date there has been no call for the hangman's knot.§

Nonetheless, the presiding sentiment was that an example must be made. Pressure to execute was even brought by Premier Sir J. W. Downer QC, but even for him and the vengeful South Australian population, 10 executions at one time was too many to bear.

---

* *North Queensland Herald*, 20 May 1911, 'The Sketcher. Graves on the Outer Edge.'
† For the full story see Pugh 2019.
‡ *NTTG*, 3 March 1893.
§ *NTTG*, 3 March 1893.

Eventually, eight of the Aborigines had their sentences commuted to life imprisonment. Only Flannigan and Wandi Wandi were to climb the gallows steps.* Dashwood would not be swayed about these two. He said of Flannigan:

> … I do not consider any further leniency should be shown…
> The evidence given at the trial left no doubt in my mind as to
> his guilt… I believe he has a wicked and depraved disposition.

Charlie Flannigan

Charlie Flannigan was the son of an Aboriginal woman and an Irish man. He came from Queensland and had grown up working as a cattleman. In the Territory, he was the jockey who had won the 1887 Palmerston Cup, but mostly he travelled the stations looking for cattle work.

On 15 July 1893, Flannigan was hanged at Fannie Bay Gaol for the murder of Samuel Burns Croker at Auvergne Station. Croker was a pioneer cattleman in the region. He had ridden with Nat Buchannan in the early days and at the time of his death was the station manager.†

On the night of his death Croker and Flannigan were on the station veranda playing cribbage with 'the stake of a stick of tobacco a game'.‡ Three others were also there; a man named McPhee, the cook, Joe Ah Wah, and a witness named Barney, who was to give detailed evidence later.

From what was said at the trial, Flannigan appears to have shot Croker very calmly. He arose during the third game, took a drink of water from a cask on the veranda, and then went to the saddle shed, returned with his rifle, and shot his boss twice. Barney said he heard Croker sing out 'I am dead' before the second shot. The body was

---

* Including these two, there have been 10 legal hangings of convicted criminals in the Northern Territory since settlement. Mr Justice Dashwood oversaw more than half of them – with six men hanged during his time as Resident.
† Auvergne Station is about 50 kilometres west of the current N.T. town of Timber Creek.
‡ *NTTG*, 9 December 1892.

buried the next morning, sewn into a blanket by Flannigan himself, whilst he 'displayed a good deal of brutal levity and divested himself of much coarse profanity in referring to the dead man'.*

Flannigan then rode to Halls Creek, surrendered himself to the police, and was taken to Darwin by steamer. His motive for the murder was never discovered and it was never sought during his six-hour trial. He was tried by jury in front of Mr Justice Dashwood, representing himself, but he brought no evidence, and appeared indifferent throughout. His indifference continued in Fannie Bay Gaol for the four statutory months required on Death Row before his execution. When asked by a clergyman, Flannigan said he was 'sorry for the life he had led but hoped it would be all right where he was going' although he was not sure whether he would 'become a stoker in Hell or come back with wings on!' According to *The Advertiser*, he:

> ... freely acknowledged his guilt and manifested no fear. He walked to the scaffold with a firm step, saying he was going 'to die hard'. The execution, which was the first that has taken place in the Northern Territory, was carried out without a hitch, death being instantaneous.†

The authorities were relieved. It was important that everything went well – they had put a lot of effort into not messing up their first hanging to avoid any 'unseemly hitches and a revolt of public sentiment'. The gallows were second-hand and had been sent from Adelaide Gaol.‡ They were:

> ... erected in the yard between the cells and the infirmary. So that there might be no mishap, the beam and rope were tested several times, with as much as double the weight of the doomed man. That fatal act, the drawing of the bolt, was practised, too, until perfection was assured. Beneath the trapdoor a deep excavation had been made to prevent the

---

* *NTTG*, 21 July 1893.
† *The Advertiser*, 17 July 1893.
‡ These gallows were replaced with a second set that were destroyed in the 1937 cyclone. Both these gallows were in the open as all prisoners had to watch the execution. The third gallows, which were only used in 1952, were built inside the infirmary building and are still on display.

man's feet touching ground after the drop; and across the front of the structure, below the platform, a screen of calico had been tacked.

Punctually at 9 a.m. the prisoner was led from his cell, with his arms pinioned but his legs free, attended by Mr. Norcock and guards. He was halted for a few minutes in the dining room close by, while the needful formalities of identification of prisoner and his delivery to the Deputy-Sheriff were gone through. Physically, he looked strong and healthy. He had spent a good night, and actually slept up till half-past-7 o'clock. He partook of the usual breakfast, and just before going forth to his doom enjoyed a smoke. Whilst the transfer from Gaoler to Sheriff was being made the half-caste betokened not the slightest concern. He never once betrayed a sign that he was going to his death but stood up in his place as stoical as an Indian, and when the Deputy Sheriff had taken him over and the signal was given to adjourn to the scaffold, he walked out with the firm step of a man going to freedom rather than of one about to be killed. Up the steps to the platform, he ascended with the same unalterable coolness, and placing himself on the trapdoor, he stood erect and for a second or two surveyed the yard and those in front of him while the hangman bound his legs with rope. That being done, the noose was adjusted, and the black cap drawn over his face…

Then the signal was given, the bolt was drawn, there was a clanging of bolts for an instant, and the spirit of the murderer flashed into eternity. A drop of 6ft had been allowed and death was instantaneous, the only thing noticeable after the body dropped being a slight muscular trembling in the feet. The neck was not torn by the rope, and there was but the merest discolouration visible. After the usual lapse of time, during which we were given every opportunity of viewing the body, it was cut down, and death was duly certified to by the Medical Officer.

… The body was buried in the gaol cemetery, and the lowering of the black flag wiped out the last outward visible trace of the murder of Samuel Croker and the prison and judicial associations of Charley Flannigan, the first man to undergo execution by hanging in the Northern Territory.*

Wandi Wandi

Wandi Wandi was an Iwaidja man from the Croker Island/Cobourg Peninsula area who murdered Thomas Howard Wingfield in December 1879.† Wingfield was a trepang collector and tobacco grower in partnership with Edward Robinson. Together, they employed about 30 Iwaidja men, but Wandi Wandi was not one of them.

Wingfield kept the wages for his employees in his storehouse; flour, rice, tobacco, and rum. Perhaps unsurprisingly, Wingfield's initial trouble started with the rum. An employee named Mayuna arrived one morning to sell some jungle fowl eggs for which Wingfield paid with five sticks of tobacco and rum. Mayuna rapidly drank the rum, wanted more, and returned to the homestead, drunk, to demand it. Annoyed, Wingfield set his dogs on him and took out his revolver, possibly just as a threat, but when someone else threw a spear (later claimed to be at a pigeon) near the homestead. Wingfield was startled and he shot Mayuna dead on his veranda.

All that day the call for revenge grew among the Iwaidja. Wandi Wandi was chosen to act on the tribe's behalf, and he killed Wingfield as he slept that evening – hitting his head three times with a tomahawk. In a letter sent to Alfred Searcy, E.O. Robinson recalled the shock of arriving home:

> ... Wingfield was killed by the natives while I was in Port Darwin. It was a knock for me on my return to find nothing but the cat to welcome me, the dwelling ransacked, and the poor old chap buried in the sand about six yards from the house. Part of his face was exposed, and the fowls were pecking at it. I had only two black boys with me, and the venture was given up.‡

Wandi Wandi was arrested and tried for murder, but as the

---

* *NTTG*, 21 July 1893.
† aka Wandy Wandy
‡ Searcy, 1909.

Territory court was not entitled to try a capital offence at that time, he was found guilty of manslaughter and sentenced to 10 years in prison with hard labour.* He soon escaped but was caught and punished by having to spend the first 12 months of his sentence in irons.†

After 10 years in prison, Wandi Wandi could speak English and had become a Catholic. He was released to take up residence at the Rapid Creek Mission with Father Donald McKillop where he stayed for some months before returning home to his countrymen.‡ He soon got into trouble. In 1892, he and nine others were arrested for the slaughter of the entire crew of a Malay fishing prau:

> ... Six aboriginal natives named respectively: Wandy Wandy [sic], Capoondur, Ingeewaraky, Dooramite, Mintaedge, and Angareeda were charged with the wilful murder of six Malays at Mandool, near Bowen Straits ...§

> .... Wandy Wandy... made the following statement, which we render as near as possible in his own pidgin-English: I sit down at Wanmook: all about blackfellow go along Mandool; Capoondur first time go: him go first along beach and find 'em proa; other blackfellows come up behind; Capoondur then said he been find 'em Malay him been break 'em proa; then all blackfellow say 'Come on, we go down and see 'em'; all blackfellows go and see them and I come up behind; the Malays made signs to take the parcels and we all went a little way and got dinner; after we have dinner we take 'em everything away and walk; Malay and me go easy; two fellow, Goolardno and Marakite, go first time and him run away; then me hear Mangerippy sing out What for you run away;" then all about blackfellow run away; then we go back where make 'em camp before; me sit down; Goolardno yabber me first time "You and me kill 'em all about" and all blackfellow say "All right, kill 'em;" then me sit down little while and Goolardno yabber longa me; he say "You take away that revolver and knife and I kill 'em"; then I sit down little bit and by and by get up and catch 'em that revolver and one

---

*   *NTTG*, 14 May 1881.
†   *NTTG*, 21 August 1880.
‡   *NTTG*, 23 March 1889.
§   *NTTG*, 18 November 1892.

knife; then me run away a little way; Dooramite catch 'em two
fellow gun and bow and arrow and sit down longa me; then
blackfellow kill 'em all about Malays; Goolardno kill 'em two
fellow first and Capoondur kill one fellow; then Mintaedge
kill another one; Angareeda and Marakite kill one fellow …'

The court found that Wandi Wandi was the ringleader of the group and although he had killed none of them personally, he had disarmed the Malays before they were attacked. The actual killers had their death sentences commuted, and they were imprisoned, but Wandi Wandi was sentenced to die, and he was told his execution was to take place in his own country in front of his clan, as a warning to the tribe†.

Eight months later, Inspector Foelsche, John Little (who then counted 'Deputy Sherriff' among his roles), and a few troopers, took Wandi Wandi to Malay Bay for his execution. They erected some gallows on the edge of a campground used often by the Iwaidja and the prisoner was executed on 25 July 1893:

… The drop was 6ft 6in, and death was instantaneous, not
even a tremor or movement of the body of any kind occurring
after the drop fell… The body was left hanging for twenty
minutes and was then cut down and buried at the place of
execution. The gallows was left standing as a warning to
natives, Malays, and others.‡

Moolooloorun

Two men from the Roper River district, near Elsey Station, were arrested in August 1894 for the murder of a Chinese man. The victim was never named but Nyanko and Moolooloorun gave clear confessions to Mounted Constable Stott. They had seen the tracks of two Chinese men and followed them along the road to catch up with them. Moolooloorun had then cut a stick 'all-the-same nulla' and

---

*   *NTTG*, 13 November 1892.
†   Pressure to carry out the execution came from Premier Sir John Downer, QC, in Adelaide, *NTTG*, 11 August 1893.
‡   *NTTG*, 11 August 1893.

then had approached the men asking for tobacco.

After being refused, Moolooloorun hit one man with the nulla nulla and crushed his skull. Nyanko hit the other on the back of the head but, although he fell down, he managed to get back on his feet and run into the bush and was never seen again. Nyanko believed he had died, though he had never seen the body. The victims' belongings (blankets, calico, mosquito net, and a few sticks tobacco) were then gathered up and kept, although their clothes were burned the next day.

Both the killers were open about their actions, telling many in their camp how the murders were committed, and it didn't take long for the word to reach Mounted Constable Stott at the Roper River Police Station. At the murder trial, Stott reported that he found the body about a month after the murder:

> ... in consequence of something I heard from Billy, I went to a flat three miles east of Mole Hill on the 8th July; I saw signs of a struggle and the grass was all beaten down and smeared with something that looked like blood; I followed a path which went from this place about 20 yards to the north; it led me off the road, and I saw the remains of a Chinaman, the body was lying on its back, head to the north; the legs and arms had been partly eaten away by wild dogs, and the body was much decomposed, looking as if dead about three weeks; the fore part of the skull was all broken in, and there was a crack from the base of the skull right down.
>
> ... on 13th July I arrested Nyanko on west side of Red Lily swamp; the blacks were corroboreeing... Nyanko speaks English; told him the charge and cautioned him; he made a statement, which I wrote down at the time; he said "Me killem, along here (patting the back of head); Moolooloorun and me; sleep one fellow night along Mole Hill; go back along Chinaman; one fellow Chinaman been run away along bush; me blanket, mosquito net, and one fellow tobacco; Moolooloorun one blanket, shirt, tobacco, money plenty."
>
> ... on the 27th July, I arrested Moolooloorun... he made a statement to me, as follows: "... me two fellow bin follow Chinaman and killem along road... This blanket and calico

belong to me; I bin catchem along dead fellow Chinaman;
this one blanket (referring to the one Nyanko was lying on)
bin take from Chinaman that go bush; I bin take dead fellow
Chinaman's stick, Nyanko bin take stick from Chinaman
that go along bush; two fellow stick sit down along river;
Chinaman along bush no more got tucker and blanket;
him walk nothing; Chinaman bin too much finish tucker,
only a little me bin tobacco me get 'em like that (3 sticks);
Nyanko all the same; black-fellow too much talk; me and
Nyanko follow Chinaman's track; he kill 'em a little bit on the
ground – Nyanko bin kill him the side of the head: two fellow
Chinamen been tumble down and me run away frightened;
me one fellow sleep; plenty blacks go back along Chinaman;
me and Nyanko pull dead Chinaman along bush'.*

Little is recorded about Nyanko, but Moolooloorun was a leader among his tribe with the reputation of being the tribe's rainmaker. Mounted Constable Stott had known him for five years. The jury took only a few minutes to return with their verdict of guilty, and Justice Dashwood then took no time in sentencing them both to death 'in the usual manner'. Five months later the Executive Council met to discuss the sentences and Nyanko was shown mercy:

... It has been decided that in the case of the younger prisoner,
Nyanko, his sentence shall be commuted to imprisonment
for life, but that in reference to the other the law must take its
course.†

The date for the execution was fixed and, in keeping with the policy of executing Aboriginal people where the murders had occurred (to teach them a lesson) Mounted Constable Stott went a few days earlier to 'assemble as many natives of the tribe as possible to witness the execution'. Deputy-Sheriff John Little and party then took the condemned man by train to Pine Creek, then overland to Crescent Lagoon on the Roper River.

Moolooloorun was hanged on the bank of the lagoon in front of 59 of his countrymen. His death was instantaneous. The emotions of

---

* *NTTG*, 10 August 1894.
† *NTTG*, 28 December 1894.

his family and countrymen are not recorded, and the *Times*, like other newspapers, kept their sympathy for John Little:

> ... No doubt the Deputy-Sheriff feels more contented in mind now than he had done for a week or two previous to the execution. There is no comfort to be derived from a duty which compels you to travel a journey of 300 miles with a murderer in tow for the purpose of hanging the convicted one at a specified time on a specified date; and in wet weather, too, when annoying delays might occur any day. Then, besides weather condition, there was also the possibility, a vague one, perhaps, of the prisoner escaping, or of the hangman deserting. As, however, none of these disasters overtook the party, and as the convict was executed in the most approved style, the Deputy-Sheriff should return to his headquarters in a fine state of mental complacency after his 600-mile journey.[*]

Chung Yeung and Lem Kai

Two Chinese men, Chung Yeung and Lem Kai, were hanged at Fannie Bay Gaol on 10 August 1899, for the murder of Chee Hang at Yam Creek. The accused apparently never did any work and lived by thieving, and the *Adelaide Observer* described their crime 'as one of the most diabolical [murders] ever perpetrated in the colonies'. Their victim, Chee Hang, apparently accused one of his killers of stealing gold, and he was subsequently shot while out fishing.

Chung Yeung and Lem Kai confessed to the crime, but what made it particularly abhorrent was their action in chopping up and cooking the body afterwards. It was unrecognisable:

> ... So completely did they carry out their gruesome task that not one bone was left unbroken, and only the heart remained intact.[†]

The murder of Chee Hang may not have been the only killing conducted by these two. Another Chinese man had been found burned to death in his hut. At the time, the authorities had concluded

---

[*] *NTTG*, 25 January 1895.
[†] *Adelaide Observer*, 5 August 1899.

he had fallen asleep with a burning opium pipe, but members of the Chinese community thought otherwise, and were 'well satisfied with the death penalty, which they consider richly deserved'.*

Finding a hangman was a problem, but Deputy Sherriff John Little recruited a prisoner from the gaol by offering him early release as a reward. The bodies of the executed were buried in the grounds of the gaol, though knowledge of the exact location has since been lost.

Other killings

There were more than 10 other murders during the 1890s, although none of the perpetrators ended up on the hangman's noose. Some were committed by persons unknown, particularly in the Victoria River and Borroloola regions. Of those that reached trial most, like Ahmed Ben Hassan, who stabbed another Malay in a fracas, had their death sentences commuted to life in prison. It was the same with Warrima and Wanchill, who killed Ah Kim in 1892 near the Daly River, for a 'mosquito net and blanket'.† Warrima was about 16 years old and was originally sentenced to death for the murder, while Wanchill was given a 10-year sentence of hard labour for manslaughter.‡

One story is different. In 1898, two buffalo shooters named Thomas Moore and Kenneth Mackenzie were killed on the King River by two young Aboriginal men named Copperang and Narbaloora. Robert Tuck, the employer of all four men, managed to get to Darwin via the *Cygnet*, a few weeks later and related the story:

> ... On arriving at the huts, I asked the camp lubras what was the matter, and Malaba said 'Been shoot him two fellow.' I asked them where they were shot, and she took me round the back of the hut and showed me some blood on the ground. She said, 'Tom been fall down here,' and a few feet away she showed me some more blood and said, 'Mack been fall

---
* *Singleton Argus*, 12 August 1899.
† *NTTG*, 11 November 1892.
‡ See Judge David J. Bevan's List of murder trials 1884-1913 (in McLaren 1878, pp364-368).

down here.' I asked where the remains were, and she said 'Blackfellow been put him alonga hole.' The hole was about a hundred yards from the huts. They (the two lubras) took me to the grave where the bodies were (both in one hole).*

The story of the murders was plain enough. Tuck claimed he had no idea of the motives behind them, but they were revealed during the 1899 trial:

> ... The evidence showed that the white men lost their lives because of their unwarranted immoral interference with lubras, and that the prisoners were animated by motives of revenge.†

Copperang and Narbaloora were found guilty of murder. Both men were sentenced to death, but public opinion was against it and mercy was recommended:

> ... on account of the great provocation which the blacks had received. According to the evidence of Lucy, a half caste aboriginal from Borroloola, Tom Moore, 'to whom she belonged', brought three lubras to a place named 'Our Ham' after a trip up the Liverpool River. Two of these were named Jungle Lily and Biddy. Moore took Jungle Lily to his hut, and McKenzie took Biddy. As Jungle Lily tried to escape during the night Moore tied her up, and later on he gave her to another white man named Tuck, who handed her over to Copperang 'because she all the time cry'.
>
> The same witness stated that when Jungle Lily was first put in the boat on the river Moore put steel wire on her legs, but did not tie up the other lubras, and that she cried all the time. In cross examination Lucy avowed that Moore was all the time good fellow along black fellows. A lubra named Malaba, whom Moore had captured on Melville Island, stated that the white man beat her and Lucy all the time, but did not beat Jungle Lily.
>
> Robert Tuck, a buffalo-hunter of Malay Bay, gave evidence that Jungle Lily did not stay in the camp against her will. He denied that he handed her over to Copperang because she made so much noise, but simply because he did not want her

---

*   *NTTG* 16 December 1898.

†   *NTTG*, 21 July 1899.

anymore.

According to the evidence the murders were committed outside the victims' huts with rifles which the prisoners had obtained. They were arrested on December 27 by M.C. Stott. Evidence was given by natives that Nabaloona fired at Tom Moore, and that Copperang shot McKenzie in the temple. A blackfellow named Nalorman, who saw the shooting, deposed that Moore had been growling at the natives for not fulfilling his orders, and that he had knocked one of them down and was beating him when Nabaloona fired and killed him.*

The recommendation for mercy was considered at an Executive Council meeting that included the Governor. The Council found 'the evidence showed that the crime was the result of gross cruelty towards the natives, including the seizing and outrage of women belonging to the tribe of the men who shot Moore and McKenzie'.† Copperang and Narbaloora were indeed shown mercy. They were 'released to their tribe'.

Shocked, the *Times* couldn't believe it: 'The screaming idiots of the metropolis have had their way,' they wailed, 'they might as well have given them a 'licence to murder'. The *Times* went on to suggest, with bitter sarcasm:

> … we may now hope to see the murderers presented with rifles and ammunition so that they may again have the means to check with a bullet any undue familiarity that may be exhibited towards them by the whites of their district.‡

Other killings were listed by Judge David Bevan, in a list he compiled of Palmerston's murder trials in 1913.§ They were mentioned only in passing by the newspapers. For example, one from 1899 involved a Middle Eastern man who died as the result of a fight:

> … On Wednesday afternoon, about 1.45, several colored [sic] men who had congregated in a shop in Cavenagh Street (China Town) Palmerston, got into a hot argument, which

---

* *South Australian Register*, 2 June 1899.
† *Express and Telegraph*, 25 July 1899.
‡ *NTTG*, 25 July 1899.
§ See McLaren, 1878.

speedily culminated in a serious quarrel. One of them, more exasperated than the rest, drew a sheath knife, and stabbed an Arab in a fearful manner. One of the wounds was in the fleshy part of the left-arm, making a terrible gash, and the other was in the back, the blade penetrating to the lungs, which were partially severed. The victim was half dragged, half carried to the police station, where he was attended by Dr. Goldsmith. Upon making an examination the doctor was certain that the wounded man could not survive his injuries, and his dying depositions were taken. He expired shortly afterwards. Two men were arrested in connection with the affair…*

The interactions between Aboriginal people and the newcomers were complex. Elsie Masson, who wrote *The Untamed Territory* in 1915, was an observer in court for the murder trial of nine men in 1913. Her words are worth repeating because they show a rare understanding of how frightening the entire process must have been for people with no previous knowledge of the European law, or any of the languages spoken around them:

> … The witnesses were established at the native camp at Kahlin Beach, where they sat all day in a stupor of fear, terrified at the strange blacks chattering strange tongues all around them. The nine prisoners – nine strong young aboriginals of splendid physique – were marched to Fanny [sic] Bay gaol to await their trial.
>
> A white man or two, a Chinese dhobi with his bundle of washing, were loitering on the stone verandah, gazing through the wide windows into the court, with its white walls, brown seats, and big red punkah. Facing the door was the dock. On a seat before it sat four of the prisoners, clad in the regulation prison dress of blue shirt and khaki trousers marked with the broad arrow. They held in their hands the end of an ankle chain and gazed sullenly at the floor or out of the door on to the free blue sea. The others were seated in the dock, over the top of which were just visible five close-cropped, egg-shaped heads, five sloping black foreheads, five pairs of eyebrows. Beside the prisoners stood two gaolers; nearby a Protector of Aborigines; facing them were the Jury. The two counsels for

---

* *NTTG*, 17 March 1899.

the Crown and for the prisoners, sat at a table in the centre, while the Judge, in wig and gown, presided overall.

The two constables… told the story of how they had dug up from the grave at King River the body of the murdered man…[*]

---

[*] Masson, 1915. (Masson, 1915).

Darwin: Survival of a City

Chapter 13
Health

In 1882, Protector of Aborigines Dr Robert J Morice, announced the diagnosis in Palmerston of a disease that he was familiar with from working in Ceylon and China: leprosy! Leprosy, or Hansen's Disease, is a condition caused by a slow-growing bacteria. It can affect a victim's nerves, skin, eyes, and the lining of the nose if left untreated. In modern times it can be cured, especially if diagnosed early, but in the nineteenth century it was a major source of fear and loathing.

The victim discovered by Dr Morice in 1882 was Chinese, so Government Resident Edward Price promptly organised passage for him on the first ship back to China and hoped that that would be the end of the matter for Palmerston. Not so. Two years later Acting-Government Resident Gilbert McMinn sent Dr Morice, Dr P.M. Wood, and V.V. Brown to a house in Chinatown suspected of housing the sick. They found three Chinese men with the disease, and five more the next year. They were deported too, while a sixth man died. It was clear that something had to be done, not least because the captains of ships began to refuse to carry the victims as it was not good for business.

Parsons wanted to get them out of town. He planned an isolation hospital for them on Mud Island, directly across the harbour from Palmerston near East Arm. It was an 'out of sight, out of mind' solution which led to a 'saga of human suffering and personal tragedy' that remains a stain on Territory history. Hence, the 'leprosarium'

known as Mud Island Lazaret was established in 1889 when a Chinese patient was dumped there all by himself.

The man was given a tent, a fishing line, and a few sheets of tin from which he was to build his own shelter. The boat that was used to tow him across the harbour was set on fire rather than brought back – such was the fear of the disease. The outcast was then visited once a week by medical staff, but their only care was to throw packages

Figure 69: Mud Island Lazaret, c 1890 (SLSA B 9761).

of food and bandages on to the beach from the safety of their boats. Parsons promised buildings, but these were never built. A hulk, to be moored off the island, was suggested, to no avail.

In April 1890, a second Chinese patient was banished to the island, but the first refused to share his hut with him, so a bark hut was quickly built for the second man. The disease spread, but people hid their symptoms and travelled out bush to avoid detection. Several Chinese station cooks were found to be sufferers. Most of the cattle stations employed Chinese cooks and gardeners and, as there was easy fraternisation between the Chinese and the locals, the disease spread into the Aboriginal population.*

The first white man diagnosed with leprosy was 63-year-old teamster, Marcus Baker, an American by birth, who had arrived in the Northern Territory in 1872. Dr Percy Wood diagnosed the disease in 1885, but Baker did not go to Palmerston hospital until October 1887 – and that was because he had been seriously injured by a nail in his boot and without feeling the injury. Government Resident Parsons was taken to see the patient and told of the need for isolation, but Parsons refused to believe it was leprosy, especially when a Colonial Surgeon from Adelaide, who had never set eyes on the patient, wrote that he considered it was not *true* leprosy. He thought it to be *elephantiasis anesthetics*, a disease of a 'non-contagious character'.†‡ Parsons refused to accept that a white man would have leprosy, and when Baker died in June 1889, after nearly two years in the hospital, he publicly denied any knowledge of him.

Many sufferers went undiagnosed but, in 1890, the first Aboriginal victim was brought in for isolation at the Lazaret. He came from Elsey Station, south of Katherine, and had clearly already suffered for years. He was shipped off to Mud Island and a year later was in the last stages of the disease. The *Times* wrote: 'the Black Leper must soon succumb to the ravages of the terrible malady.'§

There are no records of Chinese women contracting leprosy in Palmerston. None of the Chinese cooks and gardeners in the cattle stations had their own womenfolk with them, and very few Chinese women were among the miners on the Pine Creek and Katherine

---

*   Kettle, 1967.

†   *North Australian*, 15 June 1889.

‡   There is no doubt among modern physicians who have read Wood's description, that it was, indeed, Hanson's Disease (Kettle, 1981).

§   *NTTG*, 30 January 1891.

goldfields. Those most likely to catch it were Chinese bachelors, some of whom traded opium and alcohol in exchange for favours from Aboriginal women. As this was against the law, many Chinese were gaoled, and most cases of leprosy were diagnosed in Fannie Bay Gaol.

Lepers were despised. However, the 'leper station' was not a prison. Some victims were well enough to escape from it:

> ... It will probably be news to many of our readers to hear that the Chinese leper who was located at the leper station – (excuse the joke!) – a few weeks ago has vanished from that solitary abode, and the authorities at the present time "dunno where 'e are." Some aver that he has gone for a walk back to the mines, others that he was surreptitiously conveyed by his friends on board a northern-bound steamer and is by this time safely lodged in the land of his nativity. Whatever has happened to him he has certainly disappeared, and the station is again tenantless, and, we trust, will be so for a very long time to come.*

In 1896, Dr Thompson studied the spread of the disease and found that there were many more sufferers than previously thought. There was no medical system to cope with them, and most were sent home with little follow-up after diagnosis. Only the most afflicted were sent to the Mud Island Lazaret.

Government Resident Dashwood met some victims in his travels to the East Alligator River region in 1894:

> ...I was surprised and alarmed to find several undoubtedly suffering from leprosy; in one case the fingers of both hands were gone, merely the stumps remaining; in another the toes had all decayed away; and others disfigured about the face... I was informed by Mr. Cahill that he had seen, during the few months he had been in the district, over fifty natives affected in the same way.†

Townsfolk complained that Aboriginal lepers might come into town and spread their disease, so the police were given powers to arrest any who did.

---

* *NTTG*, 21 February 1896.
† Dashwood, *Government Resident's Report 1894*.

Ah Ping was an aging resident of Palmerston for most of the 1890s. Afflicted with Hansen's Disease in the latter part of the decade and ignored, he was eventually rounded up and sent to the Lazaret in 1902. By then, he was an elderly man with advanced venereal disease and leprosy but, to the *Times*, he was 'the loathsome looking Ah Ping':

> Ah Ping was an old Chinaman whose shocking condition has for long past been a subject of frequent public comment, his face being almost eaten away by some horrible disease which, however, the late Government Medical Officer, always maintained was not leprosy.
>
> Whether Dr. Goldsmith was right or wrong in his diagnosis, the fact remains that the man was in such a repulsive state from disease of some kind that to permit him to hold continued unrestricted intercourse with his fellow beings for so long has been little short of a scandal, and a reasonable regard for the public safety should have led to in his isolation many months ago. His examination by the acting Health Officer, on March 19th, ended in an order being made for his deportation to the leper station on the opposite side of the harbour, Dr. Seabrook expressing the opinion that although the loathsome looking Ah Ping was suffering principally from venereal disease, he also exhibited symptoms of leprosy. He was therefore, as previously stated, conveyed across to the leper station on the 19th March, and left to the solitary contemplation of such signs of human life as are visible from that rather distant and isolated situation. Apparently the unfortunate wretch soon wearied of this tantalising occupation, and wisely determined to make an end.*

Ah Ping was unceremoniously dumped on the island with a box of provisions and left alone for more than 10 days. When a medical officer named Riddell went to check on him, with a fresh stock of provisions, he found that:

> ... the door opening inwards struck against something, and on looking inside Riddell was horrified on discovering the putrid body of Ah Ping, clothed in trousers and shirt, hanging by the

---

* *NTTG*, 4 April 1902.

neck by a piece of rope suspended from the roof of the hut.*

Ah Ping's body was disposed of by fire. Nobody would go near his putrefying corpse, so his hut was piled high with driftwood and set ablaze, and Ah Ping was cremated while hanging from the rafters.

The reputation of Mud Island went before it. In 1902, another Chinese victim, Ah Kim, who had been diagnosed while in gaol, had such a fear of being incarcerated on the island that he leapt to his death from the boat. The poor man:

> ... determinedly evaded all attempts at rescue by diving beneath the surface until he had filled himself with salt water and sunk like a stone to the bottom.†

In 1906, Dr Ramsay Smith wrote of Mud Island: 'The Leper Station at Port Darwin is unsuitable for any being of the human species'.

Other diseases

Smallpox arrived with Chinese workers who came from Hong Kong in 1886. Government Resident Parsons, then newly in the position, ordered an isolation camp to be set up at Emery Point a few hundred metres from the hospital, where today's Larrakeyah Army Barracks sit. Initially nine Chinese patients were cared for without loss of life.

There was another smallpox outbreak among the Chinese in 1887, but by then Dr Percy Wood had vaccinated many of the local population and isolated the afflicted at Emery Point. The doctor then argued the need for better hospital facilities, less crowding in the gaol, a quarantine facility, better sanitation in the town and steps to improve the health of the local Aborigines, but he was ignored by the Government Resident.

Until 1886 the prisoners in Fannie Bay Gaol were provided a choice of menus. The Chinese ate Chinese food and the Europeans and Aborigines a more western diet. In 1886, to save money, Dr

---

* *NTTG*, 4 April 1902.
† *NTTG*, 4 April 1902.

Wood suggested that all prisoners be fed Chinese food – rice was cheap, and readily available. Unfortunately, before the year ended, an Aboriginal man had died of beriberi, a vitamin B deficiency that suggests he was fed white rice and little else.

From then on, there were deaths from beriberi among Chinese, Aboriginal, and Malay inmates nearly every year in the gaol, plus others from among the Malay crews in pearling luggers. In 1895, six men died of beriberi in Palmerston hospital without anyone getting seriously concerned. The disease's connection to poor nutrition was not understood and it was not until 1899, when Dr Goldsmith demanded a better diet for the prisoners, that it was brought under control.

The hot, humid cells in Fannie Bay Gaol were crammed full of men who had been caught supplying alcohol to Aborigines, and the Aborigines who had drunk it. Many prisoners were guilty of assault, and others languished in gaol because they could not afford the fines that had been imposed by the magistrates for minor civil disturbances. With the prisoners being guarded by just two warders, they were locked in their cells from 6 PM to 6 AM, or longer if the warders were late. Gaoler George Norcock complained bitterly that he was understaffed, and eventually a third warder was employed, which meant that work parties could be taken out to do the hard labour they were sentenced to.

It is no surprise that Fannie Bay Gaol was a source of other diseases associated with over-crowding. Cellmates shared a bucket as a toilet, and anyone who was sick remained in the cell – there was no infirmary for many years. Many Chinese prisoners, who were victims of poverty and overcrowding in their home country, already suffered tuberculosis, so the people incarcerated with them were soon exposed. Poor ventilation and overcrowding in the gaol ensured that many short-term inmates would leave with an infection and take it back to their communities.

Some of the inmates were there because of an addiction to

opium. Ailments 'due to deprivation of the drug' included insomnia, diarrhoea, and nervous afflictions. Addicts were also prone to catching any minor ailment that happened to be going round.*

A few European inmates died from tuberculosis. As this was embarrassing to the white government, it was often called 'phthisis', or 'miner's phthisis', but it was essentially the same thing, contracted for the same reasons – overcrowding in the goal.

In the 1880s, families from the Alligator rivers region were described as 'some of the finest physical specimens of humanity'.† Most of the Wulna men, for example, 'were over six feet tall with correspondingly good physique'. The arrival of the European and Chinese settlers in nearby communities and goldfields soon changed all that. Inspector Foelsche, who studied the local Aboriginal tribes and saw illnesses among them, noted the pock marks of smallpox, and in 1891 he also recorded malaria, coughs and colds, boils, ringworm, syphilis and venereal disease, neuralgia, and other ailments.

In 1890, whooping cough (pertussis) was introduced by European children to the community and it swept through the country between the Daly River and Katherine, killing many children. In the Alligator rivers region in 1899, Dr Goldsmith reported leprosy, whooping cough and measles had attacked most of the people of the local tribe. In 1905, Dr Ramsay Smith found that a tribe known as Manassie from that region had completely died out – their extinction hastened by disease.

The maintenance of good health in the small population of Palmerston was a vital role of the Government. In 1897, there were only two nurses (plus two untrained wardsmen) on the hospital staff: the matron, Miss Maria Davoran, who continued in that role until her death in 1906, and Nurse Birkett. They were joined in 1898 by Nurse Jean McWaters. The medical officer was a young Dr Frederick Goldsmith, who was to have a long career in the north. Goldsmith

---

* Goldsmith, 1894.
† Kettle, 1981.

later expressed how impressed he was with the way the nurses coped during the Great Hurricane. He was less impressed by the roof of the hospital, which had always leaked. Unfortunately, even after the repairs were made, it continued to leak, because second-hand iron was used, with old nail holes soldered.

They were busy at the hospital, but apparently not overloaded. In 1898, for instance, Dr Goldsmith found the 'institution to be in first class working order' and only 80 patients were admitted into Palmerston Hospital during that year:

> … Of the patients admitted, forty-four were Europeans, of whom 4 died; nineteen were Asiatics, of whom five died; and there were 16 aboriginals, with no deaths. *

Interestingly, the causes of the four Europeans who died in 1898 were recorded as cancer of the uterus, abscess of liver, strychnine poisoning and dysentery, and the Asians died from necrosis, tubercular ulceration of intestine, accident, and bedsores.

---

* Goldsmith in *Government Resident's Annual Report*, Dashwood, 1898.

Chapter 14
The Overlander

An anonymous man, calling himself 'The Overlander', published his diary in a nine-part series in the *Northern Territory Times and Gazette* in early 1890. It told the story of his journey across the continent by train and horseback at a time when 20 miles per hour was a *whirling* speed. He was a keen observer of the country and the telegraph stations along the line, and a participant in the 'ruby rush' from Alice Springs. He started and finished his journey by train (Darwin to Pine Creek, and Oodnadatta to Adelaide) and was a fervent believer that the 'great Transcontinental Railway Line' would soon make travel by horseback obsolete. He was happy to describe the overland route for readers of the *Times*:

> … Starting from Port Darwin on the north by the 8 a.m. train, the traveller passes through a tract of most uninteresting country, the land on each side of the line being poor and stony, and the timber invariably stunted by centuries of bush fires, the only redeeming feature in the landscape being the frequent creeks and waterholes on the line of route.[*]
>
> Here and there a good patch of land will be seen upon the margin of a running watercourse, but the general appearance of the country is not such as to tempt a farming community. The first stopping place of any importance on the journey is the Adelaide River, 75 miles from Port Darwin, and even in the driest time of the year, this is a pleasant running stream. Over this river a fine iron bridge has been erected, at a

---

[*] *NTTG*, 17 January 1890.

sufficient height to avoid the enormous floods which occur during the rainy season. Passengers for the mining districts are allowed twenty minutes stay at this station to enable them to obtain refreshments, after which they are whirled through the country at about 20 miles an hour until the Pine Creek Station is reached. This station is about 146 miles from Palmerston, and is the present terminus of the line, but it is hoped that another year will find the extension of the line to the Katherine authorized, if not actually in course of construction. I have purposely avoided any allusion to the mining districts on the line of route, such as the Howley, Union, Mount Wells, Yam Creek, and Pine Creek, as your readers are kept fairly posted in the news of your mines every week, by writers who are better able to express an opinion than I am. From Pine Creek to the Katherine, a distance of 70 miles, I accomplished on horseback, although there is a weekly mail service by buggy, for those who prefer that mode of travelling.

The country is somewhat more undulating than the road from the Port to Pine Creek, and several stony ranges of hills have to be crossed. Similar to the road from Palmerston to Pine Creek, the grasses and under-growth along the track still retain their tropical character, being tall and coarse, and are not of much value for stock until the rank grass has been burnt off by passing bushmen, who take every opportunity to thus make room for a splendid second crop of young and tender feed, upon which both horses and cattle thrive well. The country after passing Pine Creek, bound South, improves in character, and the timber, which is chiefly gum, is thicker and heavier, especially on the banks of the Cullen, Fergusson, and Edith Creeks.

The Fergusson, which is distant 22 miles from Pine Creek, is a dangerous creek to cross in the rainy season, and several foolhardy travellers have paid the penalty for their rashness in trying to cross it when flooded, with their lives. The banks being boggy and steep, it is always wiser to camp for a few days until the river goes down, in preference to risking the loss of their cattle, and probably their own lives. The Cullen and Edith are the next important creeks to be negotiated, and both of them are dangerous during flood. While upon this matter, pardon my saying that lives have been lost at nearly all these creeks, for which the callous negligence of the Government has been chiefly to blame, in not having either provided punts or wire cables for the assistance of travellers, and, worse still, neglecting to erect tidal poles, by which strangers could tell the depth of the water. 27 miles beyond the Edith the Katherine River is reached, and after crossing the innumerable miserable little creeks and watercourses on the road, it is a treat to see a fine stream, some 150 yards wide when in flood (as I saw it). At this river, a useful boat* is kept by the Telegraph Department, and I need hardly say that it is a perfect boon to travellers.

During the height of the wet season the Katherine is really a magnificent river, and it would be a bold swimmer who would make the attempt to cross it when in flood. When I first saw the stream, I considered it the grandest sight I had seen on my trip through the Continent, but I was told that in the year 1879 the water rose considerably higher, in fact up to within a few feet of the Telegraph buildings. About six years ago a new Telegraph Station building was erected, to replace the old building which had been made to serve as house and office since the construction of the line, and a portion of the old building is now utilised as a kitchen, storeroom, &c. The station is prettily situated on the Southern side of the river and is as comfortable a place for a weary traveller to drop into, as could well be found in Australia.†

'The Overlander' then travelled south through Elsey Station, Daly Waters, Tennant Creek, and Alice Springs to the railhead at Oodnadatta. From there, he whirled '20 miles an hour on the narrow gauge' through to Adelaide.

An unknown number of other overlanders also crossed the

---

* Boats like this were placed at several of the rivers. Rusted fragments of the punt eventually placed by the Ferguson River still sit in the bush where it was left by the last traveller to use. Also, the Katherine River punt can be seen at the excellent Katherine Museum.

† The Overlander's story is well worth reading. Only a part of the Top End section is reproduced here as it runs to about 16,000 words. For the full text see http://www.derekpugh.com.au/stories, or the original in the *Northern Territory Times*, between January and March 1891.

continent, perhaps looking for work or adventure, but if their stories were never published they are forgotten.

The overlander with the highest profile in those years was undoubtedly a man whose role as Queen Victoria's representative in the colony was guaranteed to give him publicity. He was the Governor of South Australia, Earl Kintore, whose story was told in Chapter 2.

Chapter 15
Palmerstonian Souls

Banjo Paterson

Travelling authors who passed through the northern capital of the 1890s appear to have developed a remarkably consistent view of the population. Andrew 'Banjo' Paterson, who visited in 1897, was one of the most disparaging of the writers. Paterson saw 'a curse on all N.T. undertakings' with an 'Eastern flavour over everything'. He deplored the squandered waste of money, the burgeoning debt, the never-ending cry for more funds and the lethargy that suggested that this was all temporary, because 'everything good is always going to happen after the wet season.' The problem was, he wrote:

> ... there is always a wet season just past or coming. If it is past, they wait 'till the ground dries' and by the time it *is* dry they think the next wet season might come early, and they – wait!*

Paterson said there was only three topics of conversation in Palmerston, the 'city of booze, blow and blasphemy' – the 'cycloon' of 1897, Government Resident Dashwood, and Paddy Cahill, the buffalo hunter:

> ... The inhabitants sit about the shady verandahs [sic] and drink and talk about one or all of these three. They start drinking square gin immediately after breakfast and keep it up at intervals till midnight. They don't do anything else to speak of, yet they have a curious delusion that they are an energetic and reckless set of people.

---
* Paterson, A.B., 1898.

Despite all this, and a continuing list of criticisms and gripes, he concluded that he would give his 'weary soul' to be back in Palmerston. The hospitality of the inhabitants, the sights, and smells of the exotic, with a 'cycloon' 'humming on the horizon' continued to call him:

> ... the man who once goes to the Territory always has a hankering to get back there. Someday it will be civilised and spoilt; but up to the present it has triumphantly overthrown all who have attempted to improve it. It is still 'the Territory'.

Long may it wave!

Jerome Murif

Jerome Murif, the cyclist who arrived in Palmerston soon after the Great Hurricane of 1897, found Palmerstonians to be a 'laughter-loving and generously hospitable people' whose lives were 'rounds of light gaieties and small pleasures. A picnic, dance, a sports day, or a concert, is ever an absorbing topic'.* Murif found that most of the European residents he met were civil servants, and therefore had to be 'non-political' and this was a hindrance to the Territory's progress. 'Unmuzzle them', called Murif, because 'so long as they are not heard from, so long must the Territory continue as a heavy weight'.

Murif praised the Chinese population but saw many difficulties. The Chinese were workers, and as such had ousted Europeans from occupations such as hairdressing, tailoring, boot making and cooking. One of their vices, he complained, was the loud monotonous humming of paper kites launched high in the air above Chinatown, at the southern end of Cavenagh Street.

'Every visitor' he wrote, 'gets a crick in their neck from looking skywards'.

A spiritual 'oasis in a religious desert'

Palmerston's reputation as a friendly, hard-drinking, opium-soaked, lazy place, did not mean that that town was free of religious, god-

---

* Murif, 1897.

fearing, people. As in most nineteenth century British communities, religions were numerous and ubiquitous. Despite the attempts of the Jesuit missionaries to convert them to Catholicism at the Rapid Creek Mission during the 1880s, Larrakia naturally stuck with their traditional beliefs.

The Chinese population were a mixture of Taoists and Buddhists, and the Chung Wah Temple, established in 1887, can still be found in Woods Street today.* A few were Christians, supported by a Chinese Methodist missionary. Many Europeans clung to their traditional creeds – mainly through the three Christian churches in town, and there were a few Jews, such as the Solomon brothers, who were without a place to worship.

The first Christian church building in Palmerston was originally owned by the Congregational Union in Adelaide, who sent a flat-packed church kit to the Pine Creek goldfields in 1872. It arrived on the schooner *Linn Fern*. It was supposed to be erected by Alfred Gore but, before the building arrived, Gore contracted malaria and returned to Adelaide. As a result, the church never reached Pine Creek. Eighteen months later it was still lying on the beach near the Fort Hill Camp.

Around that time, a 33-year-old Methodist minister named Reverend Archibald James Bogle arrived in Port Darwin on the S.S. *Taruria*. He and his wife at first lived under a tarpaulin and ran their first service under a tree on the Esplanade, on 14 August 1873. Later they used the veranda at The Residency, and then a room at one of the hotels. After one of the services, someone mentioned Gore's church, and curious, Bogle wandered down to the beach and discovered it still lying there, flat-packed, and unclaimed. At his suggestion, the Methodist's then bought the building from the Congregational Church for £175, and it was erected on Mitchell Street.

On Sunday, 2 November 1873, the community celebrated the church's official opening. The *Times* reported that:

---

* The temple is called the 'Hall of the Ranking Sages'.

> ... the structure is of wood covered by an iron roof and will accommodate about 200 persons. There are plenty of doors and windows and the ventilation is therefore sufficient. No bell has yet been added to the building, but as a substitute an iron bar has been suspended to a tree outside and this is struck upon by another iron bar when the congregation is to be called together.*

This building served the community for nearly 25 years and indeed, it was the mainstay of Christianity for the whole community. Palmerston was one of the 'least-churched' communities in Australia, complained the *Times* in 1895, but luckily:

> ... the Wesleyan is the one bright oasis in a religious desert... The Methodist persuasion is the only sect here that can feel happy in the possession of an uninterrupted course of religious instruction.†

Unfortunately, when the Great Hurricane of 1897 hit the town, the church never stood a chance. Totally destroyed, it needed to be replaced and this happened in a remarkably brief time after the storm: a new building arrived in kit form on the S.S. *Australian* in June 1897, and it was ready for its first service by 16 August. The original building was mourned because it 'ranked at the time of the storm as one of the oldest erections in the township, having been in use for about a quarter of a century',‡ but the new all-metal construction, on the same site in Mitchell Street, was larger and greatly anticipated. The structure was prefabricated in Adelaide by A. Simpson and Sons. On arrival, it cost £15 to erect, plus £7 for the floor. Its congregation, including community leaders such as Inspector Paul and Charlotte Foelsche, the redoubtable 'Granny' Tuckwell, and others, ensured its success.

At its opening:

> ... special services were arranged morning and evening. The Rev. Mr. Trewren delivered telling addresses on the subject

---

* *NTTG*, Nov 14, 1873
† *NTTG*, 18 October 1895.
‡ *NTTG*, 11 June 1897.

of a Church Membership and Church Attendance, and at the conclusion of the evening service he administered the sacrament to all those who chose to partake of it.*

The *Times* was pleased:

> ... The building, which is entirely of iron, is a great improvement on the old structure, having seating accommodation for about 120 people, is heat proof and has a specially designed system of ventilation, whereby the church is kept cool in the hottest weather. The walls are painted French grey, a colour which harmonises very prettily with a delicate shade of sky blue on the interior of the roof. The pulpit and platform are enclosed by a cedar railing behind which the choir sit, facing the audience, on both sides of the organ, which is immediately in rear of the pulpit. We should say that the new building is a great acquisition to Palmerston, well fitted for its purpose, and being capitally planned is substantial enough to easily withstand even a repetition of the recent cyclone.†

Missionaries

Missionaries in Palmerston came and went. The most prominent for a time were the Austrian Jesuits who built Saint Joseph's Mission at Rapid Creek, 11 kilometres outside the town of Palmerston (in the current suburb of Millner). In 1882, Father Anton Strele and his colleagues pitched tents in the bush and started clearing land, building, and planting seeds. Larrakia and Wulna people were soon attracted to the settlement and more than 10 men were employed by the missionaries. The men and their families, including dozens of children, were happy to move in.‡ A school was opened in 1883, and the future for their souls was looking bright.

Unfortunately, the proximity to town, with its opium dens and moonshine shanties, meant that soon the mission was little more than a baby-sitting agency. In huge financial difficulty, the Jesuits decided

---

* *NTTG*, 20 August 1897.
† *NTTG*, 20 August 1897.
‡ *NTTG*, 18 August 1883.

that they would need to go further afield where their 'flock' had not yet been spoiled.

Rapid Creek Mission closed in December 1891 and Father Donald McKillop* was sent to Serpentine Lagoon on the Daly River to set up a new mission. As Vice-Superior Joseph Conrath wrote in his 1891 report to the Government Resident, their mission was to 'settle the aboriginals on the ground and turn them into a farming population' to bestow 'Christian civilisation on them'.†

The Daly River Mission always suffered from extreme poverty and with a strong and vibrant religious culture already, few of the Mullak-Mullak (Malak) people from the Daly River region were willing to be converted to Christianity, though some used the mission as a boarding school for their children. McKillop went to Adelaide in 1893 to ask Catholics to support the mission, but little help was forthcoming, despite his promotion of his people:

> … The natives under our care … are tractable, intelligent, and teachable; superior to the southern blacks, as can be seen by the configuration of their heads and the cast of their features… our system of education is simple and effective, we have an intelligent people to deal with; they are not dull and idle as so many people believe aboriginals to be, in fact they are superior to the average Australian black. Their features are more regular and display more intelligence…‡

McKillop remained at the mission until mid-1896, when he was withdrawn to Sydney suffering from kidney stones and neuritis. He never returned to the north, so was not present when a huge flood hit the mission the following year.§ The writing was on the wall, and the mission was closed in 1899:

> … The visit of the Rev. Father Miltz to the Jesuit Mission station on the Daly River has ended in a decision to break

---

* Incidentally, originally from Melbourne, Donald McKillop was the brother of Australia's only saint, Mary McKillop (Saint Mary of the Cross).
† See Dashwood's 1891 annual report.
‡ *Register*, 20 June 1893
§ Griffith University: *Jesuits in the Northern Territory*, 2020.

up the station and abandon all further Christianising efforts in that district... Father Miltz considered the alternative of removing the station to higher country to escape the destruction caused by floods, but he had reluctantly to confess that the conditions were against favourable occupation in whatever part of the district they might shift to.*

The site was soon taken over by Mr and Mrs J.H. Niemann and their two young daughters in furtherance of his 'meat-extract' business. As children, Alice and Kitty Niemann may have left a greater impression on the local people than a decade of missionaries: the two little girls could 'chat away with the greatest ease to the natives in their own language and, in fact, appear to speak it with greater fluency than their native English'.†

In Palmerston, in February 1889, a small Roman Catholic Church was formally opened and blessed by the Very Reverend Father S.J. Strele, Administrator of the Diocese of Palmerston, assisted by the Reverend Father McKillop and Father O'Brien. It was a 'pretty little building' with an excellent choir 'secured to aid in the usual ceremonial'.‡

Eight years later the church was destroyed by the Great Hurricane of 1897. It was rebuilt by May, but a committee for its replacement took subscriptions from the congregation throughout 1898:

Catholic Church Notice

OWING to the destruction of the Church and properties, the Committee will be thankful for subscriptions for the purpose of re-erecting the church and buying new properties.

---

*   *NTTG*, 7 July 1899.

†   *NTTG*, 29 June 1900. Incidentally, Mary Niemann wrote 'The Adventures of Alice and Kitty' that outlined their years in the NT. It was published in 12 chapters in the *Melbourne Leader* (1 May through 3 July 1913). The family spent six years on the Daly River site and the girls grew up to become expert linguists in several different tribal dialects. They then moved to Pine Creek and 'Harry' returned to his original profession of chemist. In 1908 Mary was newly appointed as the schoolteacher at Pine Creek NT (*NTTG*, 24 January 1908) and opened the school with 10 students. She was born in 1876 in Armadale, Victoria and died in Adelaide in 1943 at the age of 67.

‡   *North Australian*, 2 March 1889.

Any amounts forwarded to the undersigned will be gratefully acknowledged.

D.E. KELSEY, Hon. Sec., and Treas.[*]

The grateful acknowledgment through later newspaper editions tells us who some of the subscribers were. They included prominent hoteliers such as Ellen Ryan, and public servants such as D.E. Kelsey.[†]

There was another Christian mission in Palmerston during the 1890s. From 1887, led by Brother Loie Foy, this mission worked among the predominantly Taoist and Buddhist Chinese community in northern Australia with some success: a few Chinese babies had been baptised and a few Chinese weddings were performed in the Wesleyan Church by Reverend Bradbury. On Foy's recall a Chinese minister, Reverend Joseph Tear Tack, was appointed about the same time as Reverend Henry Trewren and his wife, Mary Anne, arrived in Port Darwin in 1896 to take over the Wesleyan Church. In July 1896, 40-year-old, Chinese-born Reverend Tack arrived in Port Darwin from Ballarat in Victoria, with his wife, Emma Lee Young, and their five children.

The two reverends worked together: in November of 1896, a bilingual baptism was reported in the *Methodist Journal*. 'A baptismal service of a novel and interesting character was conducted in our church' wrote Percy Kelsey:

> ... Three Chinese converts were baptised. The service was conducted by Rev. H. Trewren in English and by the Rev. Tear Tack in Chinese. The attendance composed of yellow and white faces was good and during the service the Chinese portion of the congregation sang heartily two verses of *Bringing in the Sheaves* which Mr Tear Tack had taught them. Each of the new converts expressed a strong desire to faithfully serve the Lord Jesus Christ...[‡]

Reverend Trewren departed in 1898 and was replaced by Reverend Sampson Dyer Stephens, who was so enamoured by the 'all

---

[*] *NTTG*, 18 June 1897.
[†] *NTTG*, 13 May 1898.
[‡] In James, 2002, p 103.

pervading, busy, quiet' Chinese that he began to learn their language and gave as much support as he could to Reverend Tear Tack:

> ... Brother Tear Tack's strong point is his impenetrable consistency. Men may come and men may go but he goes on forever. His countrymen respect him, and he is often in request to assist them in legal and other matters. Brother Tack is especially to be commended for his examples of moral conduct and I believe his unconquerable steadfastness has done a great deal of good.*

Reverend Tack transferred to Cairns in 1900, and died there soon after, aged 41. Reverend Stephens was replaced by Reverend Greenwood in 1901. For three years Greenwood was happy to run services for both the Methodist congregation (in the morning) and a growing Church of England congregation (in the afternoon). The latter were busy raising funds for a church of their own. It would become the Anglican Cathedral.

In 1899, Andrew Lennox, an Anglican missionary, arrived at Kapalga, a few hundred kilometres east of Darwin near the West Alligator River. At first, he set up camp near the billabong, but later leased a strip of land from just south of the billabong to the coast and called it the Northern Territory Native Industrial Mission. It only lasted a few years. In 1903 they transferred to Greenhill Island, about 70 kilometres across open sea from the mouth of the South Alligator and close to Cobourg Peninsula, but Lennox wrecked the mission's lugger and fell out with the Anglican Bishop over his Greenhill Island plans. The Adelaide council withdrew its support, and the mission was abandoned.†

---

*   In James, 2002, p 108.
†   Lennox, 2016.

Chapter 16
A Royal Commission for a White Elephant

By the 1890s, many South Australians were worried about future financial security and tired of the constant expense of their northern territories for little return. In 1895, the Government relented to public pressure and announced a Royal Commission 'to enquire into and report upon all matters relating to the Northern Territory with a view to the further development of its resources and to its better government'. The commissioners never visited the Territory, but they called 69 witnesses during their 35 meetings and discovered what everyone in Palmerston already knew.*

One of the major issues in the community was that most of the land in the settlement had been bought by speculators in 1869, most of whom remained absent landlords and charged exorbitant rents. This meant that there were large undeveloped areas and empty blocks that could not be used within the town and the original surveys had not allowed for sufficient government possession for offices, schools, and other infrastructure. There was also often confusion over the survey results.

The Commission was held in Adelaide and Queensland, far from most Territorians – consequently, it was a farce.† Of the 69

---

* The Commissioners were Hons. W. Haslam (chairman), F. W. Holder, J. Warren, J. V. O'Loghlin, V. L. Solomon, M.P., W. Gilbert, M.P., and W. O. Archibald, M.P.
† See Fletcher 1988.

witnesses, 29 had never been to the Territory at all, eight had visited briefly, 10 had been resident for less than two years and seven more between two and five years. A third of them were Queensland sugar workers with no experience in the Northern Territory. Fourteen were wageworkers who had spent time in the Territory, but only seven had owned businesses there. According to the *Times*, the Commission 'deserved to be laughed at'.

The highest profile interviewee was Government Resident Dashwood. He was optimistic about the mining and pastoral industries particularly but said a lack of government policy on the Territory's development, low financial support for the industries, and sustained mismanagement was holding the Territory back. He wanted an injection of £20,000, which would lead, he thought, to a 'prosperous settlement'.

Dashwood enthusiastically promoted the building of the transcontinental railway following the American land-grant system. He believed it was the best way to open up the country, and 'there was no doubt that the construction of the line would add to the value of large tracts of land which for many years would lie idle'.[*]

The Commission's recommendations became a part of the *Northern Territory Crown Lands Act* of 1899, but it was otherwise unremarkable because few of the recommendations worked to stimulate development of the Territory. Several recommendations concerning the pastoral industry may have had a positive effect: it was recommended that cattle owners receive favourable rent reviews after they made improvements on their leases. They could also request 5000 acres but needed to agree to develop it within a nominated time.

Grog

The commissioners interviewed a number of people who were a part of the northern colony's early days. From them, yet again, we hear of the importance of alcohol in the Territory. Surveyor General George

---

[*] SAAP, 1895.

Goyder, who had not been anywhere near the Territory since his survey in 1869, was asked about the employment of European labour in Palmerston:

> ... I found... that unless the men had a stimulant early in the morning they could not eat their breakfast, and also that they could not eat their dinner unless they first had a stimulant... with stimulants men can work on the surface of the ground well but take that away and they utterly fail.*

Goyder's stimulant was, of course, alcoholic – much of the surveyors' work of 1869 was carried out by teams of men who were always slightly tipsy.

Palmerston remained a 'great place for drink, especially square gin, which was cheap, but if a man took care of himself, he would not do so badly,' the Commission was told by W.F. Fox, a blacksmith. With the proper amount of stimulant, he suggested, six Europeans could do as much work as 20 'coolies', but they would need six months holiday in the south after an extended period of work to recuperate.

Government Resident Dashwood wrote 'Whether in the mines or in the fields, Chinese labor was the best. The Chinese were temperate, were hardworking, gave no trouble, and all other things being equal, it was the best labor for the Northern Territory'.

Governor Kintore had said as much in 1891. He felt that Europeans were completely unsuited to working in the tropics and 'coloured' people were necessary for the Territory to progress.

White Elephant

The term 'white elephant' had been used to describe the Northern Territory since before Goyder's survey in 1869, but as the cost of keeping it rose, so too did the calls for letting it go. Even getting there was expensive.

The Ghan railway was constructed from 1878, seventeen years before the Royal Commission, and although it looked northward,

---

* SAAP, 1895.

it had managed to extend only as far as Oodnadatta. By 1891, the annual interest rate for the railway debt had reached £50,000 and no one could justify the expense of sending it through Alice Springs to meet the south heading line at Pine Creek – which also carried a debt of about £50,000.

A dispatch from Lord Kintore to Lord Knutsford in 1891 shows he was already of the mind that the Northern Territory should be separated from South Australia. In his opinion it was impossible to govern the Northern Territory from '2000 miles distant', especially since the Parliament was composed of:

> … gentlemen mainly ignorant of the conditions of tropical life, and who are swayed by constituencies having little interest in, or prejudiced, against the methods and management of tropical colonies.*

Kintore was thinking of both the South Australians and the Territorians and said that he had both their interests at heart. He thought that a 're-arrangement' would serve everyone well, but wanted to eat his cake too:

> … The extreme southern portion of the Northern Territory, comprising MacDonnell ranges, must, however, be retained for South Australia. My visit to that portion of the country led me to share the hopes that are universally entertained that the exploration of that district will handsomely repay South Australia for the money expended on it. Situated as is this district, its trade can flow in no other direction than towards Adelaide, and it is only right that South Australia should reap the advantage of her enterprise, and a suitable boundary line would perhaps be found in the 20th or 21st parallel of south latitude.

The words 'White Elephant' began to appear more often in the press as the decade progressed. Naturally, some, like 'Hugh Kalyptus', reduced the issues to humour and the newspapers were only too happy to publish his, or her, poetry in 1891:

---

* *The Age*, 5 August 1871.

The White Elephant, by Hugh Kalyptus*

Parsons had an elephant,
With skin as white as snow,
But everywhere that Parsons went
The elphy wouldn't go.

He tried to fill its great big trunk
With everything so nice–
With sugar, beet, and arrowroot,
Tobacco, also rice.

The elephant would not get fat,
But thinner every day,
And people said 'twould better be
To give the beast away.

They prodded it with railways,
And pelted it with cash,
But every time the elphy moved
It came down with a crash.

It reached its trunk for everything,
And never seemed to thrive,
And Parsons found it very hard
To keep the brute alive.

It followed him to Parliament,
Which was against the rule,
And made the members laugh a lot
And call the beast a fool.

Lord Kintore went to visit it,
And try to make it go.
But found the brute too obstinate,
Pigheaded, dull, and slow.

Not many seemed impressed with it
In any sort of way,
Some recommended that it should
Be lost or sent astray.

But still this bulky elephant,
With skin as white as snow,
Went eating on and starving still,
But never seemed to go.

But Parsons he still clung
Because it was his pet.
The biggest, slowest, sulkie
That ever he had met.

So, Parsons and his elephant
Were always seen about.
And that it might be taught at
He never breathed a doubt.

Although it had so big a head
It never seemed to learn
To help itself, or do its friends
A beneficial turn.

Parsons had an elephant,
With skin as white as snow,
And every way he wanted it
The elphy wouldn't go.

---

* *The White Elephant*, by 'Hugh Kalyptus', *Evening Journal*, 8 August 1891.

Territory For Sale?

A Rundle Street tailor and member for West Torrens, Benjamin Nash, suggested selling the Territory to pay off South Australia's debts. He valued the land at £32 million sterling, which would give South Australia £10 million in change that they could use to develop their colony. He thought the Territory was a 'snare and a pitfall and a perpetual source of worry ever since it was taken in hand'.* Poor Nash died of kidney failure 10 days after losing the 1890 election, and his suggestion was never carried forward.

Like Nash and Lord Kintore, V. L. Solomon, who did win a seat in the election, thought long and hard about selling the Territory to pay off debts. In an 1893 speech he suggested that Kintore's idea of carving off the southern part of the Territory had merit.

> ... The trade of the area in question flowed naturally in the direction of Adelaide and would always do so. The Territory was debited with a large sum yearly for the maintenance of police, etc. in the Alice Springs district, for which we received little or nothing in return. If the scheme were carried into effect South Australia would secure an additional 100 million acres of territory, or about one third of the total area of the Territory.
>
> He was of opinion that South Australia should be permitted to take this land, at a fair valuation, say at 4d. per acre. Let her credit the Territory with the sum total. It would pay off all our debt and give us a clear start, and there should be a surplus of many thousands each year from general revenue account to be expended in developing our resources.†

Various other members of the South Australian Legislative Assembly grew hoarse harping over Territory affairs, and everything that happened in the Territory was to the background hum of their high-level complaints. In 1899, one member decreed that 'the serious condition of the finances of the Northern Territory requires the immediate attention of Parliament' because South Australia had

---

* *NTTG*, 14 March 1890.
† *NTTG*, 24 March 1893.

'bitten off more than it could chew.' The *Times* summarised the issue:

> ... The debt of the Territory is over two and a quarter million sterling, for a population of about 4000! It has increased £415,000 since the Kingston Government has been in office! There is a loss at the rate of £90,000 a year; in twenty-one years it will be at the rate of £200,000, and in fifty years £400,000! Mr. Grainger therefore advised that the Government should either dispose of the Territory to some company willing to pay the present debt, and relieve them of all further responsibility, or obtain the permission of the British Government to relinquish its possession.*

The White Australia Policy

The problems were complex, not least because of the political movements of the time in the march towards federation. The *Immigration Restriction Act* of 1901, which became known as the 'White Australia Policy' was still embryonic, but negative sentiments against 'Asiatics' were building across Australia. Unfortunately for the Territory, where the non-Aboriginal population of the Northern Territory was 70 percent Asian, the sentiments of the rest of Australia, where Asian people were a minority, outweighed any local feeling. Trade unions were becoming more powerful, and Australia was moving towards a basic wage and universal suffrage. According to V.L. Solomon, there were enough Asian people in Sydney and Melbourne for them to be blamed for the 'starving white men' who had to 'stand by and see Chinese employed on our public works'.†

While the Territory still needed the cheap labour that Asian workers would agree to, southern politicians, increasingly representative of the working class, were rarely interested.

> ... The real facts in the case are that South Australia carries its incubus, dooms its northern province to stagnation, sacrifices the advantage it should derive from its proper development, permits it to be looted by aliens, and for these manifold

---

* *NTTG*, 13 October 1899.
† *NTTG*, 24 March 1893.

privileges incurs an annual debt of £90,000, simply because it will not recognise that only with the assistance of low-grade labor introduced under contract is its progress possible.*

The White Australia Policy was not good for the Northern Territory. The N.T. did not just want cheap labour – it needed all it could get. So, when the Government was forced to agree to employ Europeans when available, it was an empty agreement as so few Europeans lived in the Territory. For example, when the new jetty was to be built in 1896:

> ... According to the policy announced by the Premier, the Government intend to main true to their principles antagonistic to black labour for the Territory. Yet the same Government is prepared to construct works like the jetty here with gangs of mixed Asiatics. Our members agreed to the Department putting on Europeans where available, but as they were not available at the time, and have never been available since to the number of more than a dozen, the undertaking is virtually an Asiatic one. It would have been better never to have raised the point at all than to have raised it only to make a farce of the thing.†

The racist attitudes and a strong belief in their cultural superiority meant that many white men in the Territory, rather than being threatened by the Asian workforce, saw them as an opportunity. Few people wanted them gone and it wasn't hard to game the system:

> ... A blacksmith complained that work on the overland telegraph line was given to Chinamen. The Treasurer then gave instructions that the white blacksmith should be given the work, although at a higher price. What happened? That blacksmith turned round, employed Chinamen to do the work, and pocketed the difference.

The local mining industry in the 1890s was primarily run by Chinese, and the pearling industry was Japanese, so it made sense to hold on to them as workers.‡ But even more because, as Lord Kintore

---

* *NTTG*, 13 October 1899.
† *NTTG*, 10 April 1896
‡ By 1894 there were 19 rock batteries in the goldfields and Chinese miners owned or had tributes over 16 of them. They also held a monopoly on the reefs and alluvial

noted:
> ... Remove them tomorrow, and the residents of Palmerston would be left without fish, or fruit, to a large extent without meat, without laundries for their washing; neither would there be any tailors, cooks, or domestic servants.

The politicians thought them 'desirable colonists' – Chinese population in the north was better than no population at all. But in the other Australian colonies, the Chinese were a minority and seen as offensive because they were willing to work for lower wages, which threatened the work of trade unions. Thus, anti-Chinese sentiment continued to grow.

Chinese 'restriction' bills that were introduced by various governments eventually had their effect and the Territory's status as a 'white elephant' was grounded in some of these policies. As the *Times* put it,
> ... A 'White Australia' is a good democratic election cry down south, though it means a white elephant up north, and while it is maintained, there is supposed to be a near prospect of the Federal Government taking the Territory, with its difficulties and debts, off the shoulders upon which it now presses so heavily. *

Eventually the Federal Government did take over the Territory and its debt of more than £10 million. It took a long time – the government changed several times and Andrew Fisher was in his second term as Prime Minister by the time it happened. At last, in 1911, the 'Northern Territory of South Australia' became the Northern Territory, and Palmerston shucked its archaic name for the more popular 'Darwin'.

---

gold (Jones, 1987).
* *NTTG*, 13 October 1899.

Chapter 17
The Great Hurricane

Big storms and squalls are not unusual in the Top End and even the very first settlements experienced their wrath. The British settlement of Fort Victoria in Port Essington, for example, was destroyed by a cyclone in 1839.* By 1897, most old Territorians had already experienced some of the ferocity of the tropics. In December 1893, for example, Palmerston was hit hard by what seems to have been a tornado:

> … It came up from the eastward on Sunday afternoon last, wind and rain, thunder and lightning, and a spray that looked like nothing more than sleet. It came along in a body, and long before it was within reach, townspeople who were watching it had made up their minds that it was going to be something unusual. It was truly an extraordinary storm. The whole town felt the force of a stiff squall, but it was only within a very limited radius that the severest of the wind was experienced.
>
> It first struck that part of China Town nearest the Joss House, then coursed over the old coffee palace buildings and across to Armstrong and Lawrie's, and then, veering round again, struck the Bakery and afterwards the Club Hotel, finally departing via the Cricket Oval.
>
> Old ramshackle buildings which experienced only the outer edge of the storm were not injured in the slightest, while strong buildings within the turbulent limit were either stripped of their roofs, lifted bodily of their foundations, capsized altogether, or made to shake in a manner that was

---

* For the full story, see Pugh, 2020.

terrifying to nervous ones inside.*

Four years later, on 6 January 1897, the residents of Port Darwin were again anxiously watching their barometers. When the readings turned 'unusually low, and still falling rapidly', and they could see 'dense banks of rain clouds all round', they knew they were in for bad weather. There had already been 4.4 inches (112 mm) of rain in the previous two days, but that night, for four long hours, the tiny colony was struck by the full fury of a tropical cyclone that became known as the 'Great Hurricane'.†

The news

Post and Telegraph Master John Little managed to get several messages through to Adelaide during and after the storm:

> ... 4 a.m. – Hurricane here. Barometer 28.784. Line and station buildings damaged, also considerable damage to other buildings in township. Everything possible will be done to restore communication quickly.
>
> 7.30 a.m. – Lines all broken by hurricane; nearly every building in township wrecked. Barometer rising, but still blowing very hard.‡

Information continued to arrive in Adelaide over the next few days. Journalists decried the lack of details and claimed it was impossible to describe the damage caused by the storm, but they did it anyway. Alfred Searcy, then the Clerk Assistant in the House of Assembly in Adelaide, was tracked down and interviewed for his knowledge of the port colony. Searcy had been in the storm of 1893,

---

* *NTTG*, 8 December 1893.

† Palmerston's 1897 cyclone was simply called the Great Hurricane. Cyclones were named in the 1890s, but only in Queensland, by a meteorologist named Clement Wragge, who named them using the Greek alphabet in order, after mythological characters and politicians. Wragge retired in 1908 and the naming stopped, but in 1964, the Bureau of Meteorology began using female names, starting with Cyclone Bessie, and the practice became used worldwide. In 1975, the Australian Minister for Science, Bill Morrison, objected that only female names were used and since then, cyclones have had male names also.

‡ *Adelaide Observer*, 9 January 1897.

so he spoke with some authority on what he *thought* would have happened this time:

> ... All Chinatown is of iron and wood, and there is no doubt if the wind caught the structures they would suffer very severely, as many of them are two stories high. I have no doubt that where white ants have been prosecuting their ravages for some time there would not be much difficulty in knocking the buildings down.*

Searcy was right. All but one or two shelters in Chinatown were destroyed. As more information arrived, the devastation was described in detail by every major journal of the south. The news came in Morse code, not via the Overland Telegraph Line, which had been torn from its poles in so many places it would take time to repair, but through the undersea telegraph cables to Banyuwangi in Java and Broome in Western Australia.

George Mayhew, the editor of the *Times* described the scene:

> ... strongly built houses collapsed like houses of cards; roofs blew bodily away; lamps and telephone posts were bent or torn up; immense beams of timber were hurled away like chaff; trees were uprooted; in many instances large houses were lifted bodily from their foundations and deposited ten or twelve feet away; and in short the night was one of terrifying destructiveness that made the stoutest heart quail.†

Charles Kirkland had only recently dissolved his partnership with George Mayhew and received his share of the settlement. He was now the unhappy owner of Lot 532, including the Pickford Hotel and other buildings:

> ... half my own private house was carried away and in Lot 532 only the old Pickfords Family Hotel building and a part of the store bedrooms at the rear were left standing, the roof of the stone bedrooms was utterly gone, and a great part of the walls demolished, and the main hotel building had been blown off its piles partially unroofed and was leaning over at an angle of 45 deg., the printing plant contained therein was

---

*   *South Australian Register*, 9 January 1897.
†   *NTTG*, 5 February 1897.

also damaged.*

The *Adelaide Observer* reported on 9 January:

... The distress among the residents is simply appalling, and a large proportion of the people are absolutely ruined by the terrible visitation. The bodies of ten persons who met with their deaths through the collapse of the buildings in which they resided at the time of the cyclone have been already recovered, but a great number of people are missing and have yet to be accounted for...

The following mercantile establishments have been completely levelled to the ground by the fury of the tempest: – V. V. Brown's buildings; Rundle Brothers' stores and dwellings; Aplin, Brown, & Co.'s block, consisting of wholesale store, bonded store, and dwellings; and P. R. Allen & Co.'s wholesale, retail, and bonded stores.

There are three hotels in Palmerston – Mrs. Ryan's in Smith-street, Budgen's Terminus Hotel in Cavenagh Street, and Jolly's Victoria Hotel, managed by Mr. James, and all of them have been razed to the ground.

Amongst the other more prominent buildings which have collapsed are all the Government bonded stores, Mr. Daniel's house and stores, the Roman Catholic Church, the Wesleyan Chapel, the Chinese Joss house, and all the buildings in Chinatown with the exception of about five or six.

The State school and the head teacher's residence, the hospital, its attached dwellings and quarters, the seminary of Miss Jones, a Government building formerly occupied by Mr. A. Searcy and situated in Cavenagh Street, Lewis's bakery, Armstrong's butcher's shop, Palmer's butcher's shop, the office of the Northern Territory Times, and nearly every private dwelling in the town are either lying in heaps, a confused jumble of iron, boards, and furniture, or are roofless with their contents exposed to the element.

Further inland the railway sheds at 2 ½ Mile, Parap, were levelled and the line towards Pine Creek washed away in several places. In Fannie Bay, the botanic gardens lay flattened. The gaol was torn open, and its prisoners escaped. Any boat caught at a mooring

---

* Kirkland's 'reminiscences', *The Northern Territory Times*, 18 July 1930.

in the harbour was sunk, the lucky few were blown out to sea or into the mangrove forests – some were found on the opposite side of Bynoe Harbour.* All the Government Offices were wrecked, and government business ground to a halt.

On 10 January, when the reports arrived, worried southerners heard that the weather was now fine and sunny in Port Darwin, but 'imagination could not paint the wreck and devastation':

> ... Every building in the town has suffered, and most of them are uninhabitable. The Cable Company's quarters, the English, Scottish, and Australian Bank, and the Commercial Bank, three of the largest and least injured, have been placed at the disposal of and are being used as a shelter by a number of houseless people, the hotels, owing to their damaged state, being incapable of carrying on their ordinary trade, let alone receiving an extra strain.
>
> The Government residence, the Custom house, and the police station and quarters are all badly injured, and the railway stores and houses are in the same plight. The railway employees are temporarily occupying the railway-station quarters, which were fortunately sheltered by being built under the protection of a hill. Others are sleeping in railway carriages until their buildings are again ready for their accommodation.
>
> The only private residences now occupied by their owners, but which are all more or less injured, are those belonging to Messrs. Little, Shanahan, Herbert Cleland, Kirkland, Marchant, Mrs. Finniss, Messrs. S. Brown, Palmer, Clarke, Symes, Lawrie, Sims, Ryan, James Budgen, Gregg, O'Flaherty, and Pinder.†

Mrs Tack's family were lucky to survive:

> ... we were forced to run out into the street, nearly blinded with the rain. My little children were blown in all directions, their shrieks being heart rending. I fell several times into the water, but by breathing in the dear baby's mouth, managed by God's help and will to keep her above. The little girl, about six

---

* *Adelaide Observer*, 9 January 1897.
† *Adelaide Observer*, 16 January 1897.

years of age, was found in the morning clinging onto a fence, quite exhausted and one little boy took shelter under a piece of iron that had blown off the next house. Mr Tack managed to find the other two children and kept them with him until daybreak. He got his legs cut very badly, the children got cut and bruised, and at present Mr Tack is not well at all. The baby has a severe cold on the chest. I dropped her twice in the water and had to grope about for her in the dark…'

Few buildings had survived undamaged, and most had collapsed as if made of cardboard or blown away by the storm. During the storm, families had to move from shelter to shelter as each was destroyed behind them. One family said they had moved three times. The *Times* reported that:

> … it was impossible to tell where to go with the houses disappearing in the way they were and the pitiless rain blinding the sight. To make headway at all against the wind people had to go down on their hands and knees and lie as close to the ground as possible.†

A few days after the storm, Lighthouse Keeper, Henry Christie, sent a note from Point Charles via 'native canoe' to Port Darwin. He reported that most of the trees between Point Charles and Darwin had been uprooted or stripped of branches and leaves, and the roof of one of his cottages was peeled off by the wind and blown over the cliff. The lighthouse itself had weathered the storm and stood strong, despite 'oscillating frightfully'. It was here Christie and his brother sheltered.‡ For months thereafter, Palmerston residents could see the light from Point Charles in the town – the trees, which once blocked the view, were gone.§

A section of the Stokes Hill Jetty had collapsed. It had already been weakened by Toledo worms, and cost £51,600 just 11 years earlier, so its loss was a huge economic blow to the struggling Territory.¶

---

* In James, 2002.
† *NTTG*, 25 January 1897.
‡ *NTTG*, 5 February 1897.
§ *The Week*, 22 January 1897.
¶ The jetty was finally replaced by the 'Town Wharf' in 1903. It was made of cast

The immediate needs of Port Darwin residents were the same as for any natural disaster – shelter, food, and clean water. They also had to bury their dead. The *Times* reported that 28 people had been killed by the storm – 15 of those were on boats in the harbour. Only those bodies recovered were counted – there were probably many more washed away by the tide or buried by shifting sands or tidal mud. As usual for the era, only the two Europeans who died were named by the papers – Richard Tracey, a gold miner, and M. D. Armstrong.

Armstrong lived in the Territory for 16 years and was an import/export businessman, cattleman and butcher with his business partner, William Lawrie. At the time of his death, he was 'a prominent and useful member of the community' with many 'intimate friends'. He had chaired the Port Darwin Camp Progress Association in the early 1880s and was a committee member of the Northern Territory Racing Club during the 1890s, importing horses and running them from his stable. He owned a farm at Nightcliff known as 'Armstrong's Farm' for many years, and was about to experiment with beehives, but they arrived a week after his death.* Armstrong took 10 days to die of internal injuries brought about by being 'a good deal exposed during the night of the storm and on the following day'.†

Dudley Kelsey

Telegraphist Dudley Kelsey had the midnight to 4 AM shift at the telegraph station, which meant his wife and infant son spent the night alone during the cyclone. At 3 AM the line failed, water began to flood the office, windows blew in and the 'stationery was scattered all over the floor'. The station was sheltered from the full force of the

---

iron and concrete piers with wooden decking on top. Oddly, it was L-shaped and railway carts needed to be turned on a turntable when loading and unloading. In 1922, a cattle race was installed to allow live exports of cattle and during the 1930s a small side jetty was built as a flying boat terminal. The Town Wharf was destroyed by Japanese bombs during the air attack on 19 February 1942.

* *NTTG*, 12 February 1897
† *NTTG*, 29 Jan 1897

winds by the stone walls, but the neighbours were not so fortunate:
> ... Mr Rundle, a storekeeper from the opposite side of the street, crawled on his hands and knees under the shelter of fences to report that his store had blown away.

And one of the other telegraphists, whom Kelsey does not name:
> ... was lifted clean off his feet and, had he not been gripping the fence, it is hard to say where he might have been blown.*

Kelsey didn't get home until first light. He found his wife and son† huddled together, cold but alive, and sheltering in an outbuilding which had been blown on its side. The outdoor kitchen was still standing, and Kelsey lit a fire to warm his family, dry their clothing, and heat coffee. Their four-room house was destroyed, so with the help of an Aboriginal friend, Kelsey spent the day putting two of the rooms back together, and by evening they were once again comfortable.

Non-Europeans

The balance of those killed were 'Asiatics and blacks' – Chinese and Aboriginal people sheltering in poorly built tin and timber shanties of Chinatown in Cavenagh Street and camps on the edge of the community suffered badly:
> ... In the Chinese quarter of the city, where whole rows of shops and dwellings were levelled to the ground without exception, some loss of life occurred, and when the debris is shifted the tally of deaths may be added to; but to look at the destruction one would expect to find half the population under the ruins. At the boot shop opposite the Hotel Victoria one Chinaman was found dead the next day, and at the Catholic Church, not a stick of which was left standing, two aboriginal women, who sought shelter there, were found under the ruins stiff and dead.‡

The injured were gathered up and taken to what was left of the

---

* Kelsey, (Ira Nesdale), 1975.
† Mrs Mary Kelsey (ne Freeman) was sister to hotelier Ellen Ryan. Her son was Francis Dudley Kelsey.
‡ *NTTG*, 5 February 1897.

hospital. Mr G. H. James, landlord of the Hotel Victoria, broke his arm by falling from the hotel balcony to the ground the morning after the cyclone.* R. F. Fox, an accountant who had taken shelter at the E.S. and A. Bank, was severely injured by some rocks falling on his head.† The *Times* reported that 'the exposure to the elements brought on attacks of fever, and half of the European population complained of illness'.‡

Reconstruction

After the cyclone, accommodation was difficult to find, and people took shelter where they could. Railway staff and their families slept in carriages. Inspector Foelsche and his family found space in the Eastern Extension Telegraph Company's one dry room with three other families. Reverend Tear Tuck and his family were sheltered by a 'Manilla family' and their 'Chinese brethren' gave them blankets. The population of Chinatown gathered in any dry spaces among the ruins – a few stores still stood, and there was any amount of twisted corrugated iron lying around that could be recycled into emergency sheds. All 14 Chinese fruit and vegetable gardens in Palmerston suffered terribly during the storm so there were few fresh supplies for the town for weeks.

Carpenters were in high demand. Those who already lived in Darwin found their services become more valuable. They were:

> … busily engaged in endeavouring to provide shelter for the homeless and to prevent further loss from the heavy rain now falling. As much as £3 per hour has been demanded, and not only demanded, but paid for the services of a carpenter…§

Reconstruction was slow and it meant that some men had an opportunity to leave a legacy in the buildings that they wouldn't

---

* *NTTG*, 25 January 1897.
† Frederick Reginald Fox J.P. lived in Darwin for many years. In 1913 he was running a store and other businesses in Smith Street.
‡ *NTTG*, 12 February 1897.
§ *Adelaide Observer*, 16 January 1897.

otherwise have received. One was William 'Old Bill' Drysdale, a stone mason who had arrived with his wife, Florence, and their two youngest sons, William, and Alexander[*] by horse and wagon in 1893 from Melbourne. Old Bill's work is still in evidence around Darwin. He repaired the Commercial Bank on the corner of Smith and Bennett Streets and its façade still stands as part of the Paspaley Tower. He also built the stone railway embankments near the wharf, the stonework for the railway bridges in Darwin and the stone and cement steps leading up from the wharf to the city known as 'Travellers' Walk'. Old Bill was short, so the steps he built were designed to 'suit his legs and the ladies would be able to easily climb them'.[†]

The cost of the Great Hurricane exceeded £150,000[‡] and a relief fund for residents was quickly raised with a six-man committee to administer it.[§] In the first week of February £300 was raised but, said the *Times*, £200 of that had come from locals: 'The fact is that in South Australia charity begins at home'.[¶] However, the fund continued to collect money. The Earl of Kilmorey donated £10, for example, when on tour in the southern states, and by March there was £485 in the fund.

Charles Kirkland complained that that he could not borrow a penny from the banks against his property, but found help from an old friend:

> … I found myself practically ruined in one night. My wife and I sold all our furniture and effects and let our house, removing ourselves into smaller and cheaper premises. The late Mr Paul

---

[*] Beard, 2008.

[†] In 1902, Drysdale also built the Church of England, sourcing the stone from the Nightcliff foreshore, cutting them on site and floating them around the coast to the wharf (Drysdale, 2019). A Drysdale dynasty is still in Darwin today, though 'Old' Bill left for Melbourne in 1926 and died there in 1930.

[‡] Equivalent to more than $25 million today.

[§] The committee was: Government Resident Dashwood, J.J. Lawrie (E.S and A. Bank), G.H. Sims (Commercial Bank), J.C. Colliver (Cable Extension Company), J.J. Symes and C.E. Herbert (*Advertiser*, 10 March 1897).

[¶] *NTTG*, 12 February 1897.

Foelsche generously advanced me sufficient money on my
simple I.O.U. to affect such repairs as were absolutely needed.*

Within weeks, reason returned to the shocked population. Carpenters began accepting more realistic, albeit high, wages of 14 or 15 shillings per day. Tradesmen in general were happy that there would be plenty of work for them in the months to come. Many businesspeople erected temporary shelters and improved on them as the situation allowed. The Government, always a big employer, had a team of 200 or 300 'coolies' repairing the railway lines, and teams of carpenters working on The Residency and other government buildings.

Government Resident Dashwood embarrassed the South Australian Government by asking for permission to recruit Chinese carpenters from Singapore. Politicians of the day were in support of the *Chinese Immigration Act*, so Dashwood's requests were ignored.

A few people were left destitute, and the proceeds of the Relief Fund were directed their way:

> ... It will be admitted, we think, that there are very few instances of genuine distress amongst us, but it is also just as certain that there are many cases of individual loss which will be severely felt by the sufferers. Persons who lost their little all and know not where to turn for the means to restore their property are happily not numerous, but there are isolated cases, and these should be the first attended to.†

The isolation of Palmerston from the rest of Australia meant that people had to draw together and support each other. As Kelsey said: 'all people were in the same boat and pulled together to bring about better conditions.'

Some were helped at once by wealthy friends. Eliza Tuckwell, whose boarding house, the Resolution Villa, had blown away, was helped to rebuild by V. V. Brown. She was soon in business again with a 'two roofed' house and, four years later, happy to see her daughter,

---

* Kirkland's 'reminiscences', *The Northern Territory Times*, 18 July 1930.
† *NTTG*, 12 February 1897.

Eliza Sarah, marry Mr Brown.* In 1918, Eliza was interviewed by the *Northern Standard*, and they published a short biography of her life after her death three years later. Of the cyclone, she recalled:

> ... about 21 years ago we had a cyclone. It came on about nine o'clock at night. I was stopping at Mrs. Carbury's, and a big blow came on and put out all the lights, so we got on our clothes and went outside. Mr. Carbury went over to Mrs. Brown's place. We sat under the verandah and all the iron blew off over our heads. We went over to Brown's and stayed the night, we were watching for morning light, through a hole in the roof. You may be sure we were glad to see day light. It was all a dreadful sight to see every home more or less damaged. My house was as flat as a pancake but thank God no one was killed. It was indeed a great shock as Mr. Armstrong and Mrs. Daniels† died from the shock of the cyclone.‡

Hannah Wood

Hannah Wood was a long-term resident and retired nurse who for many years had been matron in charge of immigrant ships. She lived in a little cottage she owned behind the Roman Catholic Church and when both were destroyed by the cyclone, Mrs Wood was left pinned beneath the wreckage. She was rescued by some Aborigines who saw her plight and cared for until the storm passed. Dudley Kelsey and his wife took her in and nursed her back to health, a favour that was returned later when Mrs Kelsey 'collapsed with fever' herself.

Hannah had looked after her patients in her home, and relied on the small income it provided, so she was left destitute. On 30 July she wrote a begging letter to the editor of the *Times*:

> ... Will you kindly give me space in this week's issue to appeal to my friends and the public generally, who I beg most respectfully to ask to assist me to rebuild my cottage. I think everyone knows that I lost my all. I hoped that as I am a widow and alone that the committee of the Relief Fund would

---

* Carment, Maynard, & Powell, 1990.
† Mrs Daniels was 90 years old at the time.
‡ *Northern Standard*, 23 August 1921.

have allowed me sufficient money to re-build my cottage, and to some extent restore my furniture. My house is a part of my living, as sometimes I have to take in a patient.

The committee had already given her £20 and had increased it to £35; but it was not enough to buy timber and iron to rebuild her cottage. She hated to beg but:

... if men who are in-good positions, and receiving good salaries are not ashamed to receive a sum of money from the Relief Fund, I who have lost my all, together with my health, through that terrible storm, need not be ashamed to ask the public and my friends, some of whom have known me for twenty-two years, to assist me to rebuild my home.

The letter worked. Three months later, Hannah expressed her gratitude to her friends in another letter to the *Times*:

... When I asked the public for their assistance, knowing how much everyone had lost, I was truly sorry to have to call attention to my need, and I did not think my appeal would meet with such a generous response. I am very much pleased to find that I have so many friends, and I sincerely hope that they will accept my thanks. I have also to thank those friends who have helped me to restore my furniture.

Some have assisted me with their labor, while others have sent me useful presents. I hope they will believe that I shall remember their kindness to the end of my life.[*]

The rebuilding of the town was remarkably quick. By early February the Hotel Victoria was already in a 'very finished state' and:

... Allen &, Co. have now quite a pretentious store erected again. Rundle Bros. & Co. we understand, intend erecting spacious premises, in good time; and Mr. Jolly, who arrived here on Wednesday, will proceed at once with the erection of

---

[*] *NTTG*, 12 November 1897. Hannah Wood remained poor. In early 1903 a small group petitioned the government, unsuccessfully, for her to be granted a small pension. Dashwood replied that she could be housed in the hospital instead. Hannah and her late husband were early pioneers of Palmerston, arriving in 1875, so perhaps the Resident thought she had earned some charity. Hannah died in July 1903 and was buried in the Goyder Road Cemetery. Hannah's husband, James Wood, had died of dysentery in Palmerston during August 1880.

new buildings, in the place of those blown down.*

Chinatown was nailed back together – most houses were always shanties anyway, but the shops along Cavenagh Street were substantial, two-storey buildings. The railway was repaired, and the telegraph lines restrung. The fallen trees were cleared more slowly, but as they dried out, residents had less distance to travel to collect firewood.

The Botanic Gardens, which was almost emptied of its fruit trees and experimental farm produce, grew back quickly, and its buildings were rebuilt. Nicholas Holtze's family home in the gardens had been 'blown to utter ruin', but it was repaired, and it then survived until destroyed by Cyclone Tracy in 1974. Holtze remained upbeat about the damage. He felt that much of the garden had been protected by 'a belt of native jungle between the garden and the sea'† – a lesson modern town planners could heed.

---

* *NTTG*, 12 February 1897.
† Quoted in Bisa, 2016.

Gallery
The Great Hurricane of 1897

Many images of the damage caused by the cyclone are held by the Australian libraries. They are glass plate photographs mostly taken by Inspector Paul Foelsche or his photographic protégé, telegraph worker Florenz August Bleeser.*

Figure 70: Cyclone damage to the P.R. Allen's Club Hotel on Mitchell Street, 1897 (Foelsche, LANT, ph0560-0007).

---

* See Appendix 2 for a short biography of Bleeser.

Figure 71: P. R. Allen & Co.'s private residence, located behind the store on Smith Street (1897, Foelsche, LANT, ph0560-0045).

Gallery

Figure 72: Cyclone damage, corner of Bennett and Mitchell Streets, 1897 (Foelsche, LANT, ph0560-0003)

Figure 73: Corner of Smith and Knuckey Streets. Victoria Hotel in the distance (LANT, ph0840-0001).

Figure 74: Cavenagh Street (Bleeser, nla.obj-150833079).

Figure 75: China Town after the 1897 cyclone (LANT, ph0373-0004).

Figure 76: Cyclone damage (LANT, ph0560-0047).

Figure 77: Two views of the Victoria Hotel (LANT, ph0560-0046 and ph0373-0003).

Figure 78: St Mary's Star of the Sea Roman Catholic Church, before and after (Bleeser, 1897, nla.obj-150838741-1 and nla.obj-150842782-1).

Gallery

Figure 79: Wesleyan Church in Palmerston 1873-1897 – before and after it was destroyed by The Great Hurricane (Murif Collection, 1895, SLSA B-61443, and Foelsche, 1897, LANT, ph0560-0001).

Figure 80: Jetty damage from the 1897 cyclone (Bleeser, LANT, ph1139-0015).

Figure 81: Cyclone damage to Port Darwin Mining Agency Store (Brown's Mart) 1897 (Foelsche, LANT, ph0560-0008).

Chapter 18

And Now?

For each of the books in this series I have travelled the streets of early Darwin, looking for what remains of nineteenth century Palmerston. Of course, the ravages of termites, the gales of cyclones, Japanese bombs, and the march of progress, mean that there is relatively little to see. Other historians have noted that not a single private home from the Federation era exists in modern Darwin,* and most of the nineteenth century heritage buildings that do exist (such as Browns Mart, Fanny Bay Gaol and Government House) were built in the 1880s.

While researching this book, I arranged to meet with Peter Whelan and Paddy Coleman who have lived most of their lives – more than 70 years – in Darwin. Both men have an ongoing interest in old Darwin. I met them at Eva's Café in the Botanical Gardens, because that is one of the best sites of historical interest from the 1890s.

Tourists and locals alike meet at this café. It is a delight – surrounded by the full tropical splendour of the gardens, it pumps out some of the best breakfasts and coffee in town. For history buffs, however, it is worth an extra look. Customers usually enter the café from their numbered tables on either of the modern verandas, and so bypass the front door, which encloses a small porch area. No one these days would call it a 'vestibule', but this is in fact what it was. Eva's

---
* Carment, 2002.

Figure 82: Eva's Cafe in the George Brown Botanical Gardens, in 2022.

Figure 83: The Methodist Church in Mitchell Street 1920 (LANT, ph0386-0139).

café was the church that was built in Palmerston for the Wesleyan Methodists after its predecessor was blown away in the 1897 cyclone.

The building originally stood in Mitchell Street and for many of its last years on the site, it was abandoned and rotting. It was heritage listed in 1995 as 'a prefabricated building of considerable technical and some historical significance... the structural system [was] without any known precedent'. But it turned out that heritage listing can sometimes be a double-edged sword – the building continued to deteriorate and remain uncared for by its owner, the Uniting Church. Fortunately, its value was recognised, and it was delisted, moved to its current site in the Botanical Gardens, and renovated to modern cyclone standards, in 2000.

The church was prefabricated in Adelaide in 1897 and assembled in Wakefield Street as a trial. It was then dismantled and shipped north to Palmerston. It was a new type of construction. It was almost all steel, with wall and roof framing made from angle bars, and steel faux 'weatherboards.' It was ahead of its time, designed to withstand cyclones with anchor cables attached to each corner of the roof tied into concrete footings. The roofing sheets were fixed to the roof purlins with hooked bolts, and this did indeed prove effective in future cyclones.* It was built in a remarkably short time – the church was in use just eight months after the 1897 cyclone.

Peter, Paddy, and I brainstormed the 1890s sites around Darwin that remained. There are many older sites – the stone buildings from the 1880s plus footpaths and stairways – but we had explored those for previous books in this series. 'Visiting' the 1890s was a more challenging task as little remains.

In addition to the Wesleyan Church, there is the Victoria Hotel in Smith Street Mall, which was built in 1889 and first opened its doors in 1890 as the North Australian Hotel. It still stands, though with several new roofs after successive cyclones over the past 120 years. 'The Vic' ceased trading a few years ago and has been boarded up, but with luck its owners will one day reopen this important landmark. Apart from these two buildings, the 1890s seem bereft.

---

* The church enjoyed a long history: In 1940 it was enlarged to accommodate the combined Methodist-Congregational and Presbyterian congregations which worshipped there, and it became the chapel for HMAS Melville. In 1946 it was ceded to the United Church of North Australia and used for worship until 1960. In the following years it was used as a mission store and an automotive workshop, before being abandoned.

Figure 84: The Victoria Hotel has now been closed for more than a decade.

But two living monuments from the time still stand. The first is the Tree of Knowledge, a spreading banyan tree (*Ficus virens*), which grew on Cavenagh Street next to the Terminus Hotel from the very early days – contemporary photographs show it clearly. It is still growing, now surrounded by the Darwin Civic Centre. It is a significant tree to the Larrakia people, who call it *Galamarrma*, but it was also an important site to the residents of Chinatown, who would meet in its shade. The current Civic Centre was built in 1969, closing a section of Cavenagh Street. Initial plans were altered to ensure the tree was kept safe, and the new building constructed three metres north of its original site.

Both Peter and Paddy remember playing under the Tree of Knowledge as children in the 1950s. Peter could also remember numerous concrete foundations that remained around and about the area after Chinatown was bulldozed and bombed ruins were cleared before and during World War II.

The other tree of note is a huge double baobab tree (*Adansonia gregorii*), planted in the grounds of the early Darwin Primary School in the late 1800s. In an 1895 photograph of the school, a young tree stands in the yard – perhaps this is the same tree, planted for Mrs Pett, the teacher. The school buildings were levelled during the 1897 cyclone, but a young willowy boab tree may well have survived the gales.

The heritage value of the tree is significant:

> ... The Boab tree was planted in the late 1800s and is a fine example of this species. It marks the site of Darwin's first primary school and later the Darwin High School and the Adult Education Centre. During the war a 'Daisy Cutter' bomb lay unexploded within its shade for several days prior to discovery. Since the early 1960s it has been well known to the Darwin public as a shade tree in first the Woolworths carpark and, since 1991, the post office carpark.*

A precious tree indeed. When we visited it, it was carefully fenced and shielded from the activities of the construction teams building a city campus of Charles Darwin University. A foreman told us that the tree was 'the most valuable thing on site'. When the landscaping is finally done, it will have a wooden walkway around it and will be a site of interest to tourists.

Tourism in the Top End is different to what was usual in the nineteenth century. For example, unless you're a fish, it is less deadly to the wildlife. Alfred Searcy, who worked for 15 years as a customs officer in the 1880s and 90s, was interviewed during a holiday in Adelaide in 1891, and he waxed lyrical about the virtues of the Territory. Asked if there was anything to tempt the tourist or sportsman, Searcy said:

> ...yes, we have to any extent you like... from catching a tommy rough to baiting an alligator, shooting a wee bird to a buffalo. I wonder holiday-keepers do not patronise the Territory more. It is a most lovely sea trip through Torres Straits to Port Darwin, and then there is much that would

---

* N.T. Heritage site application.

be new to be seen. The best time to go is July or August. To anyone wanting sport it would be necessary to form a party. Going up the rivers there is unlimited wildfowl and plenty of alligators. Then there are herds of buffaloes if the other sport gets quiet, and if they want things particularly lively why they have only to go to Vashon Head and have a smack at the wild cattle there. I'll warrant they will find them lively enough. To tourists nothing could be more interesting than a visit to Port Essington and see the old barracks and soldiers' quarters and the groups of magnificent tamarind-trees.*

We walked through the parkland next to the Browns Mart. Here the English, Scottish and Australian Bank, known as the 'Tin Bank', stood during the 1890s. The building eventually became the head office of the *NT Times* newspaper: seventy years ago, Paddy was one of about 30 boys who collated the papers on site, then ran into town to sell them. They were eight pence, he recalled, of which the paperboys would keep two pennies.

We spent some time in Francis Bay looking for any remnants of the pearling fleets – the luggers used to beach here on its firm gravel seafloor during low tides. These days, however, the mangroves are gone, the shore reclaimed, and nothing of the nineteenth century is obvious.

There are some remnant stretches of railway line still in place adjacent to the Stuart Highway – they were originally laid in the 1880s, but as the lines were used for more than 80 years, it is unlikely that any of them could be the original from those years.

We gave up and agreed there is little else to see from that decade. The economic doldrums the Northern Territory, and indeed all of Australia, was experiencing then is reflected in a paucity of relics. There were no major infrastructure projects in Palmerston during the 1890s, nor were there any lasting monuments or public buildings built.

Visitors might be pleased that some still stand from the

---

* *Adelaide Observer*, 3 January 1891.

previous decade (Browns Mart, Town Hall ruins etc), but others were destroyed by any of the three major cyclones to hit since settlement, or the bombs of World War II. And poor Chinatown was levelled by bulldozers.

Beautiful Darwin is, for better or worse, now a mostly modern city in an ancient land.

Darwin: Survival of a City

Appendices

Appendix 1: Our Govenor's Trip

I reprint this ballad as an example of the social commentary in verse that was common during the latter part of the nineteenth century. It was a time of the *Bulletin* magazine, the great Banjo Paterson and Henry Lawson, C.J. Dennis, and others. This poem was written in 1891 by 'A. Taxpayer' and otherwise remains anonymous. It raises questions and makes comments about Governor Kintore's trip across the continent.

Our Governor's Trip

    With the cordial approval of the Secret'ry of State,
    His Excellency, Earl Kintore, went to investigate
    The reasons why and wherefore 'our great dependency,'
    Instead of being prosp'rous, a 'white elephant' should be.

    This was the reason given, but some cruel people say
    The real motive was that he desired to get away
    From Government receptions, and all the tommyrot
    That void the purse and vex the soul of that most canny Scot.

    For he argued in this manner: 'While I'm away, you see,
    I need not spend, unless I like, a single red bawbee.
    And I shall save what otherwise I surely must have spent,
    If I undertake a journey across the continent.'

When, in time, he reached Port Darwin, and-stepped upon the shore,
The Chinamen and blacks and whites united in a roar
Of welcome to the Gov'nor who had come himself to see
The reasons why that country wasn't what it ought to be.

They bade him to a banquet, and when he got upon his feet
He talked about their cattle, and about exporting meat
To a country, somewhere in the East, whose people, if they would,
Might buy and sell and eat it, provided that they could!

And he told them how delighted Her Majesty would feel
When she heard how they had honoured him with such a splendid meal.
But he quite forgot to mention that the 'sovereign lady' could
Have never even heard of them, and, most likely, never would.

He visited their rifle-butts and he fired-God knows where
And attended archery meetings and drew the 'long-bow' there.
But at grand old Knight's reception, where the people had been led
To hope they might approach him, he incontinently fled.

And the very information he had come so far to seek,
He most unwisely gathered through the medium of a clique
Which stuffed him with its own ideas as to the steps which best
Might be taken to advance a trade in its own interest.

Then he started on his trip, but as he didn't care to view
The nature of the country the train was passing through
To while the weary hours away and his sympathies enlist
He and his companions, for sovereigns played at whist.

Halting for a little while to let the Governor see
Millar Bros' 'Number Ten' and Jensen's property.

Leaving Pine Creek terminus, he promptly took the road
Which led him, two days later, to Alfred Giles' abode.

And here a funny incident occurred, which no doubt you
Will appreciate as highly as those present seemed to do.

His Excellency was approached by a steward of the Club
Of Katherine River sportsmen, who solicited a sub.
Towards their annual races, but the Governor turned away
Said he'd 'have to think it over and would let them know next day.'

But, next day, the steward found that the downy bird had flown,
And in his place 'the doctor' sat in the camp alone.
Who when the sportsman 'bailed him up,' put his hand into his fob.
And with evident reluctance extracted thirty bob!

The staggered steward said no more, but hung his puzzled head,
And reported to his brethren how their enterprise had sped.
But they, rising to th' occasion, and taking heart of grace,
Included in their programme a 'novel Donkey Race'.

Where the winner of the 'Kintore Stakes' should be adjudged to be
The animal that came in last – and furthermore that he
Should from the fund receive One Pound, and th' unlucky moke
That came in first should get ten bob to emphasize the joke!

(Let us just remind the Governor if he would add to his prestige.
There's a good old-fashioned maxim, to wit, 'Noblesse oblige')
Then they started through the bush to see the caves they always show
To visitors who wish to see what's to be seen, you know,

But the grass was high said the Governor voting the thing a bore
Abandoned the undertaking though he called the caves 'Kintore'

And retúrning to the beaten track hastened on his way
To where, beyond the horizon, the 'Holy City' lay.

And now that we are well assured the good that can accrue
From the Governor's proceedings, and from his rushing through
The country at a headlong pace is absolutely nil,
We ask with dire misgiving -'Who is to foot the bill?'

By A. TAXPAYER, May 1891*

---

* *NTTG*, 15 May 1891.

Appendix 2. Bleeser, The Other Photographer

The two principal photographers at work in Palmerston during the 1890s were Inspector Paul Foelsche and Florenz Bleeser. Foelsche we met in Chapter 1, but a short biography of Florenz Bleeser is appropriate here.

The multi-lingual Florenz August Karl Bleeser was born near Adelaide on 5 July 1871 and died at Malvern, Adelaide on 1 November 1942.[*] Descending from one of Napoleon Bonaparte's bodyguards, his father had participated in a botanical expedition to British Guiana in the 1840s. From him, the young Florenz learned about botany and the natural world, and this became a lifelong obsession – although his career was in the Post and Telegraph Department.

Bleeser started work as a messenger boy in 1884 at the age of 13. Six years later he was promoted and posted to Palmerston as a junior operator on the transcontinental telegraph line. It was then that he began his contribution to the Territory as a photographer and naturalist. In his spare time Bleeser collected botanical, marine and insect specimens, as well as artifacts belonging to local Larrakia people. He also learned, and spoke, their language fluently.

Bleeser was a telegraph operator at Port Darwin from 1896 to 1903, a telegraphist until 1908 and was the acting postmaster at Darwin many times until he retired in 1931. He never sought further promotion as this would have interfered with his plant collecting. A large collection made by him ended up in the Berlin Herbarium although, unfortunately, it was destroyed by bombing in World War II. Nevertheless, his legacy includes many specimens in the Victorian herbarium, at least six plants named after him, including *Eucalyptus bleeseri*[†] and a rare green ribbon orchid, *Chilochista bleeseri*, and 238 glass negatives of the Top End of Australia. The latter are held in the National Library of Australia, and they include photographs

---

[*] Bleeser spoke English, German, French, Japanese, Chinese, Malay, and Larrakia.
[†] Hall, 1978.

of people, places, and events. A special collection is of the town of Palmerston after it was destroyed by the 1897 cyclone.

Bibliography

Advertiser. (1873). Northern Territory. *South Australian Advertiser*.

Anon. (1886, February 26). The Mission Station at Rapid Creek. *North Australian*, p. 3.

Anon. (1995). *Biographical information on thirty Northern Territory women who enrolled to vote in 1895, by the Northern Territory Women's Advisory Council & Genealogical Society of the Northern Territory*. Darwin: unpublished. Library and Archives NT.

Apple, R. (June 2010). Presentation by Rabbi Dr Raymond Apple AO RFD to the Australian Jewish Historical Society (NSW Branch), on 8 February, 2010. *Journal of the Australian Jewish Historical Society*, Vol. 19, Part 4.

Atherton, C. (1991). *The Northern Territory - South Australian 'White Elephant'/ Commonwealth prize: perception and reality in the federation era*. Darwin: Library and Archives of the Northern Territory: Occasional Papers no. 22.

Austin, T., & Parry, S. (1998). *Connection and Disconnection: encounters between settlers and Indigenous people in the Northern Territory*. Darwin: NTU Press.

Bach, J. S. (1955). *The Pearling Industry: An Account of its social and economic development*. (https://espace.library.uq.edu.au/data/UQ_248877/Pearling_industry_Australia_1.pdf ed.). Newcastle: Department of Commerce and Agriculture.

Barter, L., & James, W. (1990). *Mary Elizabeth Dolan*. Accessed online 30 March 2022: Northern Territory Dictionary of Biography, Vol 1.

Bartlett, M. (1990). *Port of Darwin 150 years: History of Port Darwin 1839-1890*. Darwin: Darwin Port Authority.

Beard, M. (2008). *Northern Territory Dictionary of Biography*. Darwin: CDU Press.

Bisa, D. (2016). *Remember Me kindly: A history of the Holtze family in the Northern Territory*. Darwin: Historical Society of the Northern Territory.

Boland, J. (2016). *Know Where You Stand: Fannie Bay and Surrounds; Darwin's Industrial Heartland 1870-1950*. Darwin: Fannie Bay Historical Society.

Carment, D. (1990). *John George Knight (1826-1892)*. Darwin: Northern Territory Dictionary of Biography, Vol 1: to 1945.

Carment, D. (2002). Darwin's Federation Heritage. In L. Mearns, & L. Barker, *Progressing Backwards: the Northern Territory in 1901* (pp. 87-92). Darwin: Historical Society of the Northern Territory.

Carment, D., Maynard, R., & Powell, A. (1990). *Northern Territory Dictionary of Biography Vol 1: to 1945*. Darwin: NTU Press.

Coltheart, L. (1982). *Australia Misère: the Northern Territory in the Nineteenth Century*. Brisbane: (PhD). Griffith University.

Creaghe, E. C. (1883). *The Diary of Emily Caroline Creaghe: Explorer*. Edited with Introduction by Peter Monteath: Corkwood Press, 2004.

Dashwood, C. (1892 - 1900). Government Resident's Reports on the Northern Territory. Northern Territory Archives: Printed by The House of Assembly, South Australia.

Debnam, L. (1988). *Men of the Northern Territory Police 1870-1914 : who they were and where they were*. Darwin: Genealogical Society of the Northern Territory.

Dobson, G. (2021). *Under the Banyan Tree: In search of the lost history of Australia's north coast*. (1 ed.). Tingalpa Queensland: Boolarong Press.

Donovan, P. (1981). *The Northern Territory: A history of South Australia's Northern Territory*. St. Lucia: University of Queensland.

Donovan, P. (2022, June 7). *Solomon, Vaiben Louis (1853–1908)*. Retrieved from Australian Dictionary of Biography, National Centre of Biography, Australian National University: https://adb.anu.edu.au/biography/solomon-vaiben-louis-8577/text14973

Douglas, W. (1872). *Transcript of the 1872 Private Diary of Captain William Bloomfield Douglas* (Transcibed by Russel G. Pugh 2016. ed.).

Duminski, M. (2005). *Southport, Northern Territory 1869-2002*. Darwin: Historical Society of the Northern Territory.

Edgar, S. (1986). *Lindsay, David (1856–1922), Australian Dictionary of Biography*. Melbourne: Melbourne University Press, Volume 10, 1986, pp 105–106.

Elder, P. (1990). *Dashwood, Charles James (1842-1919)*. Northern Territory Dictionary of Biography Vol 1.: NTU Press.

Erecting an OTL pole in 1925 (1925). [Motion Picture].

Fabris, P., & Farram, S. (2022). *Wild Dogs of Song: Palmerston Dingo Glee Club 1895-1905*. Darwin: Historical Society of the Northern Territory.

Farram, S. (2017). *Charles James Kirkland: The Life and Times of a Pioneer Newspaperman in the Top End of Australia*. Darwin: CDU Press.

Fielding, J. (2022, November 21). *Florenze Bleeser*. Retrieved from Northern Territory Dictionary of Biography, Volume 1, 2008: https://dcarment.files.wordpress.

com/2014/09/ntdictionaryofbiography.pdf

Fletcher, V. (1988). *The Northern Territory 1895-1900: The Royal Commission of 1895 and its results*. Thesis submitted for Masters Qualifying: History Department of the University of Queensland.

Fletcher, V. (2013). *The North/South Transcontinental Railway in Australia's Story*. Darwin: Historical Society of the Northern Territory.

Foelsche, P. (1882). Notes on the Aborigines of North Australia. *Transactions and Proceedings and Report of the Royal Society of South Australia*, Vol 5 pp1-18.

Foelsche, P. (1888). *Annual Report of the Commissioner of Police to the Education Minister*. Adelaide: In McLaren (1978).

Gaunt, C. (Fri 6 July 1934). The Lepers of Arnheim Land and Sketches. *Northern Standard*, Page 4, Viewed 7 March 2022.

Gibson, E. (2011). *Beyond the Boundary: Fannie Bay 1869-2001*. Darwin: Historical Society of the Northern Territory.

Goldsmith, F. (1894). *Health Report to the Government Resident*. Darwin: Library and Archives of the Northern Territory.

Goldsmith, F. (1899). Tropical disease in northern Australia. *Intercontinental Medical Congress of Australasia*, 106.

Gore, A. (6 December 1887). *The North Coast of Australia - A Trip to Forida Station, Part 2*. Adelaide: South Australian Register.

Griffith University. (2020, October 23). *Jesuits in the Northern Territory*. Retrieved from German Missionaries in Australia: http://missionaries.griffith.edu.au/missionary-training/jesuits-northern-territory-1882-1902

Hall, N. (1978). *Botanists of the Eucalypts*. Melbourne : CSIRO.

Helyar, G. (1990). *They Led the Way: A short account of the Lands and Survey Department of the Northern Territory 1869-1978*. Darwin: NT Department of Lands and Housing.

Herald. (1869, January 2, 9, 16, 23, 30 Wentworth Hardy and William Fisher, Editors,). The Moonta Herald and Northern Territory Gazette Hardy, W (Ed). *Issues 1-5*.

James, B. (1989). *No Man's Land: Women of the Northern Territory: Eliza Tuckwell*. Sydney: William Collins Pty Ltd.

James, B. (1990). *Darwin's Hotel Victoria - Its Life and Legends*. Darwin: Northtype Pty: for Tumminello Holdings.

James, B. (1995). *Occupation Citizen: The Story of Northern Territory Women and the Vote (1894-1896)*. Darwin: James.

James, B. (2002). Federation and Faith: The story of Darwin's Wesleyan Methodist Church in the Federation Years (1897-1902). In L. Mearnes, & L. Barter, *Progressing*

Backwards: The Northern Territory in 1901 (pp. 101-114). Darwin: Historical Society of the Northern Territory.

Jones, P. (2005). *The Policeman's Eye: The Frontier Photography of Paul Foelsche*. Adelaide: South Australian Museum.

Jones, T. (1987). *Pegging the Northern Territory: A history of mining in the Northern Territory, 1870-1946*. Darwin: N.T. Department of Mines and Energy.

Jones, T. (1990). *The Chinese in the Northern Territory*. Darwin: NTU Press.

Kelsey, D. E. (1975). *The Shackle*. Edited by Ira Nesdale. Lynton Publications.

Kettle, E. (1967). *Gone Bush*. Sydney: F. P. Leonard.

Kettle, E. (1981). *Health services in the Northern Territory : a history 1824-1970*. Retrieved from ANU - Open Research: https://openresearch-repository.anu.edu.au/

Knight, J. G. (1890). Government Resident's Report on the Northern Territory for the Year 1890. Northern Territory Archives: Printed by The House of Assembly, South Australia.

Lennox, B. (22 June 2016). Gabarlgu Kaparlgoo Kapalga - South Alligator people, three ways, A talk by Bill Lennox. *NT History Grant Talk, NT Archives*. Darwin: https://dtc.nt.gov.au/__data/assets/pdf_file/0004/367546/Bill-Lennox-NTAS-talk-script-June-2016.pdf.

Lewis, D. (2004). *A Wild History: life and death on the Victoria River frontier*. Melbourne: Monash University Press.

Lewis, J. (1922). *Fought and Won* (Facsimile copy, Gillingham Printers Adelaide ed.). Adelaide: W. K. Thomas & Co.

Lindsay, D. (1888). *Explorations in the Northern Territory of South Australia Adelaide*. Royal Geographical Society of Australasia, South Australian Branch: Retrieved 7 March 2022 <http://nla.gov.au/nla.obj-68225300>.

Little, J. (11 August 1993). *The Hanging of Wandy Wandy*. Palmerston: Northern Territory Times and Gazette.

MacKillop, D. (1892). *Letter to the Editor*. Palmerston: Northern Territory Times and Gazette.

MacKillop, D. (1893, March 20). Northern Territory Blacks. *The Barrier Miner*, p. 2.

Masson, E. (1915). *An Untamed Territory: the Northern Territory of Australia*. Melbourne: MacMillan.

McInnes, A. (1982). *Wreck of the Gothenburg*. Retrieved April 2019, from https://espace.library.uq.edu.au/data/UQ_241126

McLaren, B. (1978). *The Northern Territory and its Police Forces*. Adelaide: LANT, RC 363 Vol 1.

McMinn, G. (1870). Diary of G.R. McMinn, Surveyor and Overseer during construction of the Overland Telegraph Line to Port Darwin. Adelaide: State Records of South Australia GRG 154/9.

Morris, J. (2000). Memories of the buffalo shooters: Joe Cooper and the Tiwi (1895–1936). *Aboriginal History*, Vol 24, pp141-151.

Mulvaney, J. (2004). *Paddy Cahill of Oenpelli*. Canberra: Aboriginal Studies Press.

Murif, J. J. (1897). *From Ocean to Ocean: Across a Continent on a Bicycle: An Account of a Solitary Ride From Adelaide to Port Darwin*. Melbourne: https://www.gutenberg.org/ebooks/58206.

Murphy, K. (1984). *Big blow up north: A history of tropical cyclones in Australia's Northern Territory.*

Nesdale, I. (1975). *The Shackle, D.E. Kelsey*. Ira Nesdale, Editor. Adelaide: Griffin Press.

Newcastle University. (2022, March 7). *Colonial Frontier Massacres in Australia 1788-1930*. Retrieved from The Centre for 21st Centre Humanities: https://c21ch.newcastle.edu.au/colonialmassacres/detail.php?r=713

Noye, R. (1972). *Foelsche, Paul Heinrich Matthias (1831-1914)*. Online version 2006: Australian Dictionary of Biography, Volume 4, accessed 18 May 2022.

NTTG. (1873-1927). *Northern Territory Times and Gazette*. Darwin: https://trove.nla.gov.au/newspaper/article.

Paterson, A. (31 December 1898). The Cycloon, Paddy Cahill and the G.R. *Bulletin*, pp 303-5.

Paynter, L. (2013). *Northern Territory Women*. Retrieved from Australian Women's History Forum: https://awhf.wordpress.com/2013/02/28/northern-territory/

Powell, A. (1982). *Far Country*. Melbourne University Press.

Pugh, D. (2014). *Turn Left at the Devil Tree*. Darwin.

Pugh, D. (2017). *Fort Dundas: The British in North Australia, 1824-29*. Darwin.

Pugh, D. (2018a). *Escape Cliffs: The First Northern Territory Expedition, 1864-66*. Darwin.

Pugh, D. (2018b). *Darwin 1869: The Second Northern Territory Expedition*. Darwin.

Pugh, D. (2019). *Darwin: Origin of a City: The 1870s*. Darwin.

Pugh, D. (2020). *Port Essington: The British in North Australia 1838-49*. Darwin.

Pugh, D. (2021). *Darwin: Growth of a City: The 1880s*. Darwin.

Pugh, D. (2022). *Twenty to the Mile: The Overland Telegraph Line*. Darwin.

Read, P., & Read, J. (1991). *Long time, olden time: Aboriginal accounts of Northern Territory history*. Alice Springs, NT: Institute for Aboriginal Development.

Register. (20 June 1893). Blacks vs Coolies. Interview with a Mission Father. *South Australian Register*, p. 7.

Register of Deaths. (1870s). Medical Officer, Register of Deaths, District of Palmerston, 1872-1890. Northern Territory Archives.

Reid, B. (2022). *Protection at a Price: Protection of the Aborigines in the Commonwealth's Northern Territory, 1911-78*. Darwin: Historical Society of the Northern Territory.

Reid, G. (1990). *A picnic with the Natives: Aboriginal-European Relations in the Northern Territory to 1910*. Melbourne: Melbourne University Press.

Rose, D. B. (1991). *Hidden Histories*. Canberra: Aboriginal Studies Press.

SAPP. (1895). Report of the Northern Territory Commision: together with minutes of the proceedings, evidence and appendices. *South Australian Parliamentary Papers*, Volume 2, No. 19.

Searcy, A. (1909). *In Australian Tropics*. London: George Robertson and Co.

Searcy, A. (1912). *By Flood and Field: Adventures Ashore and Afloat in North Australia*. London: G. Bell and Sons, 1st Edition.

See-Kee, C. (1987). Chinese Contribution to Early Darwin. *Northern Territory Library, Occassional Papers*, Web. 3 Nov. 2022. https://hdl.handle.net/10070/718877.

Sissons, D. (1977). Japanese in the Northern Territory 1884-1902. In K. T. Arthur Stockwin, *Bridging Australia and Japan, The writings of David Sissons, historian and political scientist* (pp. Vol. 16, No. 1, pp. 2–50). Canberra: A.N.U. Press.

Smith, R. (2020). Water, Women, and Weapons: Northern Territory Frontier Massacres. *Northern Territory Historical Studies: A journal of history, heritage and architecture*, Issue 31: pp 15-35.

Smith, W. (17 November 1906). Report on the Diseases of the Northern Territory. *Adelaide Register*, 4.

Sowden, W. (1882). *The Northern Territory as it is: a narrative of the South Australian Parliamentary party's trip and full description of the Northern Territory, its settlements and industries*. Adelaide: W.K. Thomas.

Spencer, B. (1896). *Report on the Work of the Horn Scientific Expedition*. Adelaide: cited in http://www.ntlis.nt.gov.au/heritageregister/heritage_register.

Stephen, M. (2021). *Contact Zones: Sport and Race in the Northern Territory 1869-1953*. Darwin: CDU Press.

Tamblyn, M. (1990). *Mines, Money and Men: Top End Mining, 1895-1921*. Darwin: Historical Society of the Northern Territory.

Thompson, G. (1900). *Thompson's List of "Half Castes" in the Northern Territory 1899-1900*. Northern Territory Archives Service, NTRS 790, Government Resident of the

Northern Territory, Inwards Correspondence, 1870-1912, Bundle 10441 : NTRS 790.

Trudgen, R. (2000). *Why Warriors Lie Down and Die*. Nhulunbuy, NT: Why Warriors Pty Ltd.

Wells, S. (2002). *Saltwater people: Larrakia stories from around Darwin (Edited by Samantha Wells)*. Darwin: Larrakia Nation Aboriginal Corporation.

Wildey, W. B. (1876). *Wildey's Australasia and the Oceanic Region*. Adelaide: George Robertson.

Wilson, B. (2000). *A Force Apart: A History of the Northern Territory Police Force 1870 – 1926*. Darwin: A thesis submitted in fulfilment of the requirements of the Northern Territory University for the Degree of Doctor of Philosophy.

Wilson, H. (1994). *The Historic Heart of Darwin: the Tin Bank, Chinatown, the Terminus Hotel and the Civic Centre*. Helen J. Wilson, Darwin.

Wilson, H., & James, B. (2002). *The Settlement of Darwin and its Environs: A Brief History*. Darwin: Unpublished report to the Department of Justice.

Wilson, H., James, B., & Carment, D. (1994). *The Annotated Letters of John George Knight 1889-1892*. Darwin: Historical Society of the Northern Territory.

Index

A

Aborigines Bill 60
Adcock, Herbert xix, 7, 18, 30, 32, 41
Adcock, William 30
Adelaide Jubilee Exhibition 1
agricultural industry 126, 130
Ah Kim 201
Ah Ping 200, 201
alcohol and opium 119
Allwright, Allan Durrant 'Jack' 167
Allwright, Marie Agnes 166, 167

B

Baker, Marcus 198
baobab tree 255
B.A.T. Tennis Club 115
Benison, Larry 158
Benison, Mrs Rose Isabel 158
beriberi 202
Bevan, Judge David 191
Bicycle races 103
black boys 59, 183
Blanket Day 58

C

Cahill, Patrick 'Paddy' 98, 134, 135, 136, 209
Cavenagh Street 12, 64, 69, 70, 72, 120, 191, 210, 232, 236, 242, 254
census 73
Charles Darwin University 255

anti-Chinese sentiments 21, 42, 64, 72, 227
anti-opium movement 122
Araby, Charley 132
Armstrong, M.D. 235
Armstrong's Farm, Nightcliff 235
Arnhem Land 131
Athletics Association 99, 100, 103, 104, 105
Australian Natives Association 115
Auvergne Station xiii, 133, 179, 180

Bogle, Reverend James 211
Borroloola 42, 80, 172, 189, 190
Botanic Gardens 19, 27, 242, 251
Brandt, Otto 127
Bright, George 60
Brown, John Alexander Voules 30
Brown's Mart xvi, 3, 31, 41, 256
Brown, Victor Voules 'Daddy' xix, 30, 31, 32, 41, 97, 99, 166, 195
Bryant, Herbert 102, 103

Chee Hang 188
Chinatown 64, 69, 70, 72, 75, 120, 195, 210, 231, 232, 236, 237, 242, 254, 257
Chinese banquet 20
Chinese festivals 69
Chinese immigrants 63, 65

Chinese Immigration Restriction Act of 1888 xii, 71
Chinese market gardeners 70
Chinese miners 113, 125, 226
Chinese New Year 67
Chinese population 63
Chinese religion 211
Chinese secret societies 67
Chin Toy xix
Chock Tong, Thomas 21
Christian church 211
Christie, Henry 158, 234
Christie, Hugh 158
Chung Yeung xiii, 188
Cleopatra 113, 147
Coleman, Patrick 'Paddy' 251
Coleman, Tom 105
Congregational Church 211
Congregational Union 211
Constitutional Amendment (Adult Suffrage) Act 163
Cooper, Harry 134, 141, 142
Cooper, Joe xiii, 134, 137, 141, 142
Cooper, Reuben 142
Copperang 189, 191
Crawford, Lindsay 178
Creagh, Emily 133
Croker, Samuel Burns 180
Cygnet 189

D

Daly River xii, xiii, 28, 29, 98, 127, 143, 189, 203, 214, 215
Daly River Mission xii, xiii, 214
Dariba Nanggalinya, Old Man Rock 55
Dashwood, Government Resident 8
Dashwood, Justice Charles James 5, 7, 8, 38, 71, 126, 180, 181, 187, 220, 239
Dashwood, Margaret and Augusta 6

Davoran, Matron Maria 203
Debating Society 30
Dingo Glee Club xii, 90, 91, 92
Dolan, Elizabeth 172
Dolan, John 93, 107, 172, 173, 174
Donnegan, Mounted Constable 172
Drysdale, Bessie 114
Drysdale, William 'Old Bill' 238

E

Earl of Kintore 17
East Alligator River 131
Echlin, E.O. 34
Elliot, J.P. Henry 167
Elsey Station 198, 207
English, Scottish and Australian Bank 256

Esau 147
Escape Cliffs 40, 53, 165
Esplanade 69, 94, 104, 211
European miners 125, 126
Eva's Café 251

F

Fannie Bay Gaol xiii, 12, 18, 30, 31, 122, 180, 181, 188, 199, 201, 202
Fannie Bay Racecourse 97
Ferguson River goldfields 126
Finniss, Frederick 40, 86, 89
First Northern Territory Expedition 89
first passenger trains xi

Flannigan, Charlie xiii, 179, 180, 181, 182
Florida Station 132
Flying Cloud 111
Flynn, Barney 140
Foelsche, Charlotte 10, 14, 80, 212

Index

Foelsche, Inspector Paul xi, 7, 10, 11, 17, 22, 25, 27, 55, 65, 67, 77, 116, 170, 177, 185, 203, 237, 238, 243, 263
Fort Dundas 137

G
Galamarrma 254
Geoy Choeng Loong 69
Giles, Alfred 23, 130, 178, 261
Goldsborough, Mort and Co 56, 130
Goldsmith, Dr Frederick 62, 94, 192, 200, 202, 203, 204
Gore, Alfred 132, 211
Gothenburg 145, 164, 177

H
Hamaura, Charlie 'Japan' 113, 147
Hang Gong, Arthur 20, 21, 65, 98
Hansen's Disease 195, 200
Hassan, Ahmed Ben 189
Herbert, Charles Edward 9, 116

I
Immigration Restriction Act of 1901 225
Ingeruintamirri, Samuel 141

J
Japanese pearl divers xx
Japanese people 76
Jesuit missionaries 211

K
Katherine River Sportsmen's Club 23
Katherine Turf Club 24
Kelsey, Dudley 235, 236, 240
Kelsey, Percy 216
Kirkland, Charles 33, 34, 231, 238
Klevesahl, Martha (Dashwood) 9

L
Larrakeeyah 111
Larrakia people xi, xx, 53, 56, 63, 100, 213, 254, 263
Lawrie, William 235
Lem Kai xiii, 188

Fort Wellington 131
Foy, Brother Loie 216
Freemasons 91, 116

Government Resident Knight 18
Governor Kintore xii, 17, 19, 21, 71, 151, 208, 259
Goyder, George xi, 165, 220
Goyder Road Cemetery 2, 14, 17, 70, 241
Great Hurricane xiii, 105, 146, 164, 166, 170, 204, 210, 212, 215, 230, 238, 243
Griffiths, Walter xii, 34, 39, 40, 41, 43, 81

Holtze, Annie 164
Holtze, Nicholas 27, 66, 127, 164, 242
Hopewell, Margaret 19, 170
Hotel Victoria 237
Hugh Kalyptus 222

Iwaidja people 142

Johnstone, Charles 11
Johnstone, Matilda Cecily 14
Joss House 67, 229

Knight, John George xii, 1, 23, 64, 177
Knight's Folly, see Mud Hut 3
Knight, Walter 2
Kohinoor xi, 10, 165
Kwong Sue Tak 120

Lennox, Andrew 217
Leprosy 195
Lindsay, Government Surveyor David 131
Linn Fern 211
Little, Edith 116

Little, Edith, Blanche, Egbert, and Maud 15

M

MacArthur River 173
Macartney, John Arthur 132, 133
Macassan trepang fishermen 137
MacDonald, Albert 102, 103, 106
MacDonnell, Governor Richard Graves 149
Mackenzie, Kenneth 189
MacKillop, Father Donald 184, 214
malaria 211
Manassie 203
Mandimbula 140, 141
Manila-men xx, 76
Manulocum 177, 178
Margaret Crossing Hotel 168
Marla-oldain, Alice Rose 142
Mather, A.W.B. 105, 106
Mayhew, George Washington 34, 89, 99, 231
Mayuna 183
McKeddie, George 62, 99, 116
McMinn, Acting-Government Resident Gilbert 145, 195

N

Narbaloora 189, 191
Nash, Benjamin 224
Niemann, Alice and Kitty 215
Niemann, John Henry 142, 143, 215
non-Aboriginal population of 1888 63
Norcock, Gaoler George 202
North Australian Cycling Club 103, 107
North Australian Hotel xii, 6, 27, 169, 170, 253
North Australian League 32
North Australian (newspaper) 20, 33

O

Oenpelli 135, 137
opium dens 119, 120, 213

Little, John Archibald Graham xi, 13, 14, 17, 19, 40, 66, 116, 187, 230

McWaters, Nurse Jean 203
Meat Extract Industry 142
Melbourne International Exhibition 1
Melville Island xiii, 133, 134, 137, 139, 140, 142, 143, 190
Midge 143
Millar brothers 65, 125, 150
Miner's Arms Hotel 168
mining industry 125
Mitchell Street 211, 212
Moolooloorun 185, 187
Moonta xi, 33, 53
Moore, Thomas 189
Morice, Dr Robert 38, 195
Muckaluggee 137
Mud Hut 3
Mud Island Lazaret 196, 199
Mullak-Mullak (Malak) people 214
Murif, Jeremy J. xiii, xv, xix, 104, 105, 106, 107, 210

Northern Light 144, 145
Northern Territory Crown Lands Act of 1890 60
Northern Territory Land Act of 1872 144
Northern Territory Native Industrial Mission 217
Northern Territory Racing Club 30, 32, 96, 235
Northern Territory Times 6, 32, 33, 80, 205, 207, 232, 239
Nyanko 185, 186, 187

Overland Telegraph Line xi, 16, 22, 42, 56, 66, 79, 80, 97, 104, 106, 149, 231

Index

P

Palmerston xvii
Palmerston and Pine Creek Railway Bill 38
Palmerston Archery Club 116
Palmerston Brass Band xiii, 34, 89
Palmerston Club Hotel 170
Palmerston Cricket Club 95
Palmerston Dramatic and Musical Society 85
Palmerston Hospital 204
Palmerston Institute 32
Palmerston Literary and Debating Society 92
Palmerston Regatta Club 111
Palmerston Rifle Club 110
Palmerston Tennis Club 115
Palmerston to Pine Creek Railway 65, 150
Parap 232
Parsons, John Langdon xii, 2, 37, 150, 177, 195
pastoral industry 59, 128, 130, 131, 220
Pater, Justice Thomas 38, 173, 177
Paterson, Banjo xv, 119, 209
Patterson, Robert 56

pearl shell industry xii, 34, 39, 76, 77, 125, 144, 145, 146, 147, 226
Pett, Mrs (schoolteacher) 255
Pickford's Hotel 173, 231
Pickwick Club 92, 93, 94
Pine Creek xii, xviii, 3, 22, 28, 80, 81, 97, 98, 125, 151, 167, 179, 198, 205, 206, 211, 215, 222, 261
Playford Club Hotel 167
Playford, Honourable Thomas 'Honest Tom' 26
Point Charles 155, 157, 158, 234
Point Charles lighthouse 158
Port Darwin 211
Port Darwin Cricket Club 95
Port Darwin Rifle Club 110, 111
Port Essington 25, 53, 111, 131, 134, 135, 145, 177, 229, 256
P.R. Allen and Co 101
prostitutes 66, 76, 77
Pybus, Alfred 16, 22

R

racist attitudes 226
Rapid Creek xii
Rapid Creek Mission 184, 211, 213, 214
Redwater fever xiii, xviii, 42, 129, 130
Resolution Villa 166
Reverend Bradbury 216
Robinson, E.O. xiii, 31, 134, 137, 143, 177, 183

Roman Catholic Church 215, 232, 240
Roper River 11, 80, 185, 187
Royal Commission of 1895 xiii, xv, 76, 152, 219, 221
Royal Hotel 172
Ryan, Ellen 167, 168, 169, 216
Ryan, William 168

S

Saint Joseph's Mission 213
Searcy, Alfred 8, 57, 59, 172, 177, 183, 230, 231, 232, 255
Second Northern Territory Survey Expedition xi, 53
See Kee 70
Smallpox xi, 55, 201, 203
Smith, Dr Ramsay 201

Solomon, M. J. 30
Solomon's Mart 30
Solomon, Vaiben Louis 3, 34, 39, 156, 163, 224
Springvale Station 164, 178
Sree Pas Sair 145
S.S. *Adelaide* 173

S.S. *Airlie* 102
S.S. *Australian* 212
S.S. *Chingtu* 18
S.S. *Maggie* 8, 27, 28, 93
S.S. *Palmerston* 38
S.S. *Taiyuan* 26
S.S. *Taruria* 211
S.S. *Victoria* 20, 25
Stephens, Reverend Sampson Dyer 216
Stevens, Hildebrand 25, 57, 112

Stirling, Professor Thomas Edward 22, 23, 24
St Lawrence (Larry) 135
Stock Diseases Act of 1888 130
Stokes Hill Jetty 234
Stone House 72, 120
Stott, Mounted Constable 186
Strele, Father Anton 213
Strele, Very Reverend Father S.J. 215
Stuart, John McDouall 8, 149

T

Tack, Reverend Tear xiii, 216, 217, 234
Terminus Hotel 232, 254
The Ghan 152, 153, 221
The Northern Territory Times xi, 232
The Overlander 205, 207
The Residency 6, 7, 19, 24, 165, 211, 239
Thomond, Right Honourable Algernon Hawkins 17
Thompson, Mounted Constable George 61

Thursday Island 76, 145, 146
transcontinental railway xviii, 3, 149, 152
Tree of Knowledge 254
Trewren, Reverend Henry 216
tuberculosis 202, 203
Tuck, Robert 189, 190
Tuckwell, Eleanor 166
Tuckwell, Eliza 165, 166, 239
Tuckwell, Ned 165

U

Uhr, Darcy 97

V

Victoria Hotel xii, 116, 170, 171, 232, 253

Union Goldfield 22, 41, 167

Victoria River 29, 98, 142, 143, 189

W

Wanchill 189
Wandi Wandi 134, 179, 183, 184, 185
Ward, F.C. 85, 152
Warrima 189
Watson, John 'Jack' 133
Wesleyan Church xi, xiii, xvi, 10, 216, 252, 253
Whelan, Peter 251

White Australia Policy 75, 225
white elephant 221
whooping cough (pertussis) 203
Wingfield, Howard 134, 183
Wood, Dr Percy 201
Wood, Hannah 240, 241
Wulna people 56, 203, 213

Y

Yee Kee 69

Yet Loong xix, 20

Z

Zaleika 137

Zapopan Mine 166

Further reading

19th Century Darwin

A history from its first days – this is Darwin and the Top End in the 19th century.

Modern Darwin is a young city in an ancient land. First surveyed in 1869, it is now a beautiful, vibrant tropical city dubbed the 'Pearl of the Arafura'. It wasn't always so nice. Derek Pugh's series on the settlement of the Top End and the early history of Darwin tells the true story, warts and all, of this most distant of South Australian settlements and its extraordinary characters.

Darwin is one of the few cities in the world young enough to be photographed from its very first days. Each book in the series is well illustrated using those photographs.

www.derekpugh.com.au

Twenty to the Mile
The Overland Telegraph Line

The greatest engineering problem facing Australia – the tyranny of distance – had a solution: the electric telegraph, and its champion was the sheep-farming state of South Australia.

This extraordinary book relates how Charles Todd, leading hundreds of men, constructed a single-wire telegraph line across the centre of the continent. All in less than two years.

The construction teams erected 36,000 poles (at '20 to the mile') and eleven repeater stations between Port Augusta to Port Darwin. It was a mammoth undertaking over 3,000 kilometres, but at last, in October 1872, Adelaide was linked to London.

Communication that once took 12 weeks, now took seven hours.

> ... a book written with heart and admiration... a lasting tribute to the inventiveness and tenacity of the people behind the planning, building and execution of the Overland Telegraph – a true nation building endeavour
> (His Excellency, The Honorable Hieu Van Le AC).

www.derekpugh.com.au

TWENTY TO THE MILE

The Overland Telegraph Line

Derek Pugh OAM

Foreword by His Excellency the Honourable Hieu Van Le, AC

The British in North Australia

The ill-fated British military attempts to settle the north coast left full cemeteries. Their on-going effects on the people and the environment of the north held lessons for those who came later, but these were too often ignored - to their peril.

www.derekpugh.com.au

www.ingramcontent.com/pod-product-compliance
Lightning Source LLC
Chambersburg PA
CBHW060944230426
43665CB00015B/2055